MADE ONLY IN INDIA

What makes Darjeeling tea, Pashmina shawls, Monsooned Malabar Arabica coffee and Chanderi sarees special? Why is it that some goods derive their uniqueness through their inherent linkage to a place? In a pioneering study, this book explores this intriguing question in the Indian context across 199 registered goods with Geographical Indications, linked with their place of origin. It argues that the origin of these goods is attributed to a distinctive ecology that brews in a particular place. The attributes of their origin further endorse their unique Geographical Indications through legal channels.

Drawing from a variety of disciplines including geography, history, sociology, handicrafts, paintings and textiles, the author also examines the Geographical Indications Act of 1999 and shows how it has created a scope to identify, register and protect those goods, be they natural, agricultural or manufactured. The work presents a new perspective on indigenous diversities and offers an original understanding of the geography and history of India.

Lucid and accessible, with several illustrative maps, this book will be useful to scholars and researchers in social sciences, environmental studies, development studies, law, trade and history.

Anu Kapur is Professor of Geography, Delhi School of Economics, University of Delhi; Fellow, Indian Institute of Advanced Study, Shimla; Senior Fellow, Nehru Memorial Museum & Library, Teen Murti, New Delhi; and recipient of the prestigious Amartya Sen Award in Social Sciences. She has authored books including *Paradise in Peril: An Ecological Profile of the Kashmir Valley* (1995), *Indian Geography: A Future with a Difference* (1998), *Voice of Concern: Indian Geography* (2002), *On Disasters in India* (2009), and *Vulnerable India: A Geographical Study of Disasters* (2010).

MADE ONLY IN INDIA

Goods with Geographical Indications

Anu Kapur

Routledge
Taylor & Francis Group
LONDON AND NEW YORK

First published 2016 by Routledge

2 Park Square, Milton Park, Abingdon, Oxfordshire OX14 4RN
711 Third Avenue, New York, NY 10017

Routledge is an imprint of the Taylor & Francis Group, an informa business

First issued in paperback 2017

British Library Cataloguing in Publication Data
A catalogue record for this book is available from the British Library

Library of Congress Cataloging-in-Publication Data
A catalog record has been requested for this book.

ISBN: 978-1-138-95709-1 (hbk)
ISBN: 978-0-8153-9593-5 (pbk)

Typeset in Goudy
by Apex CoVantage, LLC

CONTENTS

FIGURES

TABLES

FOREWORD

Challenging the conventional and bypassing the stereotype at every turn, Anu invariably manages to evoke a unique theme to work on with an ingeniously devised methodology. As an earnest geographer, she has been keen to expound on the 'philosophy of place'. Constituting the basic building block of the spatial–temporal framework of reality, 'place' is in space what a 'moment' is in time.

Essentially an ingredient of a wider context of an area of mutual interaction and influence, place is a spatially defined unit with a specific location. It is the venue of being and becoming of any entity, situation or event. Anything that exists or lived through or attached a meaning which happens to be somewhere in place. No less is it a subjective experience of bonding and belongingness. An essential task for the geographer is to celebrate place and discover its quintessence.

On the bedrock of such ideas, Anu set forth to lay bare the layers of embedded inner spaces of India through a comprehensive analysis of place names, place paintings and place goods. The effort was reckoned as a lifetime project and hence it was segmented into three components to be taken up successively over time. The first choice fell in favour of place goods or 'Geographical Indications' in official parlance. Implicit in this preference was the sight on the horizon of a fresh theme and the presence of her own discipline of geography in its formulation.

Soon it was discovered that though the expression 'Geographical Indications' had started receiving the attention of scholars belonging to disciplines like economics, sociologists, law and public policy, it has not so far found a place in geographic literature. Call it an oddity of evolution of the discipline, a distinctly geographic concept which was conceived at the Paris Convention in 1883, received a more elaborate provision in the Lisbon Agreement in 1958, got a structured framework by the European Union in 1992, and was provided the force of law by the World Trade

Organization in 1998, grossly escaped the attention of geographers in research at large. Reference here is being made to the term 'Geographical Indications'. To the best of my knowledge, no book has appeared by now on the theme nor has any research paper made its appearance on the subject in scientific journals. The dictionaries of geography, more specifically the prestigious *Dictionary of Human Geography*, are yet to incorporate this term in their lexicon.

The synthesis of both physical and human conditions in an area or place finds an authentic manifestation in its native agricultural products and bovine species. Hence these are the ones which occupy the most frequent space on the inventory of Geographical Indications. Examples include French Champagne, Florida Oranges and New Zealand Lamb. In fact, the ambit of Geographical Indications extends beyond agricultural or livestock products, as illustrated by Czech Crystal, Swiss Watches, Persian Carpets and Punjabi Phulkari. Indeed the very idea of Geographical Indications rests on three pillars of quality, distinctiveness and indigeneity.

In his innovative and engrossing book, Neil MacGregor constructed the History of the World around 100 Objects, ranging from Stone Age tool to cooking pot to credit card. This is done by way of inferring the messages which each of the select objects conveys about peoples and places, environments and interactions at different times in history. Objects reflect the needs of the people involved and also represent what they deemed critical to fabricate. They also 'demonstrate the longevity and vitality of the cultural'. He claims that a history deciphered from objects is more objective since the one based solely on texts would be biased in favour of the victor at the cost of the version that the defeated one may have offered. He reaffirms his conviction by concluding that 'whether in stone or paper, gold, feathers or silicon, it is certain that we will go on making objects that shape or reflect on our world and will define us to future generations' (MacGregor, *A History of the World in 100 Objects*, 2010).

Anu's book carries similar ecology. It is based on a holistic interpretation of 199 place goods which have made an entry into the records of the Chennai Registry. There is a subtle interweaving of the site ecology, historical evolution, cultural milieu and creative aesthetics of the goods dealt with. Leaving aside the issues of appropriate pricing, market access, cost-benefit calculus and legal protection as the domain of other disciplines, this book focuses on geographic spirit on the spatial identity of Geographical Indications goods.

The most insightful and impactful are the observations she makes on the changing centrepiece of place goods as emerged over time. In a broad spectrum, these were dovetailed to the requirements of 'temple' in ancient

India, and of the 'royal court' in medieval India, and further on had their base in 'plantation estate and black (industrial) town' in colonial India. The post-independence period is too recent to create a maturation of Geographical Indications which do take time to ripen. Nothing could be more succinctly and effectively synthesized to communicate the sum and substance of different periods of Indian history through a critique of nature, variety and evolution of objects under scrutiny. The entire discussion flows organically and reflects the totality of every place good.

With Geographical Indications at the core, the book weaves an astonishingly beautiful tapestry of India's geography in time–space perspective. At places it acquires the tenor of a folk song. If you are using a marker to highlight what is worthy of retaining, you will make most of the book extensively colourful. A researcher might be left pondering as to why he or she missed exploring such a challenging theme near home.

The distinction of the book lies in signalizing a discourse on what is so much a part of everyday life but has been overlooked even by a keen observer. It is an invitation to come across something you had not met in geographic literature, and it offers a fascinating feast of information and ideas. There are profound details, refreshing reflections and lyrical expressions to enjoy.

The book is indeed a model for learning the way fresh knowledge can be produced. This involves clarity about fundamentals of theory of the discipline, propensity to identify an unreclaimed theme for research, capacity to visualise all possible elements of the object under study, talent to devise an appropriate methodology for the purpose, and a competency to build a bridge between theory and practice. All this is demonstrated through Anu's books in succession, be it *Paradise in Peril*, *Voice of Concern: Indian Geography*, *Disasters in India*, *On Disasters* and *Vulnerable India*, among others.

As a personal note to the author, I feel honoured to have this opportunity once again to prefix a foreword to her book. It will be in place here to quote from Aldous Huxley's foreword to the book *The First and Last Freedom* by Jiddu Krishnamurthi (1959). He effectively represented the essence of the philosophy of the author: 'Addiction to formulas is almost universal. Inevitably so; for our system of upbringing is based on what to think, not how to think'. Formulas lead inevitably only to blind thinking. Anu has the talent to think beyond the formulas and reinvent her approach and style in every case. Writing this Foreword was in effect a new learning for me.

Here I am reminded of Peter Drucker, the management guru of the first order in the world. He asked Jim Collins, a learner at his feet, to pen the Foreword to his book *The Daily Drucker* (2004). Such was the generosity of the genius whose writings have been hailed as 'landmarks of the managerial profession'! The present Foreword is being done in the same spirit. It is my fond hope that I was able to capture the light and energy of this meritorious treatise which is a tribute to 'place goods', or for that matter 'Geographical Indications'. To appreciate the power of place, this book is the right place to start.

March 12, 2015

Gopal Krishan
Professor Emeritus
Panjab University, Chandigarh, and
National Fellow, Indian Council of Social Science
Research, New Delhi

PREFACE

It is a truth that that which is closest and most familiar to us is what is most overlooked and often unacknowledged. This is the case with place. It is present, it manifests in a variety of ways, yet its role goes unnoticed and unappreciated. Darjeeling, Basmati, Pashmina and Mysore agarbathi are products and goods that I have long since experienced. Yet it took time for me to realise that all of them and many more are about place. I have called these and other such goods by the term 'place goods'. These are goods which are much like what is conveyed in Blake's poem '. . . a world in a grain of sand'. Through these goods one can feel and connect to the place where they were produced, grown or manufactured. The habitation of place goods is not a function of latitude and longitude, site and situation, land and landform, temperature and rainfall, soil and vegetation, skills and techniques, customs and tradition. This endless list of listables are important no doubt, but they alone and individually are not the cause for the 'origin' of place goods. Beyond these seeable, measurable, quantifiable, qualifiable traits, characteristics and elements there is 'something' more.

What is that?

At this point of my understanding all I can say is that it is the 'chemistry of all these elements' which creates an inexplicable yet intangible energy or force which I am tempted to also call the atma of place. It is not identifiable, nor is it measurable, nor discernible – yet it is pervasive and can be experienced. It manifests in the case of place good through the taste, aroma, feel, or appearance of a good. Like soul to body, this resonates place, explains place and makes place a condition of possibilities and infinite potential. Place is not an empty vessel or a meaningless entity. It has the capacity to situate, hold and give a product, good, thing or an idea a habitation. This is the inherent nature of place. Such a character allows place to slip easily into a variety of roles be it in history, politics, architecture, nomadism, regionalism, displacement, topophilia or such other descriptions. Place goods belong to a similar category of the allowability and doability of place, but they share more about place. These are the goods that courier place. In legal parlance this synthesis of place which a good carries is called Geographical Indications.

In its literal meaning, indication is a sign that 'speaks of something'; but in the present context 'indications' should not be read as a feeble word because as it emerges the goods do not display a feeble or a hesitant connect to place. Indications are a veritable storehouse and repository of information, conditions and characteristic of a place. Indications should thus be seen as a DNA or a place code. The place reveals itself in the goods and then gets rewarded as its Geographical Indications. Thus, a Pashmina shawl allows the Kashmir Valley and Kashmiriyat to be revealed in its totality. A Phulkari allows a representation of Punjab in its entirety. A synchronicity of natural resources and wisdom of use cohere to make possible a place good. In this sense place is not just a locator but a sum total of something strong and visible. I am tempted to even go to the extent to add that the Geographical Indications are not just messengers of place but in fact are Place. The malty, musty Monsooned Malabar is the coffee estate, the Pashmina shawl is the Kashmir Valley, the leaf size, aroma and colour of Darjeeling is the tea garden. Since all these and more goods are a result of their place of origin, it follows that place goods are distinct because they are territory specific. Place goods which fall in the jurisdiction of India thus belong only and only to India. It is in this spirit that evolved the concept and caption Made Only in India. Moreover due to their connect to a particular area, even within India, place goods are confined only to the exclusive region which provides conditions for their existence and development. By their very definition and characteristics these goods cannot and do not have an occurrence beyond more than one place. Because of the fact that their exclusive characteristics accrue within a particular place and are not generic and prolific in different parts of India, in this book I have chosen to address them by the phrase 'place goods'.

When the idea of this book germinated I wanted to capture a study of place in three different ways. The first is the way meaning of place gets translated into the name of the place. A name individuates and identifies a particular entity. It is claimed that we first name the entity and then only can we come to know of it. Infact whatever can be given a name is knowable. Investigating the kind of knowledge place names contain this dimension would have explored the role of place in shaping names. Identifying the durability and politics behind change of names I was keen to research how the meaning of place gets translated and embedded into the name of place.

Places have a strong identity that is deeply felt by people. This strong 'sense of place' is made up of a mix of natural and cultural features in the landscape, and generally includes the people who occupy the place. The felt experience may be strongly enhanced by the place being written about by poets, novelists and historians, or portrayed in music or art. I wanted to capture the sense of place, through different schools of paintings in India. The second theme I wanted to engage with was to capture the sense of place through the works of creative art, specifically paintings. Paintings after all were not made in a cultural void and so capture the people – place relationship. Place in painting is the gathering spot of all that has been felt and experienced. All genres of paintings clearly evoke the person-place relationship: character, mood, theme, colour and whatever happens all depend largely on setting. The aim would have been to unveil the place rooted human experience and observation captured by the artists. The third theme I wanted to work was the 'place – product' relationship, as manifested through the place goods. Morever I was clear it had to be a work on India, with geography at its core and if possible a theme that had not been worked by geographers. My motive to engage with these three themes was simple, it was to enjoy and capture the beauty, diversity and distinctive capacity of India. Fate as it now seems zeroed the priority to focus on place goods. In a way this is turned out for the best. As I was keen to wander across the landscapes in search of the best of what India created and produced. I was keen to know about the Made Only in India. What fell within my field of intention was The Geographical Indications.

The theme came to me on its own. No one suggested it to me. It was not a project handed out by any research organisation. None of the Departments of Geography in India have ever held a seminar or organised a conference on this theme. There is not a single article on Geographical Indications in any of the leading geographical journals of India. To date there is no doctorate on this theme in India. Moreover it does not find itself in any course or syllabus of the departments and colleges in India.

It is a subject which at the international level has been engaged in, in some limited manner by economists, political scientists, legal professionals and those working on aspects of trade and international negotiations. But since the perspective is anchored around the context of place at its core, Geographical Indications is truly a geographer's beat. This is because at the fundamental level Geographical Indications is about the distinctiveness in the goods because of the 'origin' of the goods. The moot assertion is that the difference in the taste, look, feel and experience of the goods is because they hail from places which are different. Place is not a mere receptacle, but is the womb birthing the good. As mother to child, the bond of good with place needs to be recognised and legalised. With these as the issues the matter under discussion belongs, expects and lends itself to a geographical inquiry.

The theme beckoned me to itself. But the work was not easy. This is because my objective was not to engage with the already present debates and discussions of the political, economic or trade negotiations which surround the topic of Geographical Indications. In this context the research articles and reports on Geographical Indications have largely, if not mainly, been authored by Europeans. Not only was research on the dimensions of trade negotiations available but more also was the fact that my bent of mind and training being such I wanted to work through the lens of place. I was keen to grasp the spatio-temporal aspect of goods with Geographical Indications, expose the diversity of India which gets revealed through these goods, outline the roadblocks to the prosperity of these goods and moreover grasp India's bond with place through these goods. It was through the study of the place goods that I chose to achieve these objectives.

I could have adopted various methods to undertake this research. First, I could have researched on a select sample of goods and detailed on an approach akin to that of a case study. The second option was to select one or more spatial units like an administrative state or a geographical region like the Himalayas and study all the goods within it. A third way was to select a single type of good, let's say tea or coffee or sarees, and study these across India. But I chose none of these three methods. Instead I opted to take cognizance of all the place goods registered with Geographical Indications (199) in addition to few more that had been place goods in the past but had fallen to oblivion because they were not looked after. The decision to select a wide and large number of goods for study yielded dividends. It allowed many places to speak, and time periods to be represented. It gave scope for cross comparisons, and it permitted a deeper insight into the Made Only in India.

Selecting the route to description, analysis and synthesis focused around different types of goods does not come easy to a geographer, who has the critical apparatus to assist an assessment of written records and is more familiar with a study of texts. Analysing empirical data to identify the spatial characteristics and differences is also part of the training of a geographer. Maps are a tool which geographers are most equipped to handle. In map reading conventional symbols, known methods of representation of data and well-set legend and scale are all handy clues. Moreover, one is aware of the distortions and the potentials of a map. But working with 'place goods' is a more challenging and difficult proposition. It demands a considerable leap of imagination and careful analysis of both the good and the place. At one point one has to take the goods to their area of production so as to fathom the difference of one place good from the other and at another moment lift them to a different time zone to comprehend when and why they came into being.

India's place goods are a juxtaposition of all kinds and shades. They hail from different altitudes and latitudes, forests and grasslands, mountains and valleys, tropical alongside those of the temperate, rural and urban, handcrafted and machine-made and those that belong to the tribals as well as the rural artisans. Within their ambit fall places for weaving sarees, decorating metals, moulding clay, casting wax idols, picking fruit and flowers, extracting oils, stringing beads, knitting baskets, producing food and many more. The place goods could be the outcome and effort of a single small family or a community to that of a population in thousands. The region of production of place good could be as small as a room to as large as spreading across an entire river valley or even spilling across neighbours. India's place goods are legendary, evolving and timeless. The range of occurrence, habitats and type confirms that place goods have no preference of site or situation, latitude or altitude, cultural or tribal group.

The signature of the place is such that goods carry the place with them wherever they go. The place of origin is the identity and marker of the goods. Therefore each place good needs to be understood as an individual entity: for Chambal Rumal culture was the way ahead, for Mysore Sandalwood oil it was the type of tree, for Kashmir saffron the soils of the Karewas became a core point of reference to begin the exploration. To grasp the difference between Eri and Muga silk, a browse through the journal of sericulture and botanical books about the worm and caterpillar was not enough; it was important to experience the feel of silk. Such acts of interpretation and analysis are essential in any study of place through goods and goods through place.

The purpose of this book was not to seek to describe particular places in detail nor a particular good in detail nor develop theories, models or abstraction, rather the concern was to grasp the various ways in which India gets recognised and represented through place goods.

To collect the information and literature to back the research the approach was that of the way of the hunter and gatherers The important libraries consulted were Indira Gandhi National Centre for the Arts, National Gallery of Modern Art, National Museum, Indian Agricultural Statistics Research Institute, Pusa, Nehru Museum and Memorial Library, Ratan Tata Library and India Habitat Centre, all in Delhi, and the library of the National Institute of Design, Ahmedabad. To assist in a study of the goods a visit to a museum or a craft bazaar, a sparing glance within a coffee table book, a detail on a tag of a product, an article in an in-flight magazine, a browse through websites were avenues that were not overlooked. When matters got exasperating, the option of Right to Information was used to get the needed information on the goods from the Registry at Chennai, India. The effort was to search for any material that would help to uncover the characteristics, reasons and issues around the place-laden goods. Given the scatter of information across a range of sources the book is a condensation of insights gleaned from all this material and beyond. There was no formal prestructured hypothesis I was testing or point I was debating. Therefore in a sense the work created a pattern that is its very own. With this exhausting yet exhilarating auto-evolved collection and reflection, the book has been organised into eight chapters. Each chapter attempts to answer specific questions.

Chapter 1, 'Geographical Indications Act: place matters' addresses facts like, What are the main lineaments of the Geographical Indications Act? Why does an indication which is geographical need legal protection? What is the criterion to select goods for legal protection under the Act? Which goods and which places have been enrolled under the Act? When and why was it made effective? What are the various nomenclatures associated with matters of good and its origin? How does it bring to fore that place matters? How are place goods defined? How do these differ from other kinds of goods? The first chapter provides a conceptual and legal base for the Made Only in India.

Chapter 2, 'Bonding: place goods' raises issues like, What is geographical in goods? What are the place properties that nourish a good? How does place worm and weave to bond with goods? In what ways does this bond get expressed? What unique characteristics do the goods acquire with this bond? This chapter familiarises and spells out the characteristics of place goods across different parts of India. The chapter takes one to the heart of the reasons for the Made Only in India.

A historical recapitulation of place goods is the more explicit focus of Chapter 3, titled 'Nurturing: place goods'. When, and why were place goods nurtured? Who were the patrons of these goods? Which were the goods? Is the concept of Geographical Indications a recent sprout in trade or did it exist in an earlier phase of history? Taking a sharp turn from the features of bonding and nurturing, Chapter 4, 'Destroying: place goods' draws out the various ways in which Made Only in India were destroyed. The questions it addresses are, Why were place goods destroyed? What strategies were adopted for their destruction? Which place goods were destroyed? What has been the impact of this destruction on India? Chapter 5 takes the destiny of Made Only in India further and analyses the forces which could bring fresh life to them.

Titled 'Resurrecting: place goods', the enquiries in Chapter 5 revolve around issues like, What are the factors which resurrected place goods?

How did Geographical Indications gain significance worldwide? What are the benefits of adopting a law of place? What is the historical treatment of Geographical Indications within the parlance of intellectual property laws? Since Chapter 5 spells the merits that ensue to adhering to a law of place, Chapter 6 sets out to chart the route of 'Searching: place goods'. Where can one search for place goods in India? How many more place goods can be enrolled? Which are the place goods that can be drawn into the ambit of the Geographical Indications Act? The closing chapter dives into the various problems and road blocks faced by place goods.

Titled 'Concerns: place goods', Chapter 7, focuses on the following questions: What are the concerns for place goods? How do trademarks, frauds, generics and homonyms trouble the prosperity and viability of place goods? What are the other serious issues faced by place goods? What is the hope for place goods? Who are the custodians of these goods? How and why should these place goods be preserved?

Finally, Chapter 8 titled 'Geographical Indications: place gathers' ties up the strings and reiterates how important it is to protect goods which carry a sense of geography and the 'graphy' of India!

With these as the core issues this very first book on Geographical Indications in the world not only grasps a new geography of India, but it looks at Geographical Indications as a study of the bond with place. The goods that are dealt with are not ordinary productions; they are distinctive and thus the pride of India. The sum of these goods equals India's representation and identity. I am tempted to add that while the Prime Minister of India invites multinational companies to manufacture their products under the initiative of Make in India and has desirable virtues, it would be equally if not more important to give attention to Made Only in India. This is because while the thrust of Make in India is to focus on select sectors of the economy for job creation and skill enhancement, the Made Only in India is about preserving and promoting creativity, skills and products that geographically are exclusive to India.

ACKNOWLEDGEMENTS

My intention was to write a book on India on a theme that took cognizance of the value of Place. Thus came to manifest *Made Only in India*, an account of the goods and produce which belong only to India because of their place of origin. The universe aligns to an intention. As it aligns it also extends its promise to create the help. A book of this kind needs a lot of support and a lot it got. A thank you is a very, very small way to express gratitude. But it still is one way.

There are a number of people to whom I am greatly indebted in various ways in the writing of this book. First and foremost I owe to Professor Emeritus Gopal Krishan. He kindly agreed to write the foreword to my book. In recent years, I have engaged and particularly enjoyed a fruitful 'place dialogue' with him. His concern and mentoring I deeply value.

As usual my students were the backbone of research; they assisted in searching, documenting and cataloguing the material as I waded through different libraries. To name a few, Barsha, Jyoti, Krishna, Krishna A., Kriti, Nishant, Manmohan, Seema, Sumit, Tanu, Vikas, Ritwika, Nidhi and Gargi. All were joyful and enthusiastic supports. When a particular piece of reading could not be accessed by me then Rishi Chatrath, Tanaya and Shabana helped archive, sift and sort. I grew more attentive after Mariam's gentle comments on my infant draft. Anuradha eyeballed the much needed editorial corrections. I thank them both. The theme of Geographical Indications has a legal dimension. To understand the court cases a young attorney Naveen Pandey was most forthcoming. I express my gratitude to Punam Tripathi. Her erudite style of checking facts, spotting and correcting errors are not the only virtues. She lived the *guru-shishya-paramapara* in a form which today is becoming rare to find.

The book benefits from other caring relationships. All the maps of the books are new and drawn from scratch. In only a few cases was an outline of a map available; many had to be constructed and drawn with descriptions. Each map benefitted immensely from the dedication of Shri Mohan Singh, the seasoned and senior cartographer at the Department of Geography, Panjab University.

An indispensable factor in making possible the book was the award of Senior Fellow at Nehru Memorial and Museum Library, Teen Murti, New Delhi. The Director Professor Mahesh Rangarajan was most supportive in providing logistics essential for research. The Fellowship for a duration of two years had to be abruptly terminated when I was appointed Professor of Geography at the Delhi School of Economics and expected to join at the earliest date. With all the joys of being appointed Professor, the displacement from Teen Murti to the University of Delhi was not easy, and it made me realise how rooted one can get, even in a short span, for it is not time, but the place which makes the bond possible. To say that I miss Teen Murti would be an understatement for much was learnt and felt in that place. Perhaps there is a destiny of place and I was to complete this book in my own 'home' the Department of Geography, Delhi School of Economics, University of Delhi. Here my faculty understood my unfinished task of writing this book, and they took special care not to burden me with academic chores. I am thankful to the various other supports at the Delhi School of Economics. The librarians, *chowkidars*, *chaiwalas*, photocopy *wallas* and the *malis* are as always indispensable in the making of every work I do. Small as their gestures may seem yet they go a long, long way in helping keep the mood of the research.

I cannot leave these pages that carry my feeling of gratitude without thanking the Vice Chancellor of the University of Delhi, Professor Dinesh Singh and his wife, Neelanjana, and daughter, Richa. My interaction with them unfolded a beautiful new landscape adding to my values of academics and scholarship.

And finally my Ma and Dad, in addition to superhuman qualities of love, patience and care they are the space in which I write. Never do they ask for anything, except of course that I should drive more carefully, switch off the air-conditioners and come home on time! The spiritual love they luxuriously provide is amazing. I do *not* deserve them.

I do not know what the book will give to the reader, but to me it has provided a journey to numerous places, knowledge of a large number of goods, a taste of variety of produce and a realization of how vast, enduring and diverse is India.

Lastly I would like to add that the book on this theme is the first of its kind; it follows no model as there is none. It is an academic work, it is an experimental work, but also a work of imagination. When one writes a book a feeling is that one has done a lot but I am aware I have done only a little, and there is much which could be done. I owe and own all errors, slips and snags, for I am a bond with place that is human.

1

THE GEOGRAPHICAL INDICATIONS ACT

Place matters

The Geographical Indications Act received the concurrence of the President of India on 30 December 1999. Among the hundreds of 'Acts' in India this alone names the discipline of geography in its title. Soaked in a true appreciation of geography, the Act has created a scope to identify, register and protect those goods, be they agricultural, natural or manufactured which draw a definite character from their 'place' of origin within India. Using legal armour, the Act states 'geographical indication . . . is where a given quality, reputation or other characteristics of goods is essentially attributable to its geographical origin. . . .' (Section (1) (3) (e) of the Geographical Indications of Goods (Registration and Protection) Act, 1999). To gain protection under the Act, goods have to check in at the Geographical Indications Registry which was established by the Central Government at Chennai, with an all India jurisdiction, on 15 September 2003. The Controller General of Patents, Designs and Trade Marks is the administrator of the Geographical Indications Act. Most Geographical Indications carry the name of the place of origin of the goods, for example Darjeeling tea, Mysore Sandal Soap and Assam tea. But names such as Feni for the cashew drink or Alphonso for a type of mango are also eligible for protection since they fulfil the condition of carrying the characteristics of their place of origin.

The Geographical Indications Act plays an important role for both the producer and the consumer. On the one hand, it shields the genuine producers of agricultural and industrial goods from other producers who deceptively claim a place-based identity, and on the other, it protects consumers from being deceived by any good which makes a false claim about its origin. The Act is designed to break through the clutter of misleading messages about the origin of a good and connect customers with those goods which carry an authentic hallmark of Geographical Indications. It thus, prevents the unaccredited users from 'passing off' their goods as those of the registered users, and so it also ensures premium price to the genuine producers of the goods, especially in the export market. The Act ensures monetary compensation against violators and imposes fines or imprisonment and thus grants and protects the rights of the authorised users of Geographical Indications. There was no specific legislation in India before 1999 to register and regulate Geographical Indications for the Made Only in India. Being a legal cover there is a procedure for seeking registration of goods under the Act.

Registration of Geographical Indications goods: The procedure for registration for Geographical Indications involves filing an application which carries a series of questions ranging from the origin of the good, background of the producers and description of the territory of production. Since Geographical Indications are being sought, a map or at least a detailed description of the demarcated area has to accompany the application (Figure 1.1).

What has to be spelt out is the role of the geographical environment in terms of both its inherent natural and human factors and production, processing or preparation in such a geographical location. Field inspections are undertaken to the region to confirm if the good in question carries properties associated with its place of origin. A visit to the area is an integral component of the process as it allows a verification of the facts presented in the application.

Each good seeking Geographical Indications is an individual. To authenticate the contents of the application, a seven-member team of experts well versed in knowledge about the good in question and also in the law of indications is constituted. The goods that seek registration are so diverse that bringing together a meaningful team at times is one difficult aspect of the process. In the case of Alphonso mango the team included three horticulturalists, the Director, Regional Food Research, and three mango growers along with the Registrar of the Geographical Indications Registry. For Patan Double Ikat Patola sarees the team included the Registrar and Assistant Registrar of the Geographical Indications Registry, Director, Market Research (Ministry of Textiles), Faculty of the National Institute of Design, Ahmedabad, and a Professor of Textile and Apparel Designing from the College of Rural Home Science, Dharwad. For Nirmal painting, apart from the Registrar and Assistant Registrar of the Geographical Indications Registry, the team consisted of a former High Court Judge, a former Vice Chancellor of Tamil Nadu Agricultural University, Coimbatore, and a member from the Craft Council of India.

Drawing a team of experts from diverse backgrounds with specific expertise ensures that the authenticity of the good and its origin is inspected, checked and verified. The consultative group submits a report to the

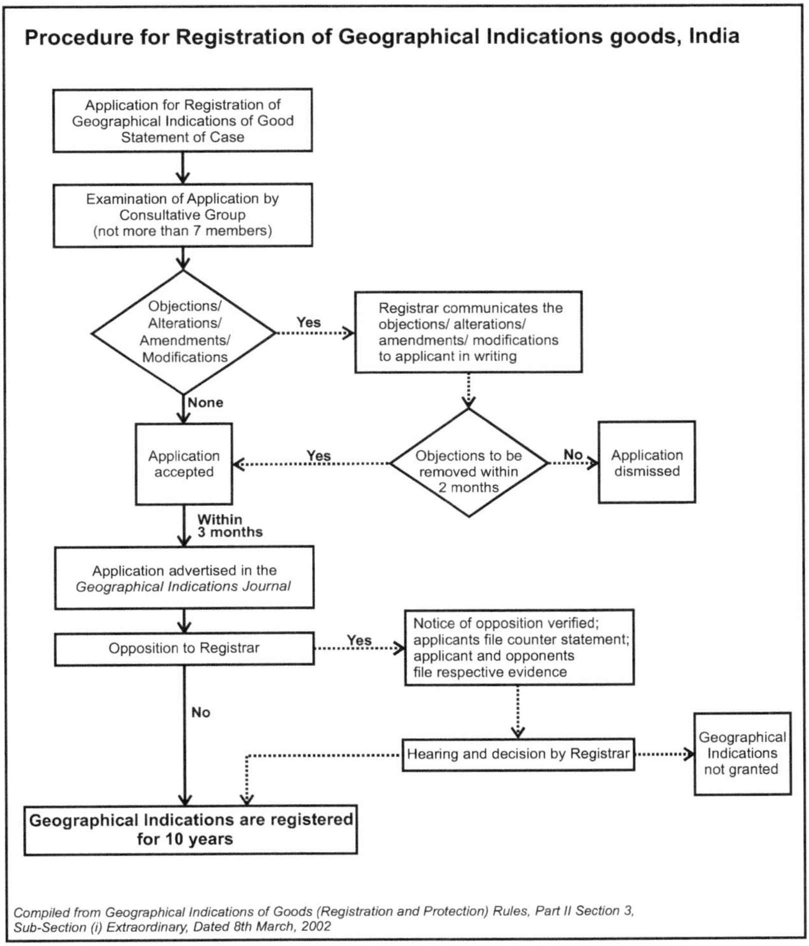

Figure 1.1 Procedure for registration of Geographical Indications goods, India

Registry with various queries, doubts and questions. When the questions raised in the report are satisfactorily responded to and removed by the applicant, the report is published in the *Geographical Indications Journal*. The latter is a bimonthly, bilingual (English and Hindi) statutory publication. This circulation of information in the public domain gives other manufacturers a chance to raise objections and submit them if there is any false claim of the origin or associated attributes of the good to a place.

Any person can oppose the application in writing within a specified time period of three months or, if needed, four months. The process of dissemination through this journal ensures that the Geographical Indications label is given to the rightful producers of the good. Considering the chain of checks and verifications, there is no fixed time for the completion of the process of registration; it can vary from a few months as in the case of Chanderi sarees to six years as for the Payyannur Pavithra ring. The initial registration is for a period of ten years, after which the applicant has to apply for a renewal.

The *Geographical Indications Journal* in India was first published on 1 July 2004, and till May 2014, the Registry had published 58 journals. Till May 2014 the Registry received 482 applications for registration of goods. Of these 482, 228 goods received a certification of origin and can lay a claim to bond with place. Of the 228, 219 goods belong to India and 9 belong to a foreign country. According to the Geographical Indications rules an applicant seeking registration for a good and logo needs to file two separate applications. There were 15 such cases with a dual registration of goods, one for the good and the other for the registration of a logo (Table 1.1).

Among the total goods that were registered with Geographical Indications, two criteria were used for selecting the goods that were to become the focus of research. First, goods which belong to India were sorted and

Table 1.1 Status of registration of goods for Geographical Indications, 2004–2014*

Status of Registration	*Total Applications*	*Indian*	*Foreign*
Not Registered	254	150	104
Withdrawn/Refused/Abandoned	10	10	0
Opposed	1	1	0
Preexamination and new applicants	243	118	125
Registered	228	219	9
More than one applicant for goods	5	5	0
Logos of registered goods	15	15	0
Single applicants for goods	208	199**	9
Total Applicants	482	369	113

* July 2004–May 2014

** The total goods registered were 228. Of these the following 29 applications were excluded – foreign goods (9), more than one applicant for the goods (5), and logos of registered goods (15). Therefore of the total registered goods 199 have been selected for study.

Based on *Geographical Indications Journal* No. 1 to 58

among these the ones which had 'passed' the test for registration were included. The first criterion is justified by the fact that the book is on India, while the ones with registration ensures that the goods have been scrutinised for being the Made Only in India. Among these were goods which had a dual registration one for the good and other the logo. In this case, though a good and its logo are officially registered separately it was decided to treat both as one, because the logo belongs to the good and vice versa and, so to speak, is not a different entity. Following these criteria, goods belonging to India, registered goods and excluding logos, meant that of the 228 goods certified with a Geographical Indications tag, this research focuses on a total of 199 goods.

Growth and spatial distribution: Darjeeling Tea was the first to be bestowed the status of Geographical Indications in India on 1 July 2004. Close on its heels came the Chanderi sarees, Pochampally Ikat and Aranmula Kannadi (mirror) in the same year (Figure 1.2, Appendix 1).

With these as pioneers, other goods soon joined the queue and the number peaked in 2008 when 54 goods bagged a position in the rolls of the Registry.

Though there has been an addition of about 15–20 goods each year, the spatial pattern of registration has been rather skewed. Spatially, of the 29 states and 7 union territories of India, only 22 have contributed to the

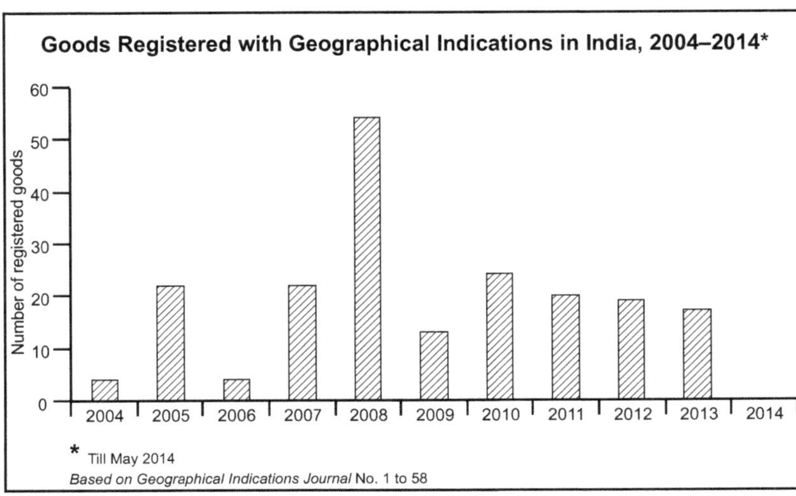

Figure 1.2 Goods registered with Geographical Indications in India, 2004–2014

pool of goods with Geographical Indications. The states of South India have shown a keen interest in registering their goods. Karnataka takes the lead with 32 goods followed by Kerala and Tamil Nadu with 23 and 22, respectively. Together these three states have a 40 per cent share of the registered goods. Another 20 per cent belongs to Andhra Pradesh, Odisha and Uttar Pradesh.

Absent from the list are states like Jharkhand, Uttarakhand, Haryana and union territories like Andaman and Nicobar Islands, Lakshadweep and Chandigarh, which have not enrolled a single good. What is interesting is that even when the address of the applicants that 'await registration' was checked a similar spatial pattern emerged. In the list of those seeking registration, Tamil Nadu tops with 20 goods, followed by Uttar Pradesh and Maharashtra. The waiting list carries no application from Jharkhand or Andaman and Nicobar Islands. This spatial distribution is more a result of lack of awareness, support and guidance to search, enrol and apply, rather than the lack of place goods within these states and union territories.

Classification of Geographical Indications: The Registry at Chennai classifies goods into four macrocategories. These are agricultural goods, foodstuff, manufactured goods and handicrafts. A dominant 69 per cent of the registered goods are handicrafts, followed by 24 per cent agricultural goods, 5 per cent manufactured goods and 2 per cent foodstuff (Figure 1.3).

India is an agricultural country, yet the range of agricultural goods that are registered is small in terms of number, spatial spread and variety. In 2012–2013, agriculture accounted for 13.7 per cent of the total Gross Domestic Production of India. Today nearly 60 per cent of the total geographical area of the country and 52 per cent of the total workforce is employed in the farm sector.

In spite of the large percentage of area and population devoted to agriculture, only 12 of the 36 states and union territories have registered an agricultural good with the Geographical Indications tag. So unbalanced is the spatial representation that only two states, Kerala and Karnataka, account for 54 per cent of the total agricultural goods, followed by Tamil Nadu, Maharashtra and West Bengal, which have registered four goods each. The latitudinal location of these states is such that the goods they have enrolled are tropical fruits like mangoes, bananas and oranges; spices like cardamom and pepper; beverages like tea, coffee; and flowers like jasmine. Complementing and closely linked to the agricultural goods are the manufactured foodstuffs. There is Nashik grapes and so Nashik wine has taken a Geographical Indications certification. There is Ganjam Kewda flower and also Ganjam Kewda rooh (Figure 1.4).

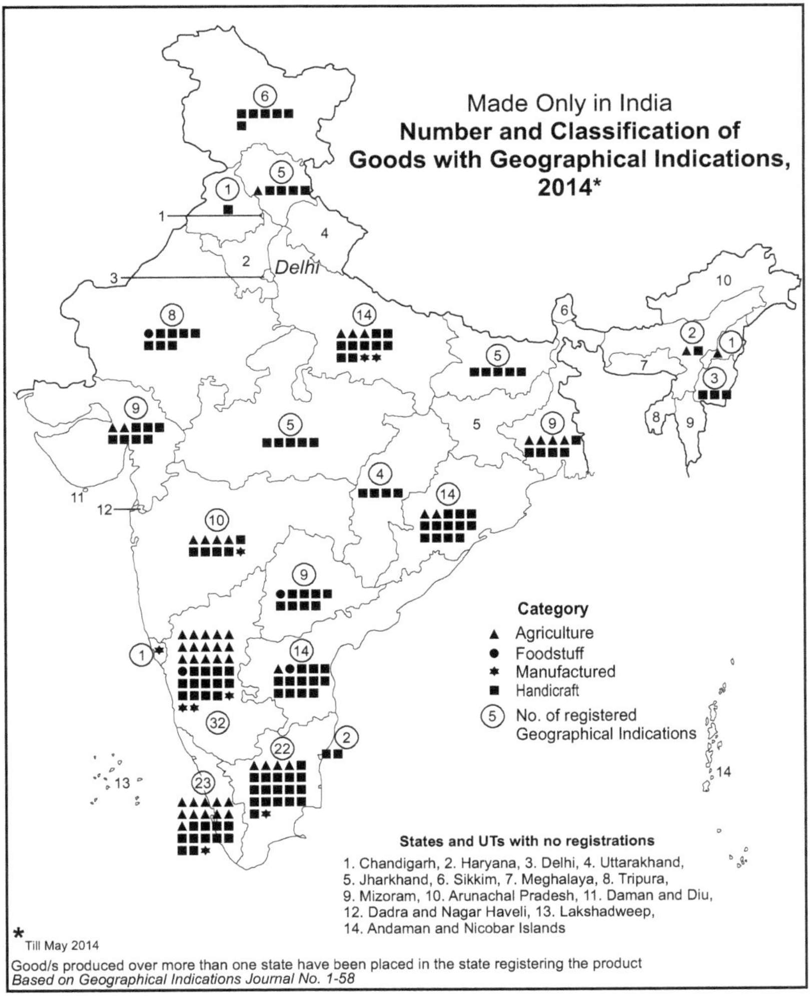

Figure 1.3 India: number and classification of goods with Geographical Indications, 2014

Source: All maps in this book are prepared by the author. Maps not to scale.

If the registered agricultural goods and foodstuff are a small number of 48, then manufactured goods are only 10 in total. In addition to Uttar Pradesh, Karnataka, Kerala and Tamil Nadu also have a marked presence in this group (Figure 1.5).

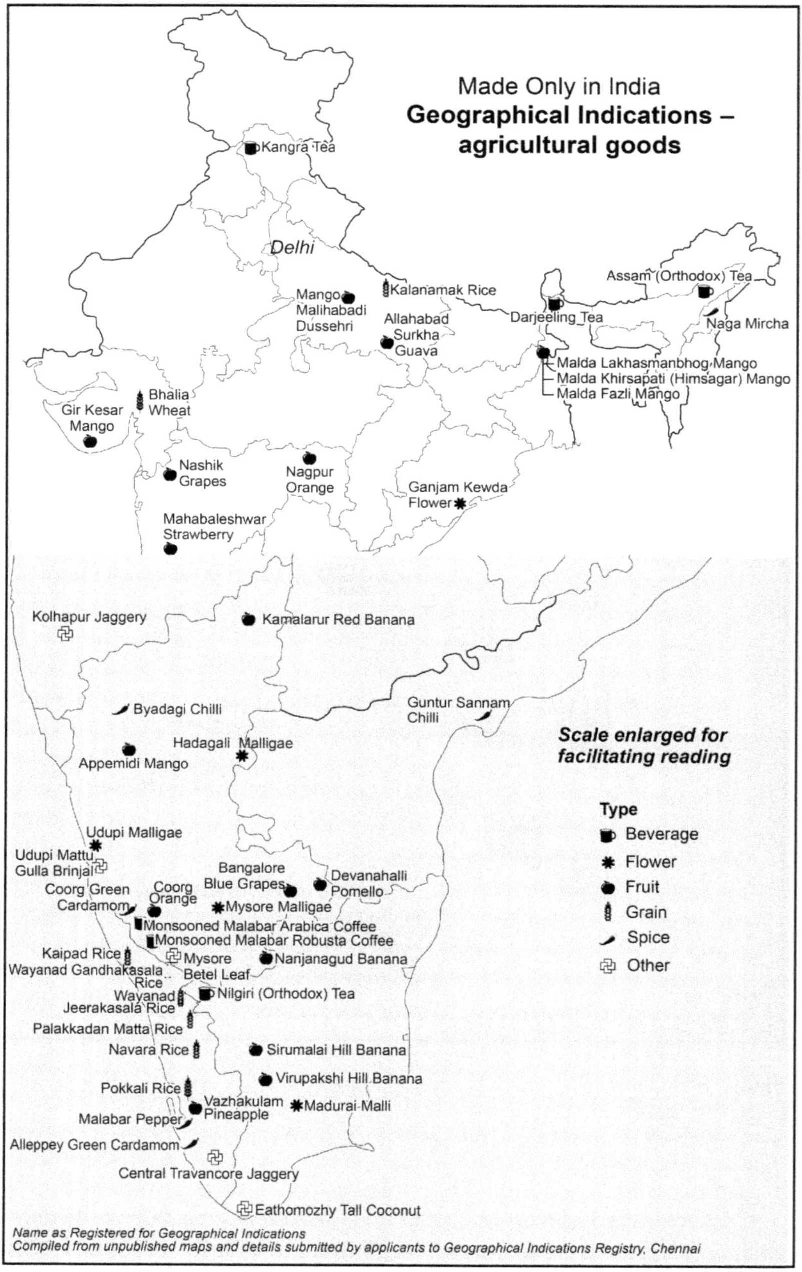

Figure 1.4 India: Geographical Indications – agricultural goods

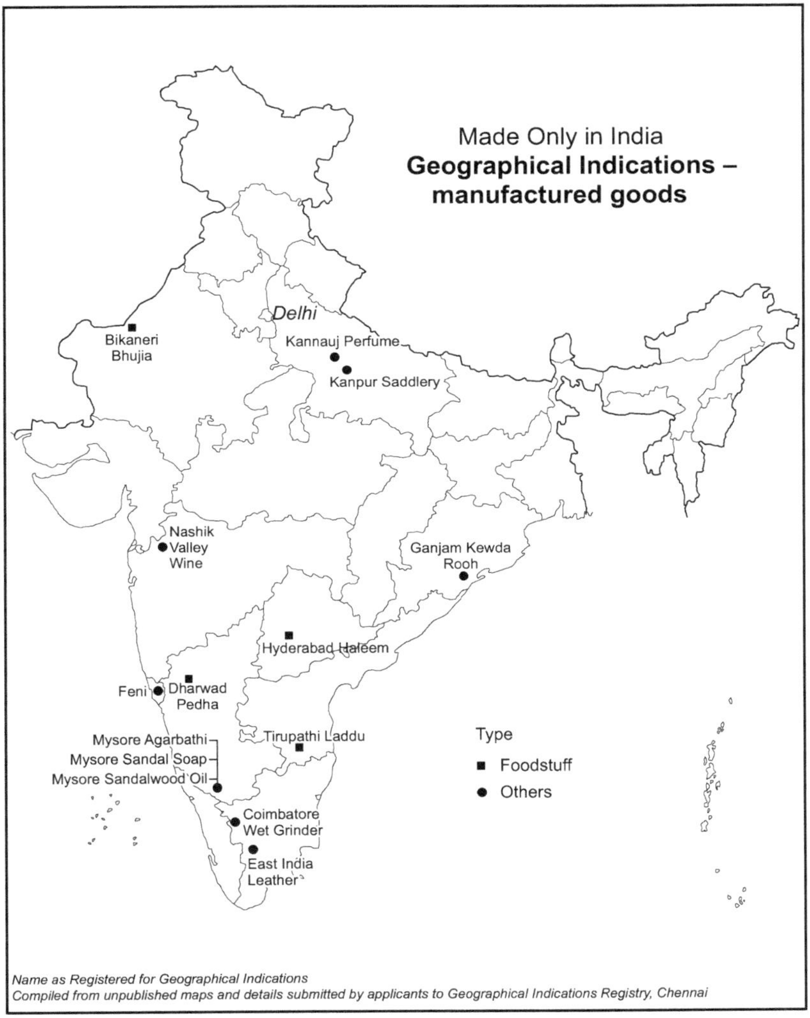

Figure 1.5 India: Geographical Indications – manufactured goods

In contrast to the small numbers in the agriculture, foodstuff and manufactured goods categories, it is handicrafts which have taken a 69 per cent share of the registration. From the total of 199 goods that are registered, a sizeable 137 are handicrafts. In terms of enrolment, 20 states and union territories out of 36 have taken a registration for Geographical Indications, but here again Tamil Nadu, Karnataka, Arunachal Pradesh, Odisha and Kerala take the lead and collectively are responsible for 65 per cent of the total handicrafts that are registered.

Handicrafts are broadly classified into textiles and non-textiles. Both take an almost 50–50 share in the registered goods with Geographical Indications. A medley of non-textile goods comprise the handicrafts. These range from dolls to baskets, jewellery to paintings, puppetry to pottery, furniture to casting of idols. To simplify the variety, the goods were classified according to their natural resource base material that is used for the craft. Among metal, wood, leather, clay, grass and paper, it was metal and wood which constituted 56 per cent of the goods with Geographical Indications. The concentration of handicraft goods again is dense in the Southern states of India (Figure 1.6).

Textiles is the second broad group within handicrafts. It alone is responsible for 80 (44 per cent) out of the 199 goods registered with a Geographical Indications tag at Chennai. It includes sarees, fabrics, furnishings and shawls. Sarees and fabrics and along with them the goods that have been recognised for their dyeing, printing and embroidery specific to an area comprise 60 out of the 80 goods registered in the textile category. Unlike in the case of all other goods almost all the states of India have got a registration for sarees and fabrics for Geographical Indications. Sarees and fabrics is the only category where the states of Southern India are no longer in the lead or the sole contributors. States like Gujarat, Maharashtra and Odisha are also in the forefront (Figure 1.7).

The broad four-fold categorisation of goods into agricultural goods, foodstuffs, manufactured goods and handicrafts by the Registry is done for 'administrative' convenience, but to provide a compressive legal coverage to the goods, the Registry classifies goods into 34 different classes. Each class is an assemblage of similar types of goods. Class 24, for example, contains textiles and textile goods, bed and table covers. Class 30 covers coffee, tea, cocoa, sugar, rice, tapioca, sago, artificial coffee; flour and preparations made from cereals, bread, pastry and confectionary, ices; honey, treacle; yeast, baking powder; salt, mustard; vinegar, sauces, condiments and spices. Of the 34 classes India has registered goods in 23 classes while for 11 goods there has been not a single enrolment (Appendix 2). In the scheme of things, while each of the 144 out of the 199 goods falls into a neat single class, there are some which transgress into more than one class (Table 1.2).

Muga silk of Assam finds mention in 5 classes – 23, 24, 25, 27, 31. It is listed as a raw silk yarn and thread for textile use; it also appears under shawls, dress materials, sarees, and wall hangings and in clothing, footwear,

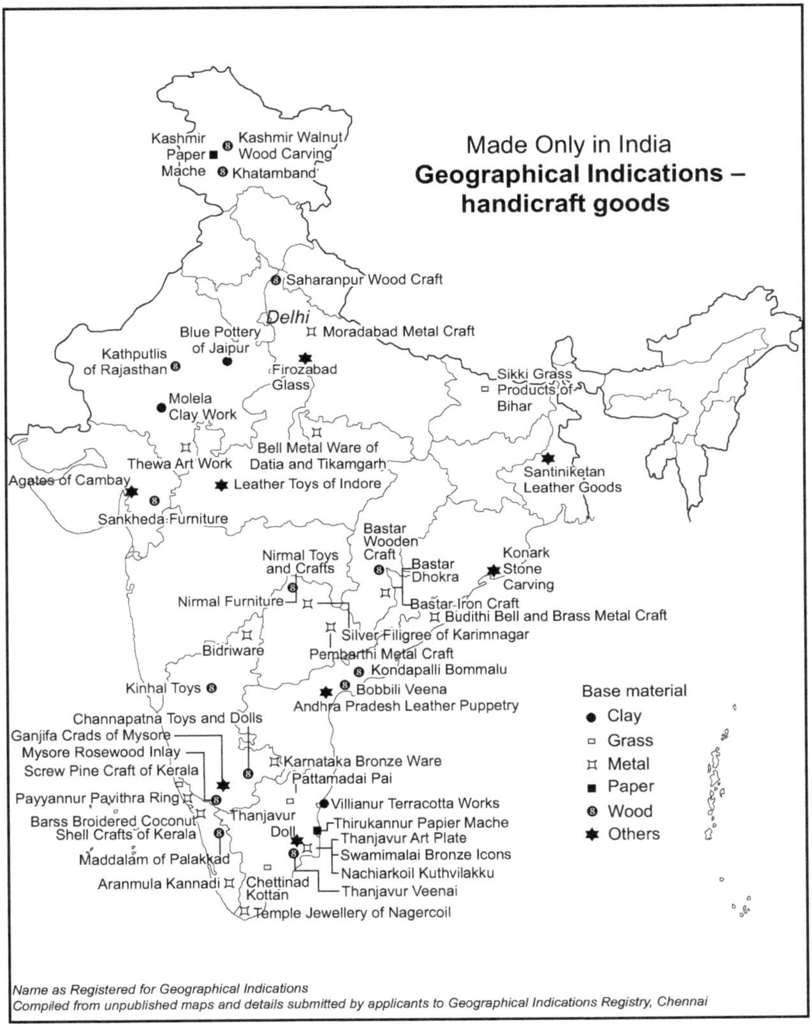

Figure 1.6 India: Geographical Indications – handicraft goods

headgear, ties, motifs, fashion wear, quilts, furnishings, and upholstery. Muga also is a type of cocoon. Similarly, Bidriware fits into two classes. One comprised of 'household or kitchen utensils and containers' and since ash trays are fashioned out of Bidriware the second class is that of 'tobacco, smokers' articles and matches'. The logic to seeking protection within

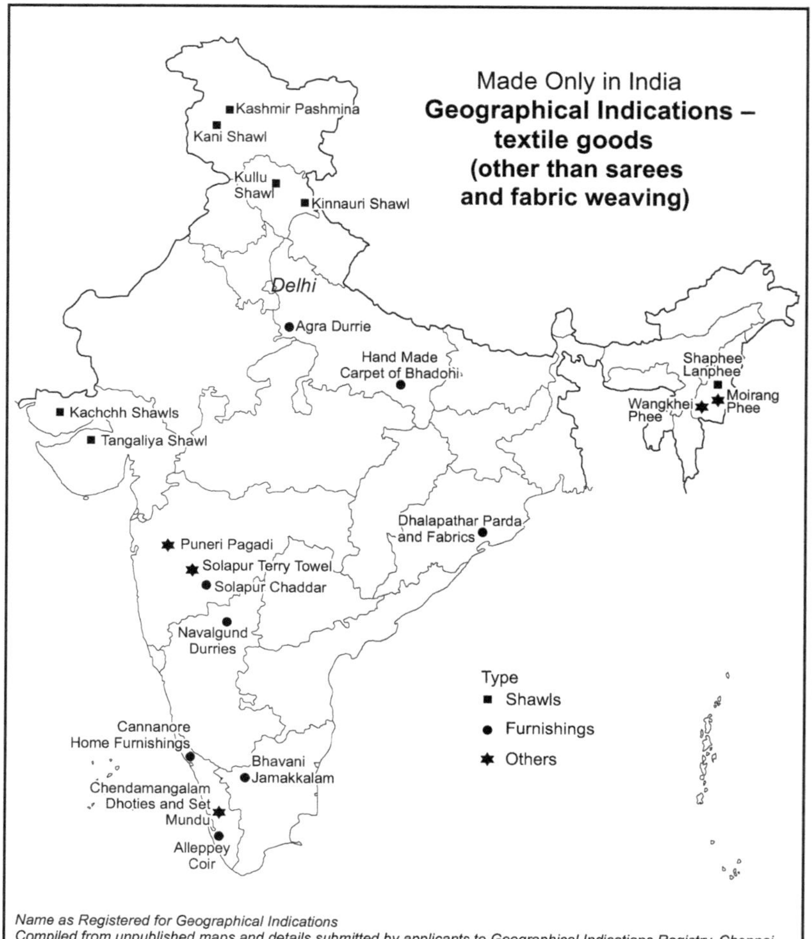

Figure 1.7 India: Geographical Indications – textile goods (other than sarees and fabric weaving)

multiple classes of the Geographical Indications Act is to ensure comprehensive protection against the misuse of the name of the good under the wings of the Geographical Indications Act.

We have so far tried to understand what the Geographical Indications Act is all about in the Indian context, what are the kinds of goods that have been registered under its umbrella which can claim a Made Only in

Table 1.2 Registration of goods with Geographical Indications in single or multiple classes*, 2004–2014**

Registration in different classes (number)	*Number of goods registered*	*Total multiples*	*Examples*
1	144	144	Coorg Orange (Class: 31); Mysore Traditional Paintings (Class: 16); Nirmal Toys and Craft (Class: 28)
2	30	60	Kashmir Papier Mache (Class: 16, 20); Bidriware (Class: 6, 21, 34); Bobbili Veena (Class: 15, 20); Mangalagiri Sarees and Fabrics (Class: 24, 25)
3	17	51	Lucknow Chikan Craft (Class: 24, 25, 26); Tangaliya Shawl (Class: 24, 25, 27); Kashmir Walnut Wood Carving (Class: 8, 20, 27)
4	6	24	Kondapalli Bommalu (Class: 16, 20, 27, 28); Nakshi Kantha (Class: 19, 20, 24, 25); Mysore Rosewood Inlay (Class: 19, 20, 27, 28); Cannanore Home Furnishings (Class: 22, 23, 24, 27); Banaras Brocades and Sarees (Class: 23, 24, 25, 26); Champa Silk Saree and Fabrics (Class: 23, 24, 25, 26)
5	1	5	Muga Silk of Assam (Class: 23, 24, 25, 27, 31)
6	0	0	None
7	1	7	Silver Filigree of Karimnagar (Class: 6, 8, 14, 18, 20, 26, 28)
	199	291	

* For details on class refer Appendix 3

** July 2004–May 2014

Based on *Geographical Indications Journal* No. 1 to 58

India certificate, what is the spatial and temporal pattern of the registration and also the classification of the goods into different class categories. It is time to acknowledge that Geographical Indications are not exclusive to India. Since legal systems differ worldwide they acquire different meanings and are addressed differently across countries.

Nomenclature for Geographical Indications: In legal parlance, the four main types of nomenclatures that are used across the world are Indication of Source, Appellations of Origin, Protected Designation of Origin and Protected Geographical Indications. Although all of them share a common texture of meaning, there are nuances which bring in a shade of critical difference. Indication of Source refers to a sign which shows that a product originates in a specific geographical region, and it includes any name, geographical or a figurative or any combination of these conveying the geographical origin of goods to which it applies. An example of a source indicator is Swiss-made chocolates.

The second expression is Appellation of Origin, which is used for the legally defined and protected Geographical Indications to identify where the 'good' was first 'grown or produced'. Appellations confirm that the characteristic qualities of the product are due to the geographical environment including natural and human. Monoi de Tahiti is the product obtained by macerating Tiare blossoms in refined coconut oil. This oil is extracted from mature coconuts gathered from *Cocos nucifera* trees growing exclusively in the coral soil in the geographic area of French Polynesia. Only 'Tiare' flower buds from the *Gardenia tahitensis* species and of Polynesian origin are acceptable. Another example is that of Parma ham. For ham to receive the name Parma, it must use pigs exclusively reared in the province of Parma, in the Emilia-Romagna region of north-central Italy.

On the basis of how close a product's link is to geography, two other nomenclatures were created by the European Union in its Council Regulation adopted in 1992. These are Protected Designation of Origin and Protected Geographical Indications (Figure 1.8).

A good seeking a Protected Designation of Origin must be able to establish that the quality or the characteristics of the product are essentially or exclusively because of the natural and human factors characterising the geographic area of its origin, covering climate, soil quality and local knowledge of production. A Protected Designation of Origin mandates more stringent conditions, as it necessitates that the entire process, including the production and processing of raw materials, must occur within the defined geographic area from where its unique properties originate. Some goods with Protected Designation of Origin are Capocollo di Calabria, a type of meat from Italy, Azeite de Moura, a type of olive oil from Portugal,

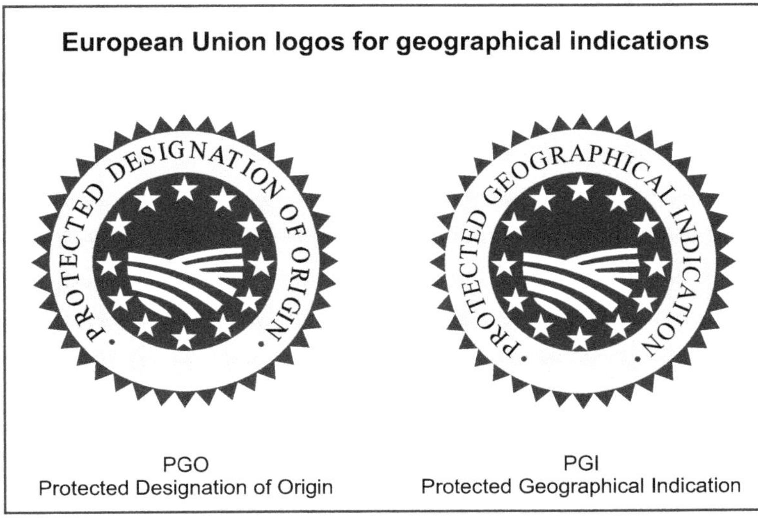

Figure 1.8 Logos of the European Union for protection to goods with place origin
Source: www.ec.europa.eu/agriculture/quality/schemes/index_en.htm

Imokilly Regato, hard cheese made with cow's milk from Ireland and Jersey Royal potatoes from the United Kingdom. In contrast, stipulations for a Protected Geographical Indications are a bit more relaxed on this count as its requirements are that to acquire unique properties only a portion of the production process is to occur within the specific geographical area. Examples of Protected Geographical Indications are Abbacchio Romano, a type of meat from Italy, Batata de Trás-os-Montes, potato from Portugal, Clare Island Salmon from Ireland and Scotch Whisky from the United Kingdom.

While these existing nomenclatures are valid within legal parlance, I have added a different expression. I choose to address goods which carry 'geography' within their ambit as 'place goods'. I believe that unlike indications, designations or appellations the phrase 'place goods' imparts a direct allegiance, meaningful association and strong affinity with a place. This phrase is not only short, easy and simple, but is also holistically expressive of the authentic bond that a good shares with a place.

Phrases such as 'goods rooted in place', or 'place in goods', 'place-based good' and 'goods carrying place' could have been considered, but somehow like a diamond in a stud, the phrase 'place goods' strongly captured the connection. The usage of the word 'place' preceding the word 'goods' and not vice versa, that is the word 'good' before 'place' is a measured decision, because it is the place that makes possible the good and not the other way round, though the role of the good in characterising place cannot be overlooked. Therefore, within this context, place goods are the ones whose distinctive attributes, qualities and reputations accrue because of their place of origin.

Difference between goods from a place and place goods: All goods are grown and/or manufactured in one or the other place. So in a colloquial sense all goods have a 'place' of origin or an 'address' of manufacture. But there is a difference between goods produced and manufactured at a place and those which are place goods. I will try to explain the difference between a good from a place and a place good with four different analogies.

The first analogy selected is the concept of cosmopolitans. A cosmopolitan belongs to the entire world and is not limited to just one part. Goods which are produced or manufactured without recourse to place are akin to cosmopolitans. These goods can be manufactured and produced across the globe. Importantly such goods do not and cannot carry or imbibe a reflection of the place they come from. Take the example of agricultural goods; it is not to say that tea can grow where wheat grows, or bananas can be cultivated in areas of strawberry cultivation but while adhering to the agro-climatic belts, what one is reiterating is that tea can and grows over large acreage, but there are some varieties of tea which carry a distinctive flavour because of their place of origin. The latter is then a place good in comparison to the former. So goods that are not bound to a specific place for their characteristics and features are cosmopolitan. They are free from local place attachments. The phrase 'free of attachment' can similarly be extended to describe 'goods which are unattached and do not carry the origin of place within their fold'.

Another illustration is that of *qalam*. In Arabic, the word *qalam* originally meant the calligrapher's reed pen. Calligraphers are esteemed in Islamic circles because their pen writes the sacred words of the Quran, the holy book of Islam. When painters were associated with writers to produce a wealth of illustrated manuscripts and elaborate albums in Persia and India, the word *qalam* came to be associated with the painters' brush instead of the calligraphers' pen. The point of reference and comparison with place goods is that when local drawing techniques and colour schemes began to influence the style of painting there emerged different *qalams*. Thus there was the Karachi qalam, Patna qalam and the Deccan qalam. Each differs in subtle ways because of their evolution within a specific nature of the region.

The *qalams* are in certain respect analogous to the regional dialects of a language, with just the subtle differences that enable those who know that language to distinguish one from the other. So a third example to comprehend a place good could be picked from the realm of language. Hindi or Hindustani is the native language of most people living in Delhi, Uttar Pradesh, Uttarakhand, Chhattisgarh, Himachal Pradesh, Chandigarh, Bihar, Jharkhand, Madhya Pradesh, Haryana, and Rajasthan. Hindi is spoken with different dialects across regions; for example, Khari Boli is spoken in Delhi and the surrounding areas of Uttar Pradesh and Haryana, Haryanvi is spoken in Haryana, Braj Bhasha in western Uttar Pradesh especially around Mathura and Vrindavan, Awadhi in eastern Uttar Pradesh, Pahari in Uttarakhand (except Dogri and Nepali), Bundeli in Bundelkhand region of Madhya Pradesh, Chhattisgarhi in Chhattisgarh and Rajasthani in Rajasthan.

This is akin to the concept of *gharanas* in classical Indian music where the identity of a *gharana* is in the style of singing which is linked to a place. The *gharana* system was greatly influenced by the gradual fall of the Mughal Empire, which forced musicians to move from Delhi to princely states such as Gwalior, Lucknow, Hyderabad, Patiala, Rampur and others where different *gharanas* developed. There can be singers who are not trained in a particular style and *gharana* and they can be equally, if not more, accomplished but they cannot claim a lineage and origin to a place. There are varied types and subtypes within a *gharana*. Thumri is a style of singing that enacts emotions mainly of romantic love. 'Thumri styles of rendering emanate from Purab (eastern Uttar Pradesh) or Punjab. The Purab style has sub-divisions encompassing Benares, Lucknow and Gaya, each of these cities has a gharana. There are subtle differences. The Benares gharana is said to be a classicized version of the songs of camel drivers. The Gaya school includes the region's folk songs while Lucknow gharanas use of Urdu poetry infuses a delicacy and refinement not found elsewhere' (Surya, n.d.).

In a vein similar to *qalam*, dialect and *gharanas* are place goods. The latter carry their *ghar* or cosmopolitans 'home', as the cause and the source of their distinctiveness, quality and identity. Place goods 'carry' place. It is the conveying and carrying of place by goods which inspired legal experts to set the label Geographical Indications and use this in the lexicon of marketing and trade. Indication is anything that serves to indicate or point out, as a sign or token. It is worth noting that the Act spells out not a singular indication but specifies that it is indication's'. The plural is important for the good carries indications or pointers which can be more than one. What and where do the indications point to? The title of the Act is Geographical Indications. And they point to one fact: that Geography Matters.

Place matters and this gives birth to the Made Only in India concept. This authenticates the title of this book.

In this research, the word 'good' refers to anything which can be produced, manufactured and traded. It can also refer to a produce or product. 'Place' is the crucible and refers to the 'ambience, milieu, environment, locale, and habitat' which creates, nurtures, supports and produces the good. Place is the base which defines the characteristics of the good. Since place has a transactional and relational association to a particular good, therefore, the latter generally refers to a specific geographical name. Documenting the bond with place, this book traces the experience of a place as expressed through the good. Moreover it tries to explore place within a good as a way of valuing place. The intention is not so much to debate the role of Geographical Indications in supermarkets and international trade but more to recognise and accord a rightful place to 'place'.

To grasp the role of place in the making of goods it would be best to step out from the dry chambers of a legal court, the Registry of Chennai and the web of terms and terminology associated with Geographical Indications and step into India and connect with the bonding between good and place. To gain insight into this bond the next chapter picks, describes and analyses a vast variety of place goods of India. It is strewn with many examples. The inclusion and reference to a large number of goods provides five main advantages: First, it familiarises one with the large variety of goods which share a bond with place. Second, the range of goods that are referred to exposes the variety of places which exemplify these goods. The third reason for drawing upon an assortment of goods is that it helped exemplify the different processes that create place goods. By presenting a diversity of goods, the fourth advantage which emerged is the role of different elements of place in the making of goods. The fifth merit of working with a large mixture of goods is that it revealed the various forms of bonds shared by goods with place. Given the fact that bonding is explored through a diversity of goods, the next chapter reads more like a patchwork quilt. The pattern and design needs to be holistically grasped to comprehend how the Geographical Indications come to define the Made Only in India.

2

BONDING

Place goods

Tea tasters confirm that the breezy taste and breathtaking aroma of the Darjeeling is an immensely refreshing experience. Its rich and full-bodied aroma with a hint of muscatel has raised it to the status of champagne of teas. Then there is the Basmati, a variety of rice whose very name translates into the 'fragrant one' (Hindi *'bāsmatī*, fragrant, from bās, meaning 'perfume', from Sanskrit *vāsaḥ*.) While Darjeeling is a star at many a taste awards, the sweet flavour of the slender kernels of Basmati gives it a front rank among over 5,000 varieties of rice grown in the world. When looking for a hot and the fiery taste, nothing can beat the Naga Jolokia. *The Guinness Book of World Records 2007* ranked the Naga Jolokia as the world's hottest chilli pepper, 401.5 times hotter than the Tabasco sauce! Naga Jolokia or Naga Mircha (Registered in 2008) is also known as 'ghost chilli pepper' or 'bhut jolokia'. The name 'Bhut Jolokia' comes from Bhutia, the tribe who originally used to gather and bring the chilli down to the valleys of Assam for trade.

Just as the Darjeeling, the Basmati and the Jolokia delight the 10,000 taste buds of the human mouth, so the 100 receptors of touch on our fingertips are judge to the unmatchable light and soft warmth of the Pashmina (Registered in 2008). The expertise of the Kashmiri artisans is in weaving a shawl so fine that it works its way through a finger ring. While Pashmina lends warmth in winter, for the scorching summer of India there are the likes of Chanderi sarees (Registered in 2004). Even when wrapped in a six-metre drape of the saree, the lightweight and sheer of Chanderi fabric keeps one ever so cool.

A human nose can differentiate from 4,000 to 10,000 smells, and a scent which appeals is the sweet fragrance of a jasmine flower! A prime member of the jasmine family is the Mysore Malligae (Registered in 2007). During the day, the timid buds of the Malligae closely hold on to their fragrance, but as the sunlight fades, they share their scent with every whiff of air which comes their way. So pure is the floral scent of the Malligae that it is believed it relieves melancholy and can lead one into a reverie. Its captivating qualities have attracted leading brands like Chanel, Calvin Klein and Lancôme to build a range of perfumes which use jasmine as their base.

Each of the above is a different good. There is the beverage, cereal and spice as also the fabric and scent. Rooted through the sense of touch, taste and smell, each of the goods transports one to a specific and distinctive place. The aromatic tea takes one to the slopes of the Himalayas in the east. The light shawl reminds us of the dexterity with which the artisans in a cold land weave the embroidery onto a shawl that is so fine that it is called Cashmere. What imparts sheer to Chanderi is the skill of separating the glue out of the raw yarn, a technique perfected by the weavers of Chanderi, a town situated close to the Betwa river of the Malwa Plateau in Madhya Pradesh. Basmati sprouts in the semi-arid plains of the Ganges, and the Naga Jolokia grows in the verdant rainforests of Nagaland in the north-east of India. The place which flashes recognition for jasmine is Pangla, a village close to the dry cool plateau of Mysore.

Each of these goods differs in look, in use and the area to which it belongs. They hail from the Himalayas, the Gangetic plain, the Central heartland and the Deccan Plateau. What unites these goods, as a flock, is that all have the repute of belonging to and carrying a sense of place in them.

To find out if goods cite an allegiance to place three small surveys were conducted in Delhi, one at a chain store of sarees and two at a tea café. The results were revealing. Nalli is a chain store of sarees and fabrics in India. Its distinction traces itself to the pioneers of Nalli, who presented King George V a Kancheepuram saree (Registered in 2005) during his visit to India in 1911. The collection displayed at their showroom carries labels like Chanderi, Coimbatore, Kancheepuram, Mysore, Nangavalli, Odisha, Pochampally and Valkakalam. Each of these is the name of a fabric and also of a place.

Aap ki Pasand or literally 'for your choice' is a tea boutique in India. In this trade since 1955, they are reputed collectors, mixers and packers of tea with outlets in leading national and international airports also. Their business profile mentions: Darjeeling, Assam, Kangra and Nilgiri tea. A visit to the *Cha* Bar, a corner that serves tea within one of Delhi's popular bookshops (called Oxford), widened the choice. The menu on offer includes cardamom, Tiger Hill, Sikkim and Cachar tea. Hailing from a specific place, each promises a different taste. Grown in the foothills of the snow-clad Dhauladhar Range of Himachal Pradesh, Kangra is muddy and strong, Sikkim carries a fruity aroma, while the roasted strong flavour comes from Assam (Table 2.1). In many a good, geography literally 'moves' into the good and flags place in myriad and tangible ways.

Table 2.1 Characteristics of tea from different places in India

Tea	*Characteristics*	*Place of Production, State*
Assam	Strong flavour, golden colour, high briskness	Brahmaputra valley, Assam
Darjeeling	Mild flavour, aromatic with high briskness	Duars (essentially hill slopes), West Bengal
Kangra	Straight flavour, muddy-coloured, strong tea	Kangra valley, Himachal Pradesh
Nilgiri	Deep-coloured tea with mint flavour	Nilgiri hills, Tamil Nadu and Kerala
Sikkim	Sweet tea with fruity aroma	Sikkim hills, Sikkim

Based on survey at *Aap Ki Pasand*, Delhi

Place 'in' goods: The affluent vocabulary of the natural environment of Kashmir inspired the rich colour palette in the *Sozani* embroidery. The majestic Chinar and Cypress trees, flowers such as the tulips, lotus and roses, with trailing creepers and leaves, are common in the design of the embroidery. The Roman emperor Nero (AD 37–68.) on receiving a Pashmina is believed to have proclaimed '. . . A fabulous shawl of many colours . . . stole from the skies, the hills, the lakes and the fields some of wondrous colours of the topmost parts of India . . .' (Mathur, 2004).

Recapitulating the role of the landscape, Aldred Baker, Professor of Textile Industries, University of Leeds, wrote, 'The surroundings of Srinagar itself are so beautiful that it would be surprising if some sort of artistic craftsmanship was not developed there. The immediate vicinity of the river is Venice-like . . . the beauties of Dal Lake, the picturesque village life encountered all along the Vale . . . create an atmosphere so entirely different from anything else, even in India itself, that it is not surprising that the people of this part of Kashmir have evolved . . . along the line of artistic craftsmanship' (Baker, 1932).

Around AD 1870, it took 30 weavers 3 years to complete the *naqsha* or map shawl of Srinagar, which measures 82 by 78 inches, and today hangs proudly in the Shri Pratap Singh Museum, Srinagar. It 'maps' the river Jhelum as it meanders through the city complete with the Dal Lake, floating gardens and boats. Reconfirming the role of place is the rich repertoire of motifs and patterns in other Kashmiri handicrafts be it in papier mache (Registered in 2011), wood carvings or silver engravings.

Resonating with the natural environment are the Todas, residents of the Nilgiri hills. They are enthusiastic honey gatherers, and so stylised bees and honeycombs form an important part of the patterns of Toda embroidery. The style of headdress, shape of the eye, style of the beard and moustache of the Rajasthan puppets or *Kathputlis* pick their cues from the people around them (Registered in 2008).

'All paintings belong to their "own setting" but this is especially true of Indian painting . . .' (Randhawa and Galbriath, 1968). Mewar region, comprising the districts of Bhilwara, Chittorgarh, and Udaipur, is a plateau of open undulating country and is partly covered with hills, rocks and dense jungles. To the west and slightly to the north of Udaipur is Bundi, and in the middle of Rajasthan between Jaipur and Ajmer lies Kishangarh, a princely state during the British rule. All these were erstwhile schools of painting from the seventeenth to the nineteenth centuries. The paintings from each of these places take a cue from the geography of their area. In the Mewar paintings the frequently appearing orange trees have been inspired by the flowering Gulmohar. What features so often in the Bundi paintings is the thick jungle along the banks of the river Chambal, which flows through Bundi. Kishan Singh, a Jodhpur prince, founded the state of Kishangarh in 1609. He built the fortress near the famous Gundalao Lake. In the nineteenth century when the Kishangarh School of Paintings was established, the area was infested with wild beasts. Thus 'the grand hunt' was a favourite theme in the paintings.

Warli paintings are a vivid expression of the daily and social life of the tribal people of the Malhar Koli and Warli tribes found mainly in Maharashtra. After close observation of nature the women used basic geometry like triangles, circle and lines to express their emotions and ideas. Phulkari embroidery of Punjab drew inspiration from village life. The embroidery carried themes like man ploughing, lying on charpoy (bed), smoking hookah, churning milk, grinding the chakki (hand mill). This is also so true for Bihar, where women stitch their experience, their sorrows and their realities into the Sujini embroidery (Registered in 2005–2007) and transform the mundane technique of sewing together pieces of old cloth into a testimony of their lives. 'We hear, we feel with our minds and our fingers translate it into embroidery' (Correspondent, 1999).

The motifs and symbols, the honeybee or the features of the human face, the flowering trees, colours in the painting are not just 'copies or imitations' of the environment but testimony to the acute observation, deep absorption and intensity of experience of a place which is translated into the goods. The details of goods provided here represent only the facet of 'appearance or look which takes and matches with the features of place'; this is the tip of the iceberg and only the surficial obvious connect to the environment. The taking from place runs deeper into the feel, colour, aroma, taste, among a host of other connects. To truly appreciate the distinctiveness of a good it is valuable to know the characteristics of the place of its origin. The sense of observation, identity and belonging to a place is not just about thinking geographically but also about harnessing geography. The bit about 'using' geography needs to be understood as a way to align with the holistic feel of place. It is after all an alignment with the sensitive rhythms of nature, its limitations and potentials within a place which allows the fragrance and taste in plants to be captured and sustained. This is the case not only with the cultivation of rice or tea or jasmine but also with the designs and detail in handicraft and any other type of good which has a Geographical Indications tag. Place goods are ones where the bond of the good with the place is seamless and deep. Moreover the foundation of the concept of Geographical Indications is rooted in the concept that because places are different goods may look seemingly similar but definitely are not the same.

Place goods – similar is not same: Similar after all is not the 'same' as Same. Same refers to being identical, or of the same kind, or bearing the same manner. But the meaning of the word 'similar' carries the element of resemblance or likeness. Take the case of similar triangles and congruent triangles. Similar triangles have the same shape, but the size may be different, while congruent triangles have the same shape, angular arrangement and size. Therefore there is a difference between *same* and *similar*. Here are a few examples to illustrate the point: Muga (Registered in 2007) is a silkworm raised in Assam, and Eri is another kind of silkworm raised here. But in colour, texture and weave, there is little common between the two (Figure 2.1).

The feeding habits of the Eri and Muga silk worms differ. Muga on the one hand feeds on the forest tree called Saur, while the Eri silkworm, on the other hand, feeds on the castor plant known as Eri. Eri does not produce a continuous filament while Muga spins a filament which can be reeled into a thread. These differences lead to nonsimilarity between the Eri cloth, which is coarse and rough, and the Muga cloth, which is finer and more lustrous.

Coorg oranges (Registered in 2005) are greenish yellow in colour and have a tight skin and a tangy taste, unlike the Nagpur oranges or mandarins (Registered in 2013), which have a smooth and glossy skin. The taste also differs. Nagpur mandarin is sweeter with a saffron colour juice (Figure 2.2).

Coorg green cardamom (Registered in 2008) has a cool camphoric fragrance and harsh taste, while Alleppey green cardamom (Registered in 2008) has a sweet floral aroma with a pleasant mellow almost fruity flavour (Figure 2.3).

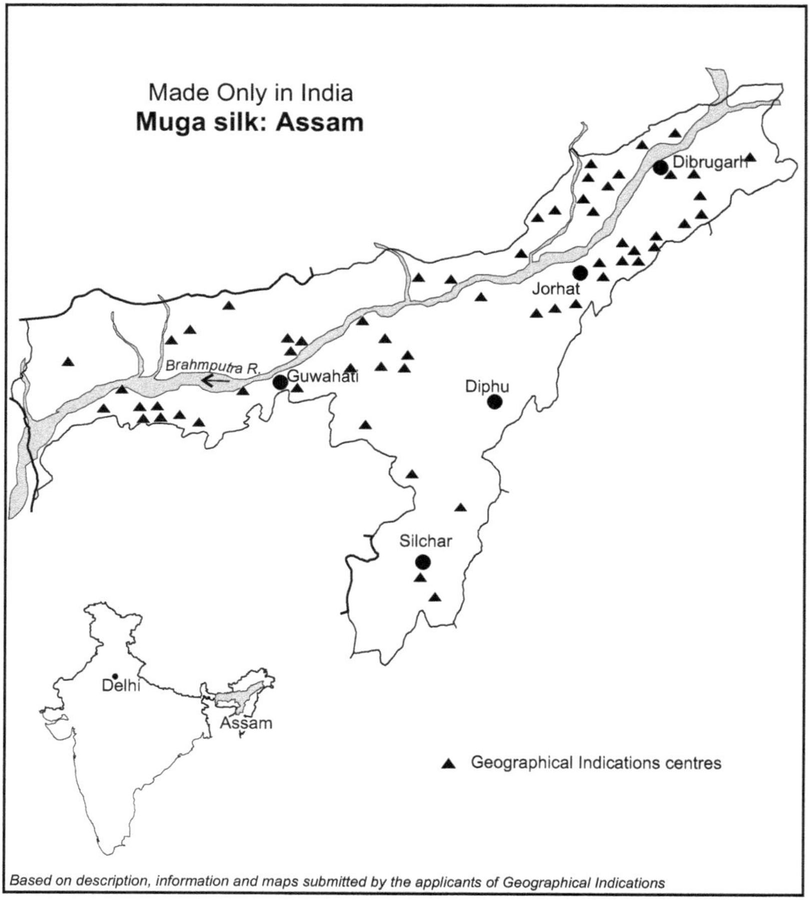

Figure 2.1 Muga silk: Assam

The orthodox variety of Assam tea has bright yellow liquor, smooth strength, and an astringent quality which gives it briskness. Nilgiri, on the other hand, has leaves that are hard, thick and leathery. It has a typical malty flavour and bright colour liquor, known for its antioxidant qualities. The prime centres of woodcraft in India are Srinagar in Kashmir, Mysore in Karnataka and Saharanpur in Uttar Pradesh. Srinagar is known for its geometric designs and motifs, Mysore rosewood inlay (Registered in 2005), for depiction of human and animal motifs, while Saharanpur uses the floral design as a link to integrate geometric and animal motifs.

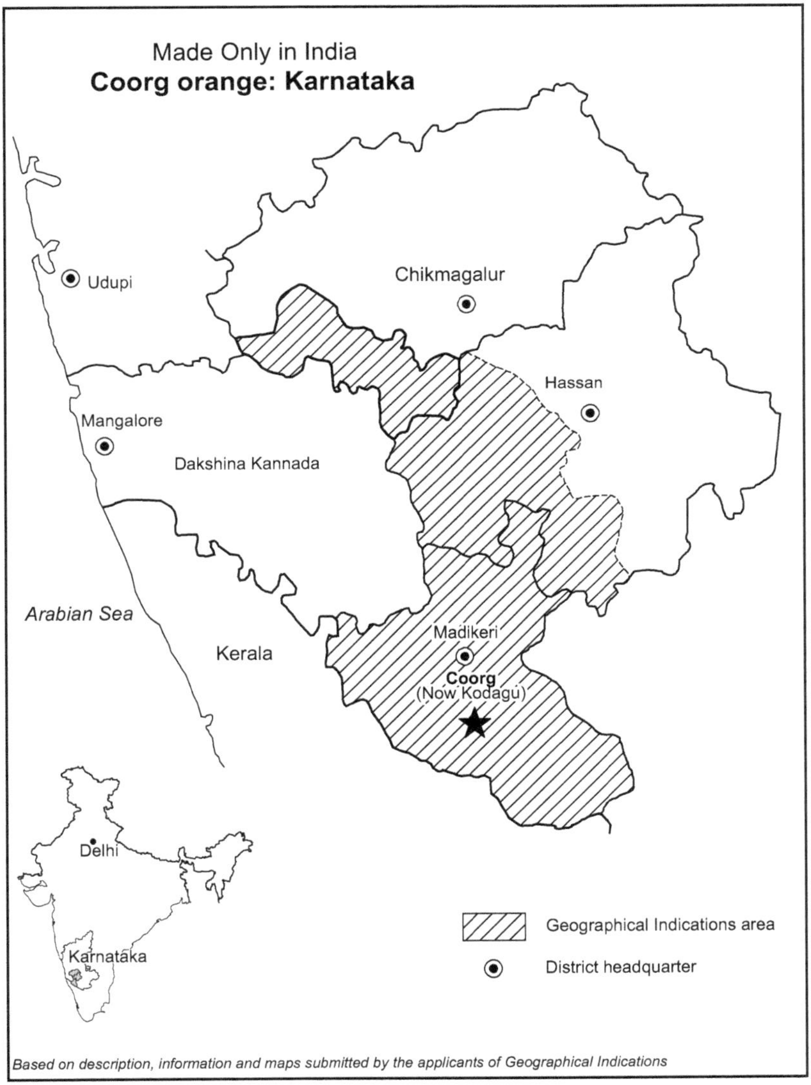

Figure 2.2 Coorg orange: Karnataka

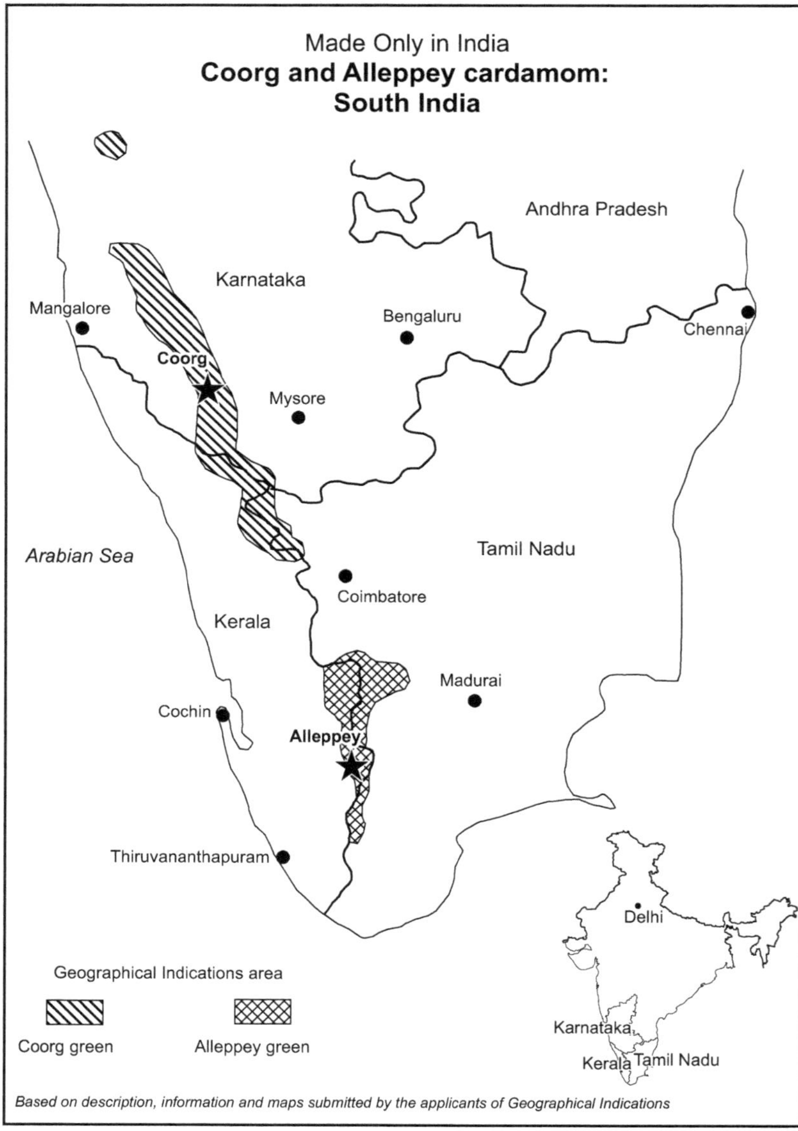

Figure 2.3 Coorg and Alleppey cardamom: South India

Filigree is common to both Karimnagar (Registered in 2007) in Andhra Pradesh and Cuttack in Odisha, yet the filigree of Karimnagar uses round wires which are intertwined to make them more tensile while in Cuttack, only one square wire is used to make this craft. Datia and Tikamgarh are both located in north Madhya Pradesh and are places famous for goods crafted through the lost wax process. The bell metalware of Datia (Registered in 2008) shows *jali* work, while Tikamgarh products are solid and plain, more figurative with only bits and pieces of ornamentation (Ghosh, 1985). The bell and brass craft of Budithi, Srikakulam, is more heavy and engraved (Figure 2.4).

The people of Kashmir and Himachal are neighbours; one occupies the Kashmir Valley and the other the Kullu Valley. They share a mountainous terrain and temperate climatic features, yet the culture is such that the shawls woven in Kashmir are intricate, detailed and of featherweight, while the ones from Kullu carry bold geometric motifs and are heavier to hold (Registered in 2005).

To a novice, miniature paintings may all look the same, yet observes the veteran Coomaraswamy (1909) that there is a 'subtle' yet sure difference between the outlines of Mughal and Rajasthan miniature paintings: while the former is precise and patient, the latter is interrupted but always swift and facile. Tanjore and Mysore paintings are both highly ornamented forms of iconic paintings designed to express and inspire devotion (Tanjore painting, Registered in 2007, and Mysore traditional paintings, Registered in 2005). The ancient pilgrimage site of Tirupati in Andhra Pradesh has been suggested as the possible place of origin of these related art forms. In both the Tanjore and Mysore traditions the paint is water-based, in both the subject matter extends beyond secular portraiture to include sacred subjects. But there is a difference: Unlike the Tanjore paintings, Mysore paintings are more subtle, the relief is not so high and the jewels worn by the subjects are represented by dots of white paint rather than embedded glass (Rossi, 1998). Therefore goods may appear similar, may also be produced in close proximity, may originate in seemingly similar habitats, yet because of the differences between places the goods are not the same. Because of the difference, one can experience many places through a single good.

Experiencing many places through one good: It is through the sensitisation of one place good that one can get to know a network of places. Thus, to know Darjeeling tea one has to also to be familiar with Assam or Kangra tea, to know Rajasthani miniature paintings is also to be acquainted with Pahari paintings or Mughal miniatures, and so forth. A place can have multiple identities, be that of a monument, historical event, type of culture or even a distinctive landscape feature like a waterfall, lake or limestone

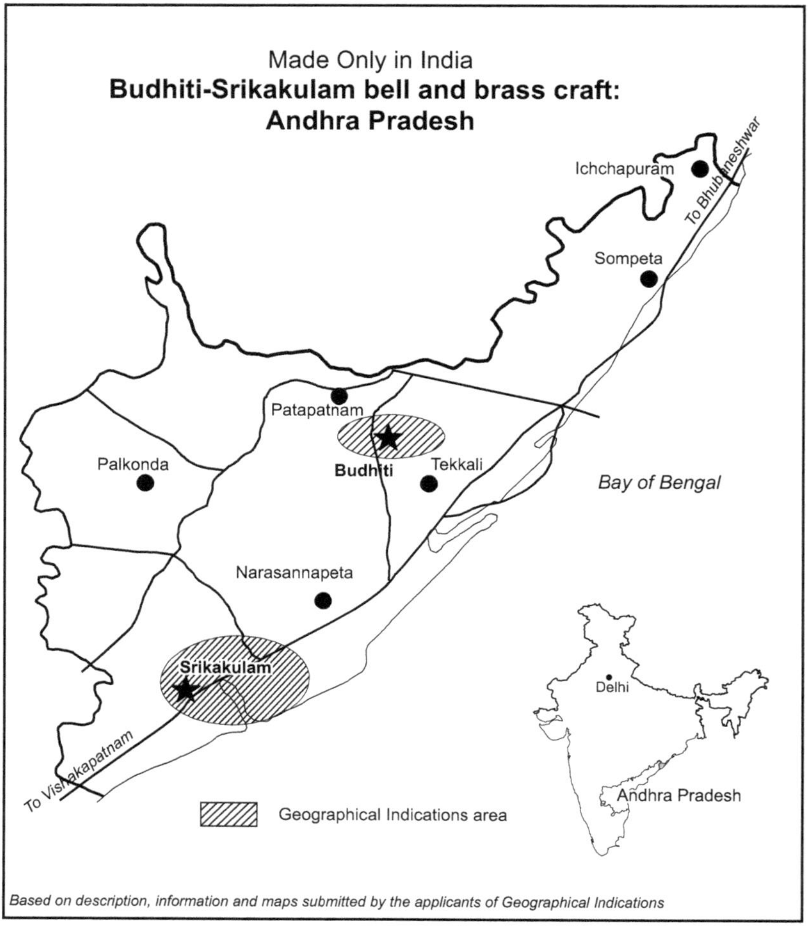

Figure 2.4 Budhiti-Srikakulam bell and brass craft: Andhra Pradesh

caves. One identity is that of a place good. Thus Agra has not only the Taj Mahal but also the Agra durrie (Registered in 2012); Hyderabad has not only the famous Charminar but also the rice biryani and Hyderabad haleem (Registered in 2010). Mysore is famous not only for the Mysore Palace, but also for agarbathi, Mysore Sandalwood Oil, Mysore Sandal Soap, Mysore traditional paintings, Mysore rosewood inlay (all Registered in 2005), Mysore betel leaf (Registered in 2006), Mysore jasmine (Registered in 2007). Lucknow is famous not only for its nawabs, who ruled during the medieval period, and their culture of politeness and gourmet food, but also for handicraft: Lucknow Chikan Craft (Registered in 2008) and Lucknow Zardozi (Registered in 2012).

The merit of good as an identity is that unlike a historical monument or a landscape feature which is fixed to a site, a place good takes the virtue of place far and wide and yet keeps its bond with place alive. There are many routes that activate the bond of connection. It is not necessary to even visit a place. A binding memory of a place can be built by watching a film, leafing through an article in the *National Geographic* magazine, surfing a travel blog or listening to an enthusiastic traveller who is narrating a description of a place at length. The ability to be transferred from good to place depends both on the skill of description and our own imaginative and empathetic inclination. The taste, fragrance or appearance of a good could lead to a recollection of place.

It is possible to sip the Monsooned Coffee and be transported to the bluish misty mountain range of Coorg where it grows under the shade trees. Savouring the Basmati, one can visualise the lush paddy growing in embanked fields with meandering water channels. The wizened craftsman hunched over a piece of shawl draped over his legs and his arms working the delicate embroidery is the image that is conjured when draping a Pashmina. The palm leaf basket reminds one of the women of the Chettiar community of Tamil Nadu holding the wrap with their feet while weaving the weft of the Chettinad Kottans.

The words, pictures and captions in an advertisement are used as vehicles to evoke a connection between the product, the specific geographic location of its region and the people concerned. The intention is to ignite the imagination and connection to place. The cartons that package Tilda rice proclaim, 'Tilda basmati rice has travelled from the foothills of the Himalayas. It has been carefully tended and harvested by hand in an area whose unique soil and climatic characteristics give the rice its exquisite and delicate flavour'.

The 'good' is the vehicle, a link of sorts to this image of far away and the place of origin of the good. The authenticity of the good and our moorings and understanding of the geography of places determine the degree to which one connects a good to a place. Goods are an identity in which place is solidified.

To confirm the authenticity of this connect is the Act for Geographical Indications. It provides a legal certification which assures that you are getting what you identify with, strongly and honestly, because the quality and reputation of the goods is a hallmark of their geographical origin. Geographical Indications are thus signifiers that Darjeeling originated from a particular region, locality or garden; the santra (orange) identified with its rustic and pockmarked exterior, and sweet and juicy pulp, is from Nagpur; Assam tea marked by its strong, spicy and aromatic flavour is from Assam; A tradition of hand embroidery called Phulkari that translates as flower work is from Punjab; Chanderi saree is woven on the looms of a town in Malwa; coffee is grown in the blue mountains of Coorg; the Molela idols are moulded from the red clay found in Molela village and Pashmina is spun, woven and embroidered in the Vale of Kashmir. A fact universally shared by each of the goods is their claim to a relationship with place.

Place is more than a construct of natural, human and divine elements

A place is a nest of different elements of the land, water, soil, sunshine, wind, plants and animals and is a lot more inextricably woven by ways, means and modes of people. Undoing the weave is a delicate process. All the applicants at the Registry of Chennai, aspiring to join the league of Geographical Indications, maintain that the characteristics of a place determine the attributes of the good. It is on the basis of a bond between place and good that each of the applicants makes a claim for registration. The applicants put forth many explanations, arguments and evidences about the role of place in 'creating' the Geographical Indications. When the explanations forwarded by the 199 registered goods for the 'role of place' in the formation of goods were culled and collated, they fell into three broad realms: natural, human and divine environment. While the two segments of natural and human have well-established acceptance within geographical literature, it is worthy to note that aspects of the Divine are often subsumed within the human facets and characteristics. However, I have preferred to treat it separately for the producers of goods themselves see the Divine as special and esoteric. The divine environment is difficult to define, and yet it carries messages of saints, and mystic revelations and so conveys a sense of environment other than that of the physical and human world.

Though these three types of environments may have been distinguished, yet in most cases the distinctive quality a good draws from a place includes features and strands of all the three environments. In the following section, an attempt is made to present some features of place to which are ascribed the distinctive characteristics of place goods. In spite of the fact that not a single factor provides satisfactory explanation for a good acquiring distinctive qualities, yet there are three reasons for elaborating the 'elements of place'. First, the isolation of these variables brings forward the justifications by the applicants for registration of the goods and thus are worth knowing. Second, what emerges is the specificity of elements which are picked within the context of place to explain the creation of place good, somewhere it is wind, at others sunshine and in another it is skills or even the blessing of the Divine. Third, the 'elements' are able to provide a more disaggregated glimpse of the bond between good and place.

Physical environment: The claim was that Coorg oranges are rich and tangy because the undulating Western Ghats that surround Coorg, soar between 600 and 1,200 metres above the mean sea level to create a special environment. The hillocks that surround Kamalapur, a village situated about 120 kilometres north of the city of Hyderabad, create an ideal environ for the cream-coloured banana to acquire a skin which is red when it ripens. It was booked in the Geographical Indications Registry in 2009.

The specific taste of the Darjeeling tea is attributed to the gentle slopes at elevations between 600 and 2,000 metres, which provide natural drainage. Famous for its Sun Temple, Konark has acquired repute for its carving because its craftsmen have access to the serpentine stone found in the vicinity of Odisha, Assam and Manipur (Registered in 2008). Climate too is an element of claim for the distinctiveness of place goods.

It is the dry climate of the Mysore Plateau which allows Mysore Malligae (Registered in 2007) to acquire its *stayty*. The broad and extensive valley of Wayanad is set high in the Western Ghats. The higher elevation and forest cover creates a cool climate which nestles the scent in the Wayanad rice (Registered in 2010) (Figure 2.5).

The humid easterly wind blowing through the Palakkad gap determines the robust earthy flavour for which the pink grains of Palakkadan Matta rice (Registered in 2007) are famous. The weather regime is claimed to determine the quality of the grapes in Nashik. Internationally, the grape regions lie between 30° and 40° North and South of the equator. Nashik is the only region in India which grows superior quality grapes south of the Tropic of Cancer. In this place the fruit begins to set just when temperature dips in November, and this allows the formation of acid in the grapes. The high level of acid in the crisp berries gives the Nashik grapes (Registered in 2010) and the wine (Registered in 2010) a rank amongst the best in the world.

A good which announces a strong connect with climate is the Monsooned Malabar Robusta Coffee and Monsooned Malabar Arabica Coffee, both of which were registered in 2008. The process of production of these two coffees is aligned with the rhythm of climate. With the onset of the south-west monsoon in early June, unwashed Arabica Cherry or Robusta Cherry is spread evenly in 4- to 6-inch-thick layers in trays and kept in godowns to allow the free flow of air. The coffee beans are raked from time to time for four to five days. After this they are packed in gunny bags,

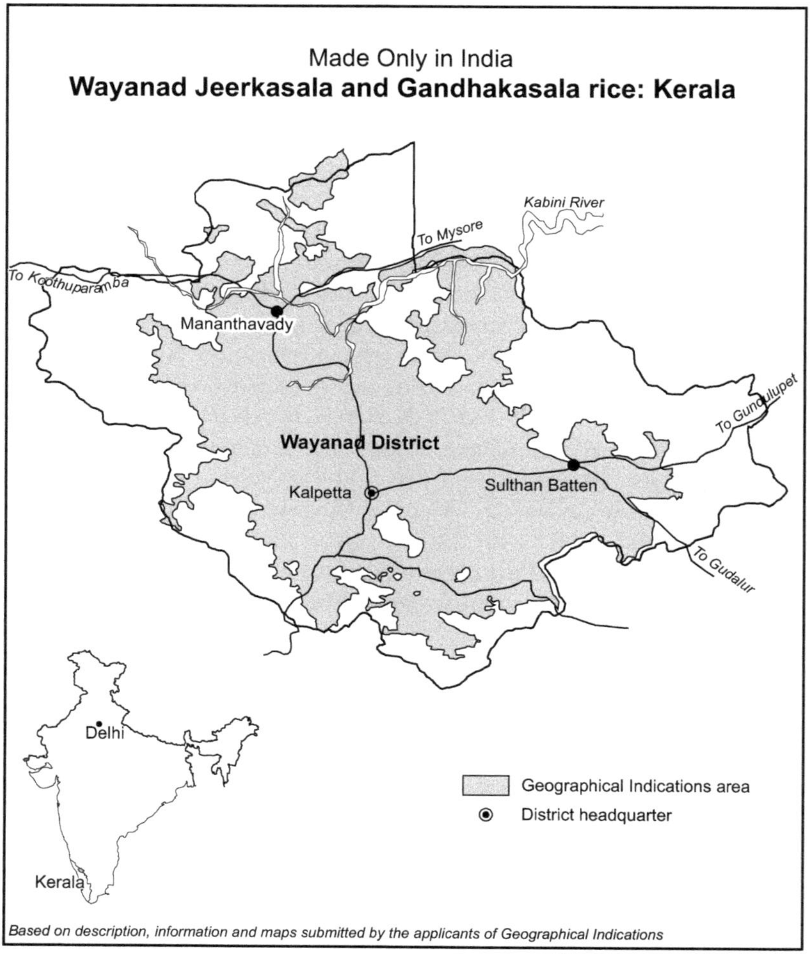

Figure 2.5 Wayanad Jeerakasala and Gandhakasala rice: Kerala

stacked in rows in such a way that there is sufficient space in between to allow the monsoon air to circulate freely around each bag. Because of the exposure of the beans for about a month and a half to air loaded with humidity, the coffee changes from a green to a golden colour. At this stage it is considered to be fully monsooned. The coffee beans are then hand garbled, and after a mild fumigation to prevent attack by weevils, the coffee is ready for the market (Figure 2.6).

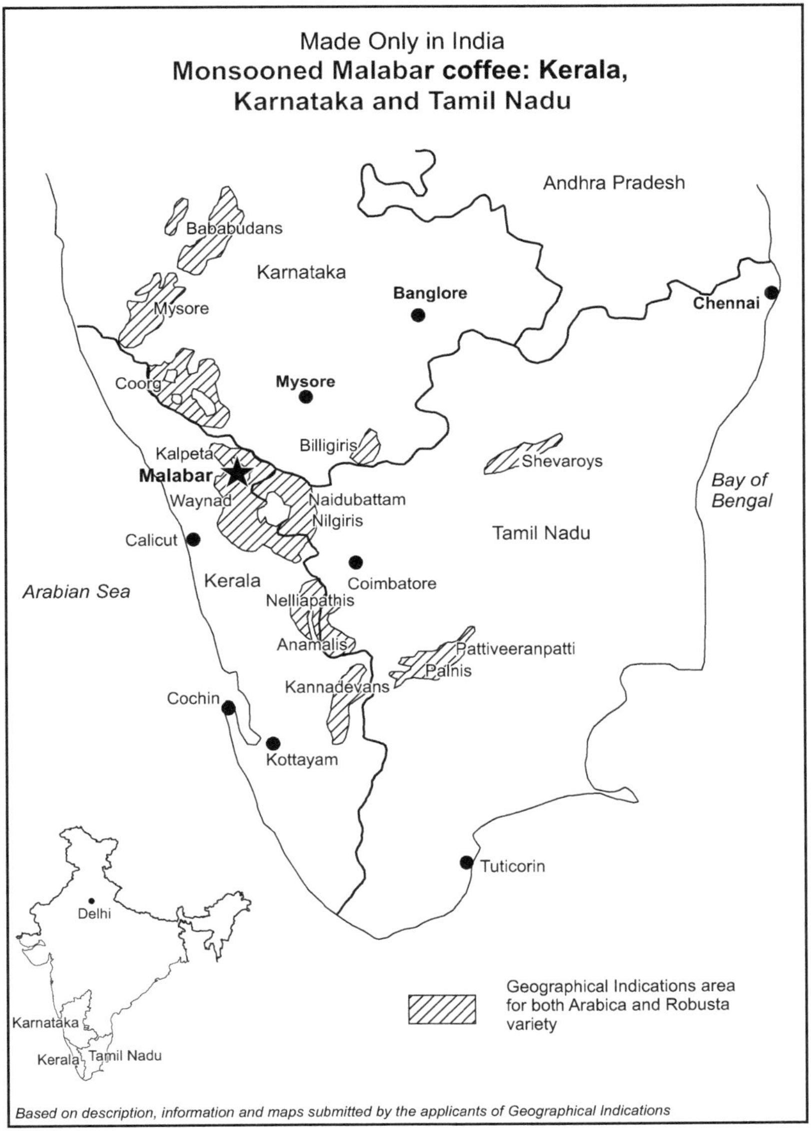

Figure 2.6 Monsooned Malabar coffee: Kerala, Karnataka and Tamil Nadu

If it were not for the monsoons, the coffee could not have acquired the reminisces of age in its flavour and taste. Such is the allegiance that 'rain in place' is carried in names of the coffee: *Monsooned* Malabar Robusta Coffee and *Monsooned* Malabar Arabica Coffee.

India supports a variety of soil regimes, and some factor this into explaining the Geographical Indications in the goods. The black or *regur* soils around Palakkad have 60 to 80 per cent clay and silt content which allows them to hold a larger volume of water. In addition the constant run-off from the surrounding rocks builds a high content of lime in the soil. These microconditions are ideal for Palakkadan Matta rice. Likewise Nanjanagud Rasabale (Registered in 2006), a variety of banana, grows only in the Nanjanagud area of Mysore. The black clay saline soils of Nanjanagud are reasons why the fruit tastes like a mix of a banana and apple (Figure 2.7).

The mango from Malda in West Bengal has a distinct flavour because it is free from the taste of turpentine found so often in the mangoes of an inferior species. 'Their flavor is due to the soil, which is lacking in saline properties'. (Three varieties of Malda mangoes were registered in 2008.) The sandy loam in Mysore and surrounding areas has a comparatively high soil pH, and because it is more alkaline, it builds the high-volatile oil and fragrance of the Mysore Malligae (jasmine).

The over 90 per cent sugar content in the Central Travancore jaggery (Registered in 2010) is attributed to the soil along the banks of the river Pampa, Kerala. The river Pampa runs so close to the coast that its banks are generally swampy and liable to flooding during both the south-west and the north-east monsoons. This flooding brings fresh silt which ensures the sweetness of the cane and ultimately of the jaggery.

Along the streams of the hilly region known as Malenadu in Karnataka grows wild Appemidi which literally means unripened mango. The frequently flooded streams keep the latex of *midi* (which in Kannada means tender, sweet, sour and soft) ideal for pickle. Appemidi's distinct flavour was registered in 2009.

Pokkali is a traditional salt-tolerant rice cultivation technique confined to parts of Central Kerala and Kaipad in Northern Kerala (Pokkali, Registered in 2008, and Kaipad Rice, Registered in 2013). In the low-lying marsh, the soil is clayey in texture and thus impervious and gives scope to build a rich organic content which makes it highly fertile. While the sea and backwater tides make these soils saline, the high and low tides occurring twice a day removes excess salts, regulates the fertility and sustains the productivity of the Pokkali and Kaipad soils.

Soil is explained as giving India some of its distinctive handicrafts, be it pottery, metalwares or textiles. The alluvium along the banks of River

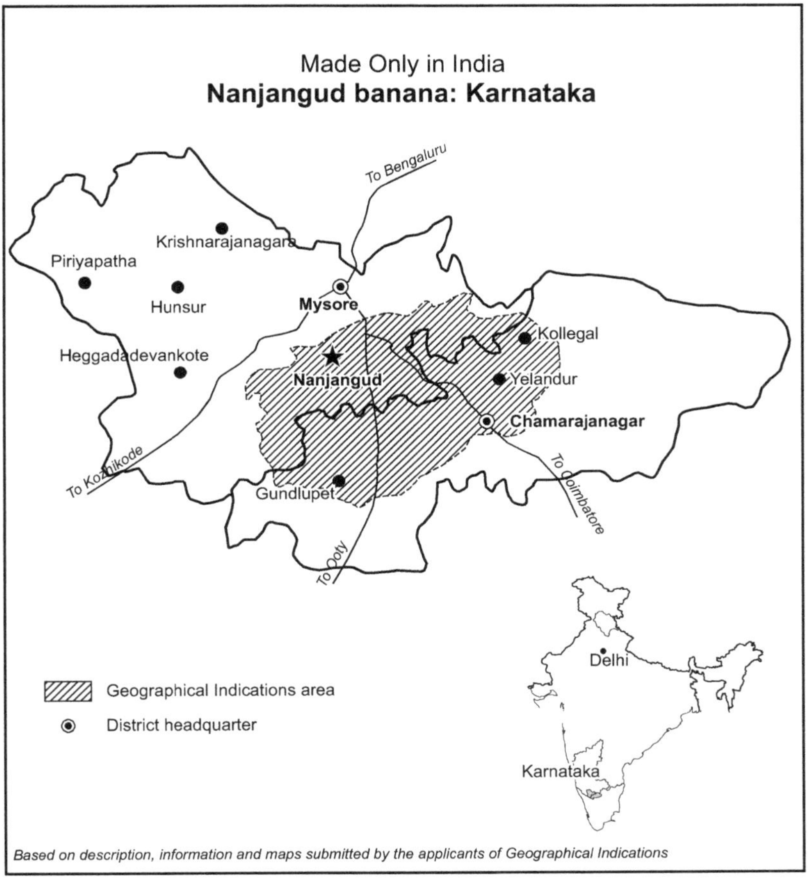

Figure 2.7 Nanjanagud banana: Karnataka

Thamirabarani, a tributary of the Kaveri, near Swamimalai, does not crack upon drying. This clay is soft and therefore malleable, a characteristic which imparts perfection to the *panch loha* idols called Swamimalai Bronze icons of Tamil Nadu, which gained entry into the Registry in 2008.

Molela, a village 300 kilometres to the south-west of Jaipur in Rajasthan, is located close to the Banas river, a tributary of River Chambal. There are around 50 potter families whose special terracotta plaques took a call with the Registry in 2008. Here potters have mutually divided specific parts along the banks of the Banas for collection of best quality clay. Brass and metalware of Nachiarkoil (Registered in 2012) acquire their sheen and shine, claim the owners, because they are able to access and use a variety of sands found in close vicinity (Figure 2.8). The sand in the river bed adjacent to Nachiarkoil is ideal for moulding and casting; the *karuman* sand which is light red in colour is for making moulds, while the *savuttu* sand of light grey colour, found in the tanks to the south and east of the village, is used in moulding wax (Census of India, 1961).

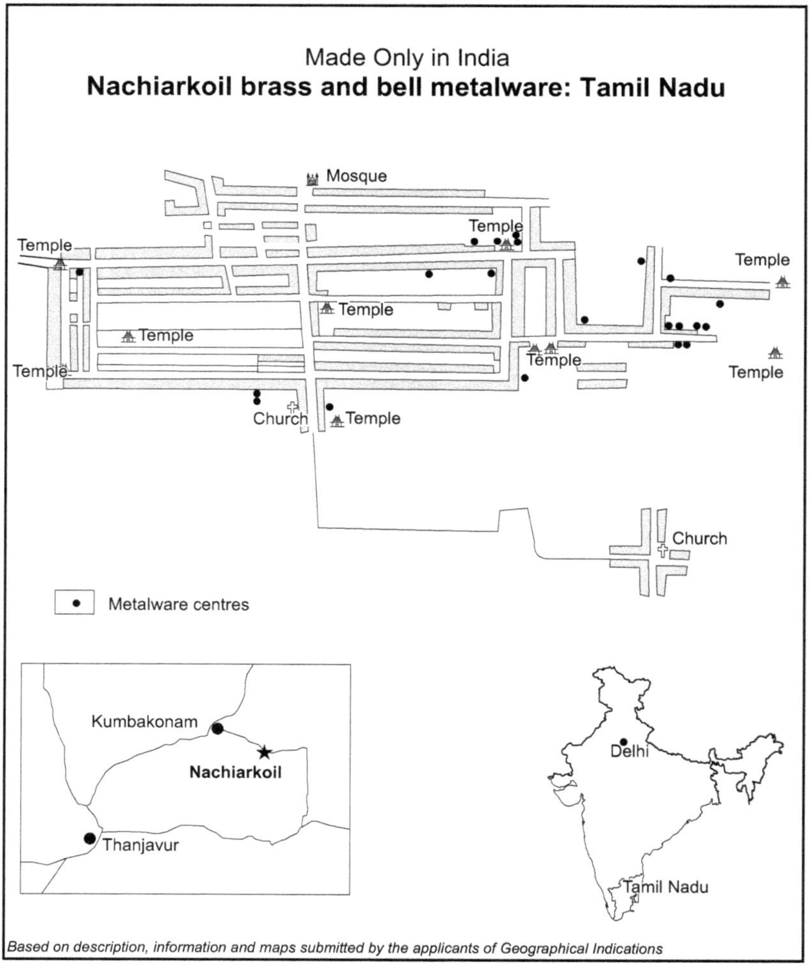

Figure 2.8 Nachiarkoil brass and bell metalware: Tamil Nadu

For Bidri, the craft of metalware, the claim is that the soil buried for centuries in the Bidar Fort built in 1427 has not been exposed to rain or sunlight for years. This soil carries chemicals which impart the unique lustre of black to the articles fashioned in Bidriware (Registered in 2005). Similar to soil, some applicants connect to the role of water in their place as a factor for the Geographical Indications in their produce.

Some of India's most famous place-based textiles owe allegiance to the river close by. It is the waters of the Palar that flow from Nandi Hills, about 60 kilometres from Bangalore, which 'brings out' the lustre in the dyed silks at Kancheepuram. The uniqueness of the Kasaragod sarees of Kerala is attributed to the high content of dissolved organic matters and minerals in its wells. This pure 'natural soft water' results in the superior dyeing. Originating in the Western Ghats, the Siruvani and Bhavani rivers traverse through the textile centre of Kovai Kora and ensure the quality dyeing of this blend of cotton and silk yarn (Figure 2.9).

The waters of River Brahmani, which flows along the industrial town of Raurkela, Odisha, is used for degumming and is said to impart lustre to the Gopalpur tussar.

Bagh, a village in Dhar district of Madhya Pradesh, is situated on the bank of River Baghini. The chemical composition of this river imparts luminosity to the vegetable dyes and enhances the red and black tones in the Bagh prints, making them different from the prints of other places in Madhya Pradesh and Rajasthan. Bagh attained a geographical tag in 2008. The fine feel and texture of the yarn used in the production of the Bhavani jamakkalam (Registered in 2005) is attributed to the vegetable dyes which come to 'life' because of the waters of Bhavani River which collects its nutrients as it travels through Kerala's Silent Valley and flows into western Tamil Nadu, before merging with the Kaveri.

The Machilipatnam Kalamkari which entered the Geographical Indications Registry in 2008 can be identified by the all-over floral designs hand drawn or block printed with natural vegetable dyes. The 'richness' in the water of the river Krishna is said to account for the brilliance of the colours. River Kapila, a tributary of the Kaveri, is recognised for its contribution to the exceptional sheen and regal look of the Mysore Silk (Registered in 2005). 'The water of the river is what gives the silk its correct denier, and is also very good for drawing out the silk thread from the cocoons,' says a senior official of the Karnataka Silk Corporation of India. River water is thus recognised to play a role in the life, colour and distinctiveness of the many textiles that India can boast of. In the scheme of what in a place gives the good its Geographical Indications, the applicants remember the plants and the animals.

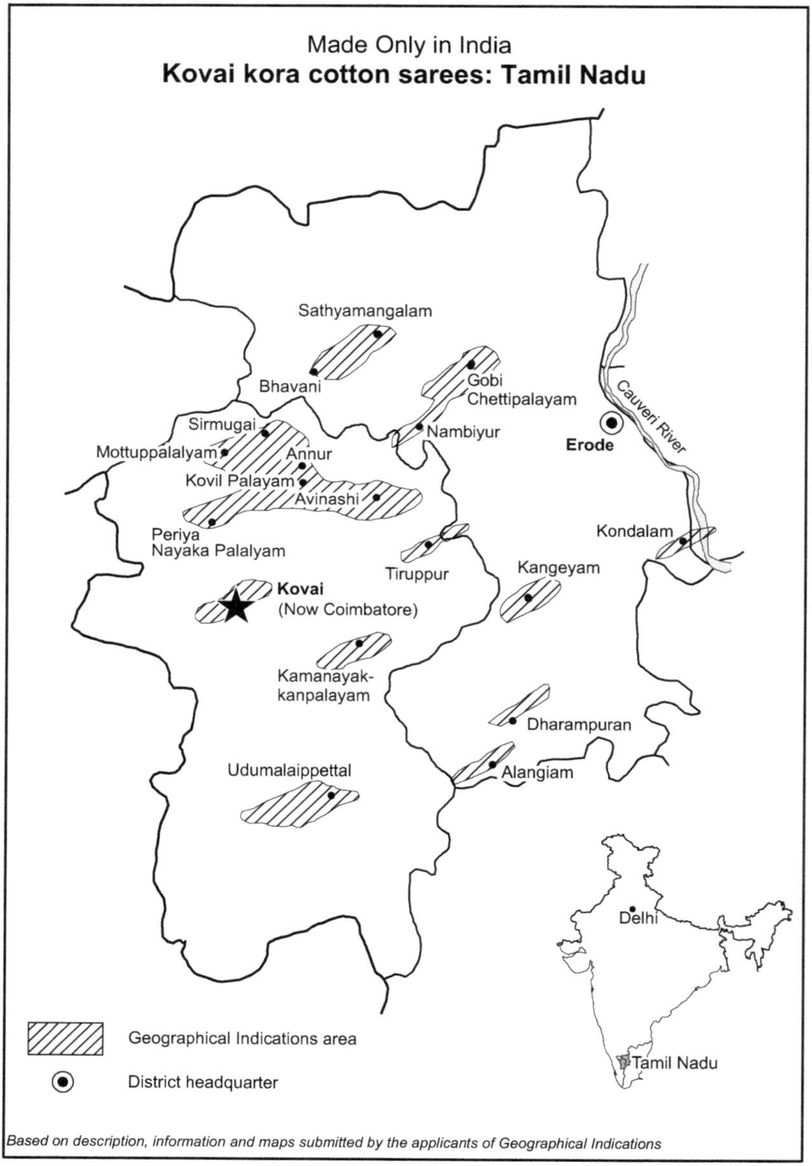

Figure 2.9 Kovai kora cotton sarees: Tamil Nadu

The people of India make extensive use of the different bio-geographical realms of the country. A special type of vegetation in the vicinity of a habitat can be a reason for the speciality a place acquires. Kondapalli Bommalu (Registered in 2007) are rural toys crafted from the tree called Tella Poniki which grows in the forests nearby. Poniki wood is light and can easily be fashioned into toys of different kinds. Also called White Sander these trees clothe the hills of Kondapalli, a village 16 kilometres to the west of Vijayawada in Andhra Pradesh. It was again Poniki which allowed Nirmal, another town 200 kilometres to the north of Hyderabad, to gain entry into the logs of the place goods of India in 2008. While the bodies of the toys are crafted from the Poniki, to add colour and decoration to the toys natural colours are extracted from the moduga tree, the bark of the pomegranate tree and the indigo, all of which grow alongside the Poniki forest. With these resources are crafted such exceptional toys and models depicting village life, that Kondapalli and Nirmal found an entry into the Registry in 2007 and 2008, respectively (Figure 2.10).

Sandalwood grows in the dry deciduous belt which runs in proximity of Mysore city. The woody aroma of the golden yellow oil from the sandalwood trees is responsible for the Mysore Sandalwood Oil as also for the blended fragrance of the biodegradable Mysore Sandalwood Soap. The availability of the sandal tree was critical in the registry of both Mysore Sandalwood Oil and Mysore Sandalwood Soap in 2005.

Screw pine is a mangrove associate which grows gregariously in the coastal belt of Thazhava in Kollam district of Kerala. Sharing a strong resemblance to palm, the leaves of screw pine are long, thin and shaped like swords, 2 to 3 feet in length, which can be twined, woven and braided to make fascinating products like mats, boxes, bags and hats. The women of the Kurava community of Kerala registered the screw pine craft with the Geographical Indications Registry in 2008.

The botanical diversity of the tropical forests around Mysore has nurtured Intarsia or the art of laying woods of different colours upon a darker surface. The work is called Mysore rosewood inlay because rosewood, locally called *kari mar*, burns with a smoky flame which smells like rose water. The Mysore Inlay uses rosewood for the background, Jack, which is yellow, Nelli, rose red, Devadaru, light brown, Ebony, jet black, and Silver oak, pink. For stark contrasts the dark brown of sandalwood, blue-grey of the tamarind, dark red of the Patagan and ash cream wood of the Guava are used. Craftsmen have used the different colours of wood to build contrast while filling the designs. This has helped Mysore build a substantial industry with a market for export (*Census of India*, 1961). The bouquet of colours makes it evident how the diversity of the vegetation influences the scope for the goods to acquire place features.

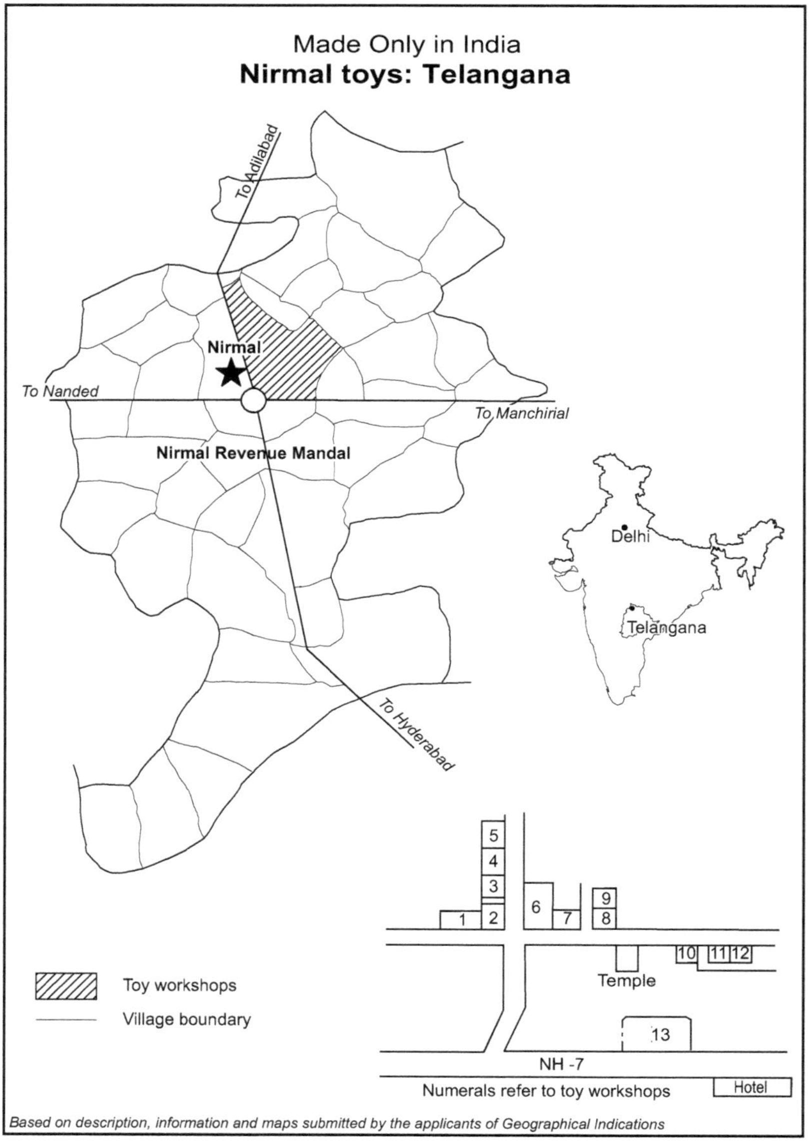

Figure 2.10 Nirmal toys: Telangana

Canopy is the critical factor for some goods. Naga Jolokia thrives within the bamboo and banana plantations. It is said that the longer the cultivation of bamboo or banana, the hotter the chillies. With its distinct pungency and fruity aroma, Naga Jolokia gained entry in the Registry in 2008. Cardamom too is a shade-loving crop. It is grown extensively in the hilly regions of South India especially in Kerala, as an undercrop in forest lands. Protected under the two-tier shade of the evergreen trees, Monsooned Malabar Arabica Coffee gets its desired requirement of a cool equable temperature throughout the year. Similarly, the Virupakshi hill banana is raised as a shade tree for young coffee in the Palani Hills in Dindigul district, Tamil Nadu (Figure 2.11).

Therefore, be it the Darjeeling tea, the Monsooned Coffee, Travancore jaggery or Mysore Sandalwood Oil, all these plants are rooted in soil while their leaves, fruit and flowers breathe the air around. Their fragrance, juice, sweetness, tenderness or pungency inevitably reflects these conditions. Physical attributes of the territory are also translated into the cause for the lustre of *zari* or gold thread, texture of fabrics, brightness of prints, fineness of idol and fragrance in soap. There is an undeniable physical geography which underpins to give the Geographical Indications to the craft, food or a fruit of India. Humans interweave these physical properties of a place into the objects or goods they create.

Human environment: It is the people of India who have directed their intention and attention in creating goods which come to mirror a place and create the made only of their country. The largest share of goods registered under the wings of India's Geographical Indications Act belongs to the sector of handicraft and confirms this factor. 'Indian handicrafts are not products of individual artists, enveloped in a shell of inward-looking egocentricity, searching for a method of intense self expression. It is an art of the people, which means that skills are not in the hands of the individuals but have seeped, spread and taken root through time, through generations, through communities, through music and dance, rituals and prayers' (Jaitly, 1990: 9). In this quotation the phrase 'taken root through time' can be appreciated as a reference to a sense of rootedness in place. Rootedness in place stems from a deep sense of affective attachment to a place. A pride of Andhra Pradesh is the Kondapalli toys. The presence of *Poniki* trees in the forests may have been a factor, but it is the nimble-fingered artisans called Aryakrishatriayas who draw inspiration from folk tales, deities or characters from the epics and have the expertise to carve toys from the light wood.

The craft of carving the Thanjavur Veenai belongs to the Viswakarma sect who maintain an unbroken heredity in making quality veenas. Wood from the fully grown Jackwood tree that is free from nodes is usually chosen

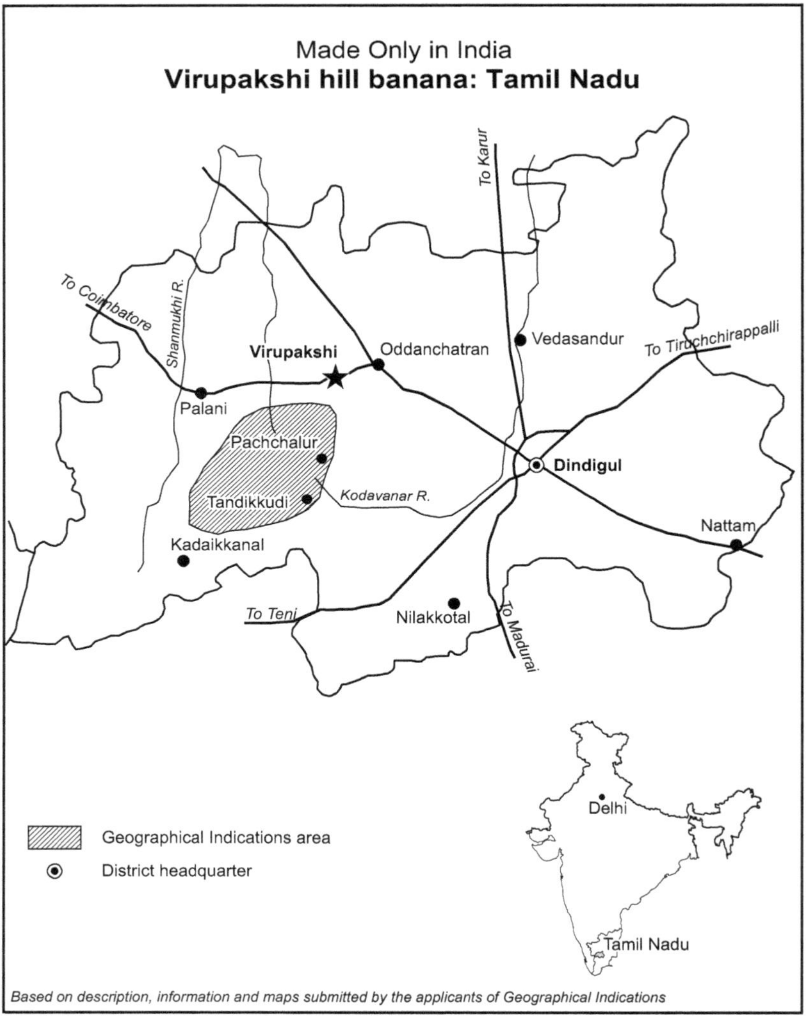

Figure 2.11 Virupakshi hill banana: Tamil Nadu

for making the veena. The body of the Thanjavur Veenai is painted and engraved with delicate woodwork to give it an elegant beauty (Registered in 2012).

The community of Gudigars are craftsman engaged in sandalwood carving in Karnataka. They claim almost with some vanity that their craft requires an artistic ingenuity which is not a common quality of all men and is definitely a 'natural gift' (*Census of India*, 1961). The fame of the Sanganeri hand-block printing in Rajasthan rests on the shoulder of Chhipas and Kharadiyes (Registered in 2009). While the Chhipas have expertise in mixing the desired ingredients for preparing the colour, the Kharadiyes or the turners use the dried woods of plants such as shisham, mango and teak to make the design for the block printing. The method of boiling the tussar cocoons, for four to six hours in an earthen pot, at boiling temperature with sodium carbonate (washerman's soda), is held responsible for the softness of the Bhagalpur silk (Registered 2012). The semi-moist cocoons are then reeled by women on their thighs. The thigh-reeling system is a traditional technique where women in their rural habitats sit on the floor and draw five to six filaments on their thigh from a cocoon. This process, locally called *kheba*, increases the strength of the fabric three to four times and keeps the yarn most lustrous.

The quality and fineness of the green leaf in Assam tea is achieved by the expert pluckers whose families have lived for generations on the tea estates in the valley or adjoining hill slopes. So is the case with betel vine or the Mysore veelyedele, where expertise is required to pluck the tender light green leaves. The Appemidi mango tree normally branches out to a height of 25 feet, although in some cases they can grow as tall as 80 feet (Figure 2.12). Harvesting tender mangoes requires great skill as the person has to carefully move through the branches, plucking mangoes with long stalks (Figure 2.12).

The Aranmula Kannadi, a metal mirror produced by a handful of traditional families in Kerala, is another case of human ingenuity (Registered in 2004). The mirror is hundred per cent handmade. The making of the metal mirror is a process that needs endurance and experience. Mud from the local paddy fields is used to make the mould. The lost wax method is used to cast the mirror. A coating of metallic powder mixed with special oil is used for the bell-metal mirror. The artisan then laboriously rubs the metal with a hessian cloth over several days. The polished face of the metal not only resembles glass but also has the same ability to reflect images clearly. Manufactured with tin and copper, the speciality of this mirror is that its quality of image is near perfect and outdoes the looking glass mirror. The expertise is such that when the scientists from the Regional Research Laboratory, Council of Scientific Industrial Research, did an analysis on the alloy they found that it is composed of 70.4 weight per cent of copper and 29.4 weight per cent of tin. Traces of zinc (0.006), phosphorous (0.02), iron (0.034) and nickel (0.052) are also reported. However, several attempts to make a metal mirror of the Aranmula quality using this composition failed even in the hands of these scientists (Pillai, Pillai and Damodaran, 2002).

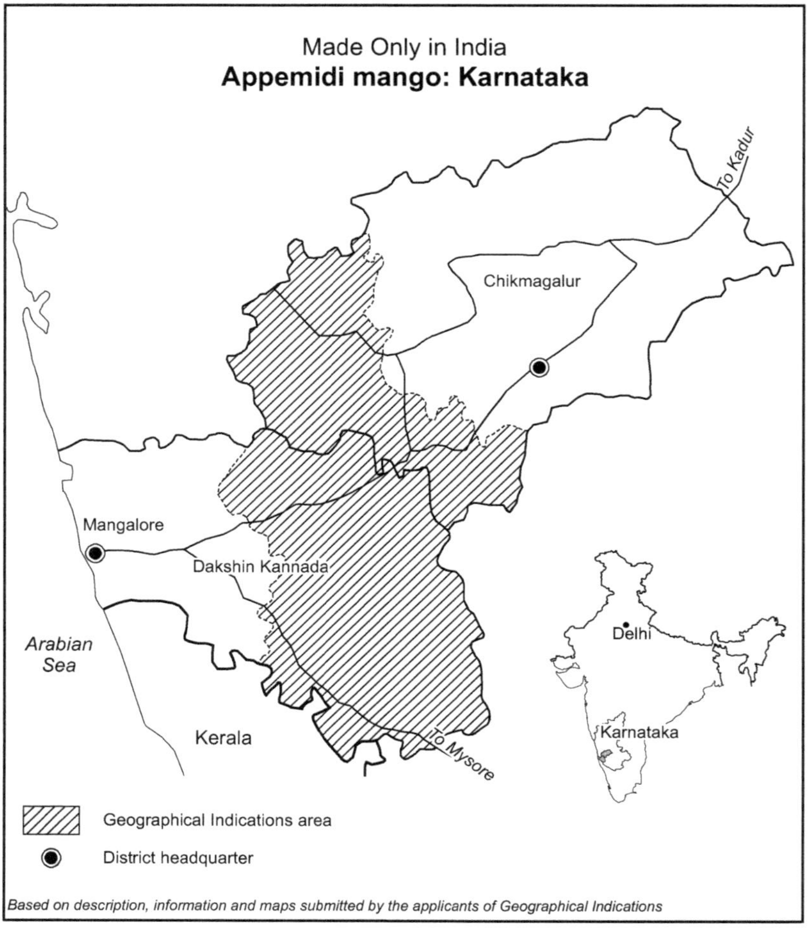

Figure 2.12 Appemidi mango: Karnataka

The kantha of West Bengal (Registered in 2007) where women darn odd pieces of fabric together or the fine chikanwork of Lucknow which comes to life after small pieces of fabric are finely stitched on to each other or the meticulous patterns which the Kashmiri shawl worker sits down to weave and embroider are evidence of patience and care with which artisans craft goods taking from their place.

The endeavour and endurance of people in different places that create textiles, handicrafts or foodstuff are reasons for the qualities in place goods that show up as Geographical Indications. Geographers classify the characteristics of place into the physical and the human environment. But in the case of applicants who have registered for role of place in the making of the goods in India, there occurs a third dimension that of the role of the Divine. The claim is that the revelation or blessing of the gods manifested at 'this', 'their' particular place which is responsible for the distinctive place good.

Divine environment: About 400 years ago, goes the narrative, the chief priest of the Aranmula temple, who was a patron of art and craft, brought in a few families of Kannansonnur professional bronze makers from Sankaran Koil, a small temple town located in Tirunelveli in the south of Tamil Nadu, and settled them in his territory. In return they were to make bell metal vessels for the temple. Soon they started making an alloy in silver that shone and reflected like a true mirror. It is said that the secret of this metal mirror was revealed to a female member of the family by Lord Krishna of the Aranmula Parthasarathi Temple (Figure 2.13).

Rajasthani string puppets or Kathputli are attached to the puppeteers' fingers directly. This demands a great deal of virtuosity (Registered in 2008). Today there are about 200 puppeteers in the Nagore district, a few in Jodhpur and Jaipur. The belief is that the Putli Bhats (as the *Kathputli Bhats* are known) were born out of the mouth of Lord Brahma and, therefore, entertaining people is their profession. Another narrative relates the origin of the craft of puppet making to the times of King Vikramaditya, one of the influential emperors of the Gupta dynasty who ruled India from AD 375 to 415. Due to his righteousness, the Gods had gifted him a throne decorated with magical figures who had the power to come alive and render advise to the king. These figures were puppets at the behest of the king and thus the origin of puppetry. Whichever be the accepted interpretation, both are soaked in the religious sentiment of the people. Similarly the themes that dominate the famous Tholu Bommalata, which literally means the dance of leather puppets, are the two epics of India: the Ramayana and the Mahabharata. The base of this art form is in the township of Nimmalakunta in Anantpur district and Narsaraopet in Guntur district, both in the state of Andhra Pradesh.

Puppetry no doubt is a traditional art form in which performers are not just wandering entertainers but also ones who spread news and information when modern forms of communication such as radio, television, cinema or the internet were not available. It is seen from these examples that puppetry in two places, one in Rajasthan, in the north-west, and the other in Andhra Pradesh in South India, using two different fabrics – wood and leather – both claim a religious association and both gained a site in the

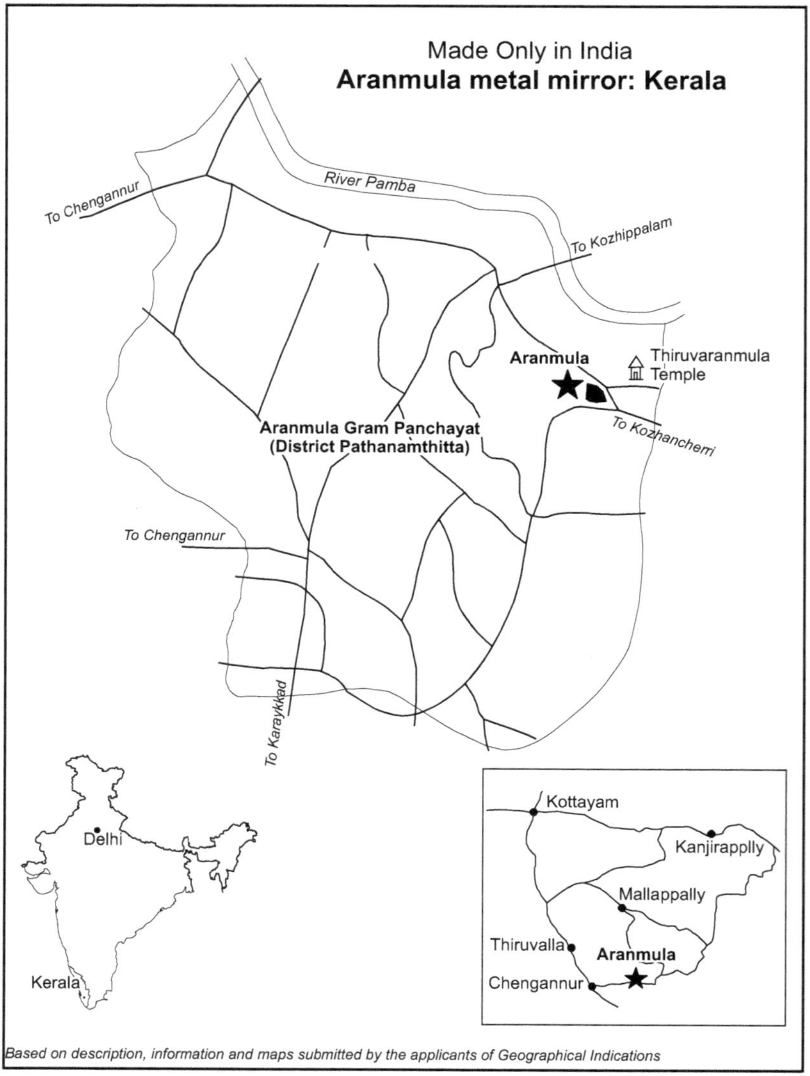

Figure 2.13 Aranmula metal mirror: Kerala

Geographical Indications Registry in 2008. So strong is the religious association, that when a Rajasthani string puppet becomes old, irreparable or beyond use, it is immersed in a river much like the Hindu practice of submerging idols of gods and goddesses (Dhru, 1990). The belief is based on the fact that the power vested in puppets can only be acceptable to the gods when the puppets are submersed in water.

A legend about the origin of the lacquer work on the Sankheda Furniture (Registered in 2008) goes like this: about 150 years ago, a *kharadi* (skilled in the craft of wood work) of Vadodara had attended upon a sage during his sickness. The sage was so impressed by the devotion that he blessed the *kharadi* and trained him in the secret art of polishing the lac which involves a coat of lacquer polished with a leaf of the *kewda* tree. The royal palette of gold, yellow, red and subtle linear work gives the furniture a unique finish.

The popular legend in Molela, a village located in the Rajasamand district, which is famous for its mud-baked plaques, is that one night a blind potter had a dream in which Lord Dharamraj, the god of death, instructed the potter to make an image of him. When the potter in turn replied that since he was blind it was impossible for him to do so, Lord Dharamraj blessed him with sight, assuring him that buyers would come on their own. From that day onwards, the potters of Molela have been making votive plaques of local gods and goddesses. The Molela plaque was registered as Geographical Indication in the year 2008.

The legend behind every Aranmula metal mirror, Sankheda lac work, Kathputli, or Molela plaque is symbolic of the way people invest faith in the Divine connect between the good and the place. The sacred is the space used to explain the distinctive features of place goods.

Many are the ways of bonding between good and place, yet a fact seems clear that in the making of place goods, there seldom are simple relationships of rainfall to soil or water to crop, colour to cloth! To say it is just soil, skills or the Divine would be a rather loose assertion of the role of place. Doubts and questions can be raised about the extent of the influence of natural factors on human activity and the extent to which man can react, respond, change or adapt to these impacts. In an attempt to explain this, geographers have coined concepts like determinism where the role of the natural phenomena are considered to influence, dominate and determine human action and activities or possibilism where a scope for change and taking a different stance is envisaged. But these are not important points of worry, for in reality, there is no sharp dichotomy between the two since the physical and the human are deftly intertwined everywhere. The factor which plays a critical role varies in each good, but in the finale it is claimed that the combinations cannot be replicated elsewhere. Darjeeling is thus not a result of slope, soil or drainage nor about the method of collection, plucking and drying, but its distinctiveness is the because of the 'sum total of what emerges from these individual parts'. An alert sensitivity to the potential resources in a place along with intent to perfect the art of exclusive production seems to be an essential factor in the emergence of place goods. The catalyst for the occurrence of this observation, intention, experimentation and perfection is not a single element or factor but the 'chemistry of place'. This is because even if all the elements of a place were reassembled piece by piece in a laboratory, the chances are that the replicated product may be *like* the good, but not be the same as the good from that place. It may be difficult to isolate the construct of place goods, but this does not/cannot rule out their existence and identity. Goods through their Geographical Indications thus reflect a connect with Place. A tribute to the relationship is evident in the name carried by the goods.

Name as a bond between good and place: The fact that goods 'owe' and 'own' their 'origin' is evident from the way place is entwined within the fold of their names in eight differing ways:

1 Place is named because of the production of a good.
2 Good is named because of its place of destination.
3 Resource base of a place is the name of the good.
4 Skills or the process of production in a place is the name of the good.
5 People of a place is the name of the good
6 Place is with the name of the good.
7 Place is the name of the good.
8 Good is without a name of place but connects to place.

Place is named because of the production of a good: When a place is seen primarily through a lens of the good it produces, quite likely the name of the good becomes the name of the place. The south-west coast of India was often referred to as the pepper coast. Traders specified that 'a diagonal cut from the straits to the Pepper Coast of south-west India took 40 days' (Thomson, 1948: 298). Cardamom acquired the status of a plantation crop in the beginning of the nineteenth century. Its cultivation spread so fast that the Europeans named the range in the backdrop of Travancore, Cardamom Hills. H. H. Wilson identifies *ruma* with Sambhar; *rauma* means salt. Alexander Cunningham mentions that Raumaka is the name of the salt brought from the hill country of Ruma. 'It is probable that the term may have been applied to the Sambhar Lake in Rajputana as well as to the Salt Range of the hills in the Punjab' (Cunningham, 1963: 158). The names Pepper Coast, Cardamom Hills or Sambhar lead us to believe that when naming a place, every criterion, be it its people, language or history, becomes secondary, and what is kept is the single utilitarian purpose it serves. Such a name is imposed more often by the 'outsider', the explorer, traveller or trader and is given to a place, not according to its topographical or navigational convenience but as a result of the importance of a place as a producer of a particular distinctive good. Such is the bonding that a place acquires a single identity that of the producer of a distinctive good. At times so dominant is the production of a particular good at a place that the latter borrows a nickname from the good. Firozabad is known as the capital of bangles, Bhadohi the carpet city, Vazhakulam the pineapple city, Bhagalpur the silk city, Kannur the land of looms, Moradabad the *peetalnagri* or brass town and Hyderabad as the city of pearls.

The allegiance between goods and their place of origin is also seen in the name of trade routes. Take the silk route which traversed from ancient China through Central Asia and India to the Mediterranean countries. On this route was hauled such large consignments of one commodity that it came to be known as the silk route or the Silk Road. The route which carted incenses from India, through north-east Africa and Arabia to the Mediterranean world was called the incense route. Similar names emerged for routes of trade across the world for opium, saffron, incense or amber. The flow of oil, wheat or even the trafficking of drugs and armaments is the contemporary counterpart. At times the opposite happens; a good is named not from the origin of production but from its place of destination.

Good is named after its place of destination: Pochampally Ikat (Registered in 2004), which took the form of cotton Teliya rumal or chokas (diamond within a square), was first used by fishermen as lungi which is a garment wrapped around the waist extending to the ankle. In the 1930s they were exported in large numbers to Burma (present-day Myanmar), East Africa and West Asia, where they were known as Asia *rumals*. An American textile, the cowboy's bandanna, derives from the Indian *bandhani* (tie-and-dye). The latter were imported as silk kerchiefs in the eighteenth century (Scott, 1993). The coarse blue salempores manufactured at Nellore, a coastal town in Andhra Pradesh, were in demand in West Africa and for years they were known as the slavery cloth. Their production suffered when the West Indian Emancipation Act, 1833, which freed Africans, who refused to wear the garb of slavery! Guinea cloth was the name given to the striped or checked calico purchased by the Dutch in large quantities from Broach and Baroda and sold in the Guinea coast of Africa (Hariharan, 2002). The natives of Kashmir distinguish the ornamentation of the shawls by different names, some of which indicate the place of destination. A special variety designed for the Armenian market was known as the Tara Armeni. In certain places the natural resources that are found in a place are so dominating in the creation of distinctive goods that they become prefixed to the name of place good.

Resource base of a place is the name of the good: Screw pine, which in Malayalam is known as Thazhappai, lends its name to Thazhavain in the Kollam district of Kerala where it has a gregarious growth. This grass that grows on the banks of rivers and streams is used to weave products like mats and bags which are famous for their finish and softness. Sikki craft is made from a special kind of grass known as *sikki* found in wet and marshy areas of Bihar (Madhubani district) and Uttar Pradesh. Popularly known as the 'golden grass', *sikki* holds a place of significance in the regional way of life. The grass is traditionally woven by the women, especially brides-to-be, who then carry the products to their marital homes as part of their dowries. The skills and techniques employed in the use of resources to manufacture a good are another connector to a place.

Skills or the process of production in a place is the name of the good: Phulkari is a traditional embroidery work of Punjab which literally means floral work as the entire field is filled with flowers (Registered in 2010). Stitched to create the veils of Punjab, the simple and sparsely embroidered ones where the pattern is dispersed at intervals over the cloth are called phulkaris, but where the embroidery covers the entire fabric it is called bagh or garden. Phulkari carries an identity only with Punjab. *Kani* is the Kashmiri name for the wooden spool which is used in the weaving of Kani shawls. The village in the Beerwah block of Badgam district, Kashmir, where Kani shawls are produced is called Kanihama. In some cases more than the natural resource or technique, it is the people in a place which take credit for the name of good with the place.

People of a place is the name of the good: The name of a good at times is associated with the people of a place who manufacture the good. Even though branded as the most 'backward' of India, some tribes have spread the fame of place and goods far and wide. Todas, a pastoral group, have developed a technique where the stitch of the embroidery follows at right angle the thread in the warp and weft of the fabric on which it is worked. As the embroidery is continuous, both the obverse and the reverse sides appear similar. Referred to as Toda embroidery (Registered in 2012), it gives the impression of a woven, rather than embroidered, pattern. In contrast to the Todas, who are a small group confined to the Nilgiri plateau of South India, there are the itinerant or Banjaras of the vast arid tracts of Rajasthan, north-west Gujarat, and western Madhya Pradesh. Banjara embroidery is noted for its lively decoration, cowrie shells, coins, cotton and woollen tassels edged with lead and glass beads. Even a single person in a place can become the name of a good. Balaramapuram, a village

15 kilometres to the south-east of the city of Thiruvananthapuram in Kerala, is famous for the weaving of traditional textiles. Maharaja Balaramavarma introduced handloom weaving in this village in the mid-eighteenth century. This weaving was listed in the Geographical Indications Registry in 2009 by the name Balaramapuram sarees and fine cotton fabrics! The allegiance exhibits where the name of place is welded with the good.

Place is with the name of the good: The sword-blades of India had a great fame: 'The Hindus excel in the manufacture of iron, and in the preparation of those ingredients along with which it is fused to obtain that kind of soft iron which is usually styled Indian Steel (*Hindiah*). . . . It is impossible to find anything to surpass the edge that you get from Indian Steel *al-hadid al-Hindi*' (Yule, 1920: 93). India ink was the name given to the high carbon content of the indigenous mixture of burning bones, tar and pitch. Applied with a reed pen, this was the common medium used for writing.

Pepper is one of the oldest Indian exports. The plant is found wild in the forests of Malabar and Travancore (Registered in 2007). The first mention of red pepper is found in a letter by Peter Martin dated September 1493. This exotic spice similar to black pepper in pungency, but red in colour, was called Indian pepper. Reciprocally the Europeans called black pepper Indian capsicum (Mahindru, 1982).

In all such cases, India steel, India ink, Indian pepper or Indian capsicum, the prefix India is indicative of the source of the good. There also are evidences where the name India is embedded within the name of the good. The phrase 'Open Sesame' is derived from the name of the Indian oil seed, *til*, or *Sesamum indicum*. Tamarind in North India is a graceful shade tree, but in South India its flowers and fruits provide a sour pulpy seed pod much valued for flavouring. Tamarind could be an anglicised version of the Arabic and Persian word *Tamar-i-Hind*, meaning dates from India. Some are of the opinion that the Arabic should be Thamar-i-Hindi, fruit of India, where *ind* is a reference to it being a native of Hind. The plant *Indigofera tinctoria* and the dark blue dye made from it are called indigo. Indigo is indigenous to India, its appellation being *Indica*, and well known as a product growing in the neighbourhood of the river Indus. Similarly, the scientific name for the Muga silkworm, *Antheraea assamensis*, carries Assam as its birthmark. Muga is an Asomiya word indicating the amber colour of the cocoon. For the unusual lustrous golden-yellow, attractive and strong silk, Assam has the monopoly of world production (Registered in 2007).

The scientific name of the tea plant which belongs to the Camellia family is *Camellia assamica*. It was discovered in 1830. Nagaland, one of India's smallest states, houses the hottest chilli in the world. The local name of the chilli is Naga Mircha or Naga Jolokia, an allegiance with the Naga tribes of Nagaland.

Textile fabrics frequently take their names from the place where they first acquired excellence, and retained them long after. 'The muslin woven in the region of Warangal, in the Coromandel Coast, was called *Oringal muslin* in London and was marketed all over Asia as well as in Europe' (Erwin, 1996). The hills surrounding the city of Salem lend support to the Sanskrit word *sailam* meaning mountain. The word *salya*, itself a corruption of the Sanskrit original *shalika*, means 'weaver' which emphasises the antiquity of Salem as a weaving centre. Most of the weaving in Salem is still concentrated in producing *saeylai*, a Tamil word for saree. Salem means the place where *saeyalis* are produced (Salem Fabric Registered in 2005 and Salem Silk Registered in 2008).

There is a mention of Vahita or Vahika country which was reputed for the manufacture of woollen chaddars (blanket) known as Vahitika in the Sutta Pitaka, the Pali collection of Buddhist writings, compiled in the fourth century BC. The description of the Vahita country corresponds geographically to the western part of Himachal Pradesh and the Kashmir territory (Chanda, 1998). Banaras is famous for its cotton or silk tussar; its well-known orange-brown dye *kashaya* gave the first colour for Buddhist robes and retains its popularity as the famous *Banaras kailhai*.

With the recasting and reorganisation of India's administrative boundaries post-1947, many earlier provinces and princely states and districts acquired names. The names of many goods today are glued to their administrative names (Table 2.2).

Mysore, the second largest city of Karnataka, comes forward with silk, paintings, oil, soaps, *agarbathis*, jasmine, rosewood inlay, betel leaf *and* ganjifa cards. Smaller seemingly nondescript areas are not left behind. The picturesque hill station of Sirumalai on the southern-most tip of the Eastern Ghats lends its name to the Sirumalai hill banana. The fibreless, tasty and fleshy Dussheri mango draws its name from a village named Dusher located between Lucknow and Malihabad in Uttar Pradesh. The one-time estate of the nawab of Lucknow, the village of Dusher is presently called Dusseheri. The name under whose banner the mango was officially registered in 2009 was Mango Malihabadi Dusseheri. Two place names in the address for one good. But overriding resources, people and technique of production a grand tribute to the relationship is where the name of place transcends into the name of good. Here the name of place submerges fully into the name of the good, in contrast to the situation where the good was the name of place.

Place is the name of the good: Darjeeling, the name of the hill station of West Bengal, became a type of tea from 1882 onwards. Bidri, a metalworking technique known only in India, takes its name from the Deccan city of Bidar. There are also goods which do not even make the effort to

Table 2.2 Places with more than one Geographical Indications good attached to their names

Place	*Number*	*Goods*
Place (State)		
Kashmir	4	Kashmir Papier Mache, Kashmir Pashmina, Kashmir Sozani Craft, Kashmir Walnut Wood Carving
Bihar	3	Appliqué (Khatwa) Work of Bihar, Sikki Grass Work of Bihar, Sujini Embroidery Work of Bihar
Assam	2	Muga Silk of Assam, Assam (Orthodox) Tea
Kerala	2	Brass Broidered Coconut Shell Crafts of Kerala, Screw Pine Crafts of Kerala
Orissa	2	Orissa Ikat, Orissa Pattachitra
Place (District)		
Mysore	9	Ganjifa Cards of Mysore, Mysore Agarbathi, Mysore Betel Leaf, Mysore Malligae, Mysore Rosewood Inlay, Mysore Sandal Soap, Mysore Sandalwood Oil, Mysore Silk, Mysore Traditional Paintings
Thanjavur	4	Thanjavur Art Plate, Thanjavur Doll, Thanjavur/Tanjore Painting, Thanjavur Veenai
Bastar	3	Bastar Dhokra, Bastar Iron Craft, Bastar Wooden Craft
Malabar	3	Malabar Pepper, Monsooned Malabar Arabica Coffee, Monsooned Malabar Robusta Coffee
Malda	3	Malda Fazli Mango, Malda Khirsapati (Himsagar) Mango, Malda Lakhasmanbhog Mango
Alleppey	2	Alleppey Coir, Alleppey Green Cardamom
Coimbatore	2	Kovai[1] Kora Cotton Sarees, Coimbatore Wet Grinder
Coorg	2	Coorg Green Cardamom, Coorg Orange
Ganjam	2	Ganjam Kewda Flower, Ganjam Kewda Rooh
Kangra	2	Kangra Painting, Kangra Tea
Kutch	2	Kutch Embroidery, Kachchh Shawls
Lucknow	2	Lucknow Chikan Craft, Lucknow Zardozi
Madurai	2	Madurai Malli, Madurai Sungudi
Nashik	2	Nashik Grapes, Nashik Valley Wine
Palakkad	2	Maddalam of Palakkad, Palakkadan Matta Rice
Salem	2	Salem Fabric, Salem Silk known as Salem Venpattu
Solapur	2	Solapur Chaddar, Solapur Terry Towel
Udupi	2	Udupi Malligae, Udupi Mattu Gulla Brinjal
Wayanad	2	Wayanad Gandhakasala Rice, Wayanad Jeerakasala Rice
Place (Other than district or state)		
Nirmal	3	Nirmal Furniture, Nirmal Paintings, Nirmal Toys and Craft

[1] Kovai is the old name for Coimbatore.

Compiled from *Geographical Indications Journal* No. 1 to 58 spell out place, yet the name allows consumers to instantly conjure up a specific place. There is also the case where the good and place connect such that even though the name of good does not carry any address, yet the letter reaches its correct destination.

Good is without a name of place but connects to place: Mention Feni and one could be transported to the white sand beaches of Goa where the cashew nut has been gathered and brewed into this alcoholic drink. When the liquor is shaken in a bottle and poured in a glass, the froth that is formed is known in the local Konkani language as feni.

Such is the attachment that certain goods continue to use the name of place, even when the place does not exist anymore. Baluchari textiles are prized for their pictorial brocades of outstanding motifs and complicated weaving technique. This group of textiles is named after the village of Balachur. The latter was situated on the banks of the river Bhagirathi in Murshidabad. However, the old village of Balachur no longer exists because its remains were flooded by the Bhagirathi (Rakob, 1995). A true tribute is one which continues when one is no more.

Logos and stamps: To strengthen identity and foster an adherence to a geographical location manufacturers also make use of logos and stamps. A map is central to the logos of Central Travancore jaggery, Bhalia Wheat, Udupi brinjal and Bangalore Blue Grapes. Along with these cartographic manifestations of the allegiance with place a subtle yet strong evidence of the bond between good and place is the goodwill which accrues both ways (Figure 2.14).

A stamp: A way in which the nation projects itself to the rest of the world is through postage stamps. Moreover the release of a stamp is a way in which a government endorses the value and distinction of a person, event or a good. Stamps are a gateway to spread the value of a product far and wide. When the archive of Stanley Gibbons, the world's largest stamp dealers, was accessed, one found in their collection stamps commemorating goods which later went on to gain a Geographical Indications tag. A stamp bearing a surhai or vessel for water, in the craft of Bidriware, was released on 16 June 1965 and Bidriware was registered for Geographical Indications in 2006. As part of the Indian Miniature paintings series a stamp of the Cheriyal painting (Registered in 2010), which carried a picture of a chained elephant, was released on 5 May 1973. On 15 October 2000 a series of stamps were released as part of a set on Madhubani paintings. The stamps cover themes like Krishna and the Gopis, and the flower girls. Among the many objectives of the first five-year Exim Policy of the New Millennium launched in 2002 by the Government of India was the one to enhance the local strength and efficiency of Indian

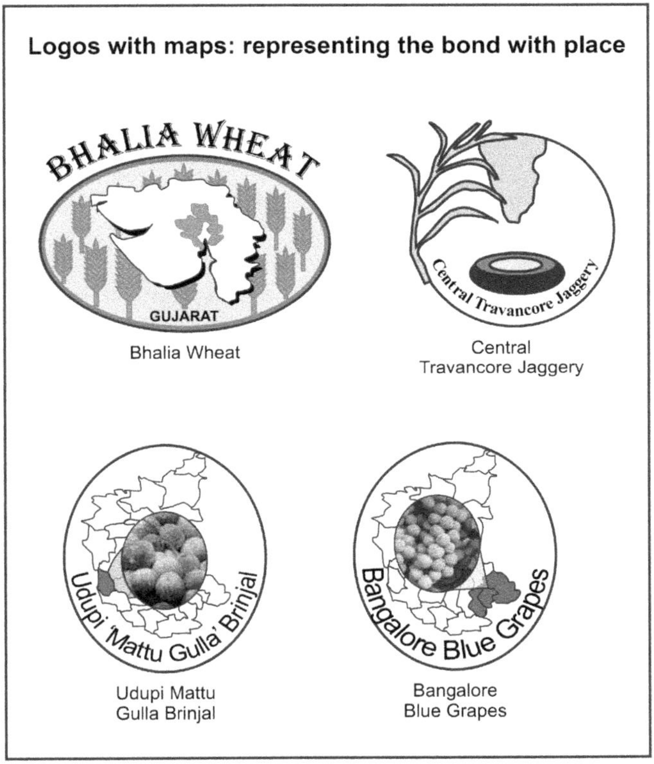

Figure 2.14 Logos with maps: representing the bond with place

Source: Bhalia Wheat – *Geographical Indications Journal* No. 38
Central Travancore Jaggery – *Geographical Indications Journal* No. 34
Udupi Mattu Gulla Brinjal – *Geographical Indications Journal* No. 40
Bangalore Blue Grapes – *Geographical Indications Journal* No. 48

agriculture, industry and services, thereby improving their competitiveness. Since the policy covered the agricultural, cottage and handicrafts and the small scale sector a few stamps were released under its umbrella (Figure 2.15).

Dhokra casting, Patan's Patola, Thewa Art, cane and bamboo artefacts found a display on stamps. Rewarding the experience of place and the good is India's first scented stamp released on 13 December 2006. When you rub the embossed stamp the fragrance which is released takes one to the dense sandalwood forests of Mysore.

Figure 2.15 Postal stamps for Geographical Indicator goods
Source: Philately Division, Indian Postal Department

Goodwill – an acknowledgement of the bond with place: Goodwill and reputation is the result of careful experimentation with resources and handing down inventions and skills from generation to generation. In this context of Geographical Indications and place goods, what is important is all this transference has transpired within a specific spatial unit. Reputation plays an important role in the confirmation of Geographical Indications, where '*a given quality, reputation or other characteristic of the good* is essentially attributable to its geographical origin' [The Geographical Indications of Goods (Registration and Protection) Act, 1999]. Reputation for a place is an offspring of years of hard work and becomes a mechanism of advertising and marketing.

A fine comb through the copious document submitted by the applicants at Chennai confirms that goodwill is claimed and attributed on the basis of the place of origin. The expressions of reputation vary from adulatory adjectives, ranks, medals and awards.

Words of appreciation: Wayanad Gandhakasala rice is *valued* for its pleasant flavour and aroma; the capital city of Uttar Pradesh has the *distinction* of producing one of the best embroideries of the world, the Lucknow chikancraft; Payyannur Pavithra ring has acquired a *valuable reputation* indicative of quality and unique skill; Kinnauri shawls are *widely renowned* for the intricacy and finesse in weaving; Malabar has always been considered to produce the *best pepper*; and qualifying the craft of *zari*, it is claimed that Surat is the *only famous centre* of production of *zari* thread and embroidery material in the world. Brass broidered coconut shell crafts of Kerala and the Thanjavur art plate are a collector's delight and enjoy the patronage of connoisseurs all over the world. Another sure sign of recognition is to gain a rank among the top products. Steven Spurrier, a British wine expert who organised the Paris Wine Tasting of 1976, rates wine on a 20-point scale. He ranked Nashik wine between 13 and 17 points, bracketing it in a category ranging from 'acceptable' to 'very good'. The vocabulary of praise varies but a common thread is the echoe of the high mark of goodwill each of them draws because of their place of origin.

Awards and medals: Tangible proofs of distinctiveness are the various awards and prizes won at exhibitions by the goods. Kangra tea bagged gold and silver medals in the Amsterdam and London markets during 1886–1895. The Bhavani jamakkalam won the first prize at an exhibition conducted at Madras in 1883 (*Coimbatore District Manual*, 1887). In 1913, Governor Lord Wellington bestowed a certificate of excellence to Dharwar Pedhas. This was followed by a second certificate on 22 October 1926 given in the Agricultural and Industrial Exhibition. The quality of

Pattamadai mats is so fine that they can be folded like a saree. The mats were sent to Queen Elizabeth II on the occasion of her coronation in 1953.

These awards and rewards are reminders that flag the distinctiveness of place goods. The bond between the good and the place is neither recent nor trivial. Many have evolved over the years. Whereas the Geographical Indications Act came in 1999, yet when the descriptions of 199 place goods registered at Chennai were searched they brought to light that India had nurtured place goods to great fame long before one had heard of any such thing as Geographical Indications.

3

NURTURING

Place goods

The origin of many place goods is shrouded. Yet a study of the 199 place goods registered at Chennai unfolds three broad phases of nurturing: the first are goods that predate the arrival of Islam, the second are those which trace a belonging to the Mughal phase and the third are goods that owe an allegiance to the colonial phase. In terms of numbers, the majority of place goods predate the arrival of Islam; another substantive group belong to the Mughals, while barely a handful belong to the colonial period. There was not a single place good registered at Chennai which belongs to the post-1947 phase. Three situations and demands seem to have reared most, if not all, the place goods. The first set of place goods were born to service the Hindu temples and were nurtured by tradition, the second were cradled to appease the appetite of the Mughal badshahs or royalty and the third group of place goods was raised by the British for military and commercial reasons. The dynamics of these three historical periods were different in how and why they nurtured place goods.

Religion nurtures place goods – case of Hindu temple: In India, the basic rite of Hinduism is worship (puja) in a temple. The temple originated probably as a small cave or hut but later became grand with stone and sculptures, and by the Gupta period, India was probably as much a land of temples as it is at present. Amidst the dense type and variety, if one was to scale into a typical Hindu temple, it will reveal a small shrine room, where the Divine is worshipped in the form of an idol. The shrine room is sanctified by special rites, after which it is believed that 'divinity' has in some sense taken abode in the temple. Since the deity is revered as a living soul, in almost all temples, the god and goddess are ceremoniously awakened in the morning with music, bathed in milk and curd, adorned with flowers, garlands, jewellery and perfume and served the best of rice and fruit. India has a hot and humid climate, and in many of the larger shrines attendants can be seen 'fanning' to cool the idol. In some temples, the most festive day is when a deity is taken for a tour in the village or town in a splendidly decorated chariot accompanied by a retinue of musicians and dancers. To the temple throng devotees from near and far, each with offerings and who in turn take home *prasad* or a token of blessing. The diverse forms and rituals that accompany worship in India make a temple a storehouse in need of a constant supply of a variety of goods. Early in India's history the temple became the life of the people, and this sustained the demand of goods for temples.

When the origin of place goods was researched many were meant to service the needs of the temple. To begin with, a Hindu temple needs an 'idol' to worship, and here comes the importance of Swamimalai. It was during the Chola period of Tamil culture from 850 to 1279 CE, that Raja Raja Chola built the Thanjavur temple. Scores of sculptors from various parts of India who were skilled in making icons were invited to this site. After the completion of the Thanjavur temple, the sculptors called *sthapathis* were engaged in building temples across other areas including at Swamimalai. The temple is scenically located on the northern banks of the river Kaveri, eight kilometres north-east from Kumbakonam in Thanjavur district. Here the sculptors evolved a distinct Chola style of sculpturing, where each of the idols is mounted on a pedestal and the measurement of each part of the idol is perfected according to *shilpa sastra* or the code for creative work (Krishnamurthy, 2009). Today, Swamimalai idols adorn temples in the United Kingdom and the United States of America. A work cherished by the *sthapathis* is the 60-feet-tall Lord Nataraja idol for the United Nations Educational Scientific and Cultural Organization headquarters in Paris. The Swamimalai bronze idols gained a Geographical Indications tag in 2008.

Lending fragrance to idols is incense, dhoop, agarbathi and flowers. Most Hindu ceremonies are incomplete without the use of incense. Fulfilling such a need and role Mysore agarbathi from Karnataka made its claim with a Geographical Indications tag in 2005. The producers of Mysore agarbathi claim that the shrubs and herbs used in the manufacture of their agarbathi are exclusive to the forests of Karnataka. Saffron is another ingredient that provides colour and fragrance. The Hindi word for saffron is *kesri or kesar*, a colour associated with Hinduism since Vedic days. Kashmiri saffron is recognisable by its dark maroon-purple hue; made from the three orange-red stigma of the purple flower of the saffron crocus, the Kashmir saffron is among the world's darkest, which hints at strong flavour, aroma, and colourative effect. Its yellow colour is valued in the tikka or tilak, a ceremony of putting a mark on the forehead, which is considered auspicious and a hallmark of pride across India.

Hindus believe that a way to please the gods is to offer sweet-smelling flowers. This gives importance to the jasmine or champa – chameli. Often called the queen of flowers, among the 200 varieties of jasmine, Mysore Malligae, a holder of Geographical Indication tag since 2007, is in demand for stringing garlands for the gods. The Udupi Malligae grown in Shankarapura and surrounding villages in Udupi district, Karnataka, are offered to many temples among which is the famous Lord Krishna temple in Udupi, built in the twelfth century. The Hadagali Malligae, grown in Hadagali taluk of Bellary district, Karnataka, are sent daily to Sree Veerupaksha Temple at Hampi and exported to different parts of India. All the three, Mysore, Udupi and Hadagali Malligae, gained a Geographical Indications tag in 2007. Easy and durable to string into garlands is also Madurai Malli, a jasmine cultivated in the districts of Tamil Nadu. Malli retains its white colour for nearly 24 hours and thus lends a stronger scent; in addition the thick nature of its petals has a stiffness which allows the scope to garland the flower according to one's wishes. Madurai Malli attained the Geographical Indications tag in 2012 (Figure 3.1).

In a temple, the gods are served the best food. An item on the menu for Lord Krishna is Mattu Gulla (Registered in 2011), a brinjal grown only in Katpadi, Mattu and Kaipunjalu in Udupi district (Figure 3.2). Nanjanagud Banana is offered to Lord Sree Srikanteshwara at Nanjanagud temple, located on the bank of river Kapila, 29 kilometres south of Mysore. This banana is grown only in Devarasanahalli and surrounding villages of Nanjanagud taluk in Mysore district, Karnataka. Then again there is Navara rice, one of the native genetic species of Kerala, which is often referred to as a 'pious grain' served on auspicious occasions. It was registered with a place tag in 2007.

Temples generated a great demand for embroidered work in the form of wall hangings and veils. Priests ordained which textiles were acceptable within the premises of the temple and silk was considered an auspicious material. Since silk was needed for rituals, customs surrounding the care and gathering of wild cocoons became ritualised. 'Silk forests' are considered sacred, and to harvest the bounty of cocoons, people, especially tribals, protect caterpillars from predators such as birds and snakes.

Among the orthodox Vaishnavites, Hindus and Jains, any form of killing is prohibited. It is because of this that silk known as *mutka* produced in Benares is of special appeal. This silk is made from moths which have completed their life cycle and broken out of the cocoons and have thus escaped alive. Because of this 'nonviolent' form of production the silk threads are short and broken and so the fabric quality of *mutka* is inferior. But in spite of being a low quality fabric, religious reasons fetches *mukta* a higher price. On religious occasions women wear silk because of the sanctity bestowed on it. Gadwal sarees, manufactured 184 kilometres south-west of Hyderabad, Telangana, are regarded as puja sarees to be worn during festivals and other

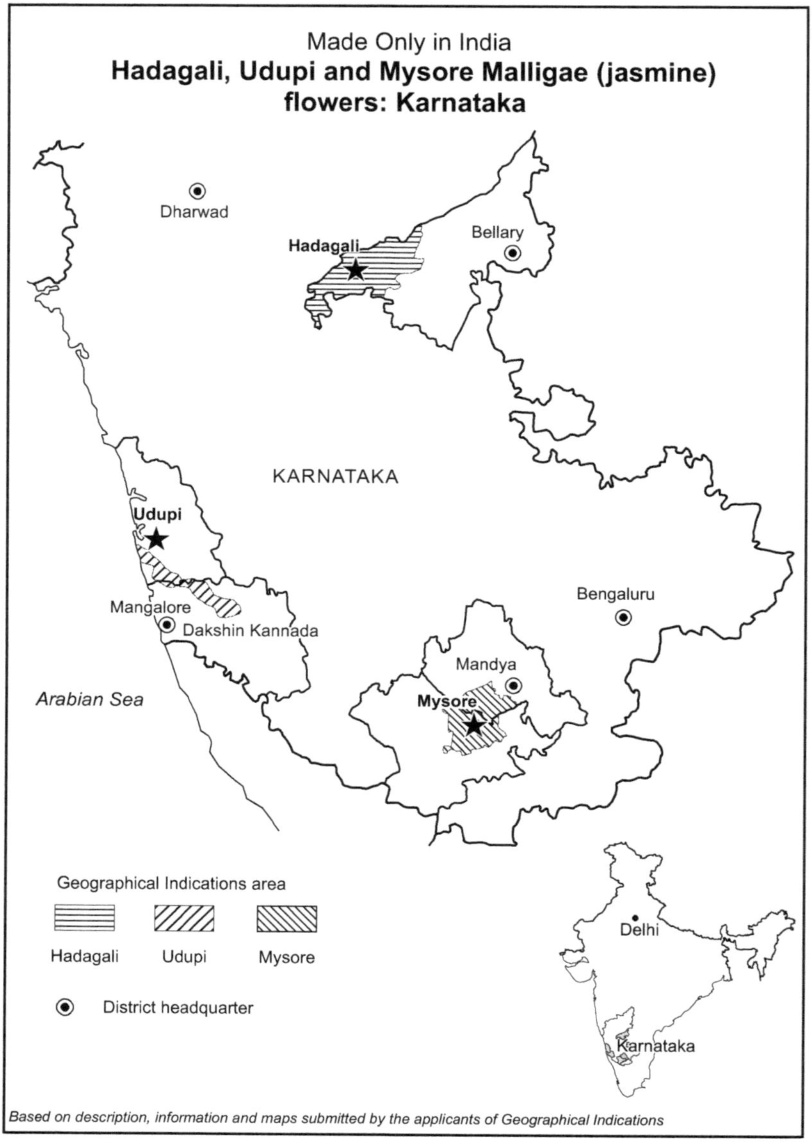

Figure 3.1 Hadagali, Udupi and Mysore Malligae (jasmine) flowers: Karnataka

traditional celebrations. It gained a Geographical Indications tag in 2010. Kancheepuram is a temple town in Tamil Nadu, 72 kilometres south-west of Chennai. The weavers here weave fabrics that 'include red silk handkerchiefs which are tied around the waist of the idols of gods during temple festivals while Brahmins performing the prayer ceremony had to wear silk cloth'.

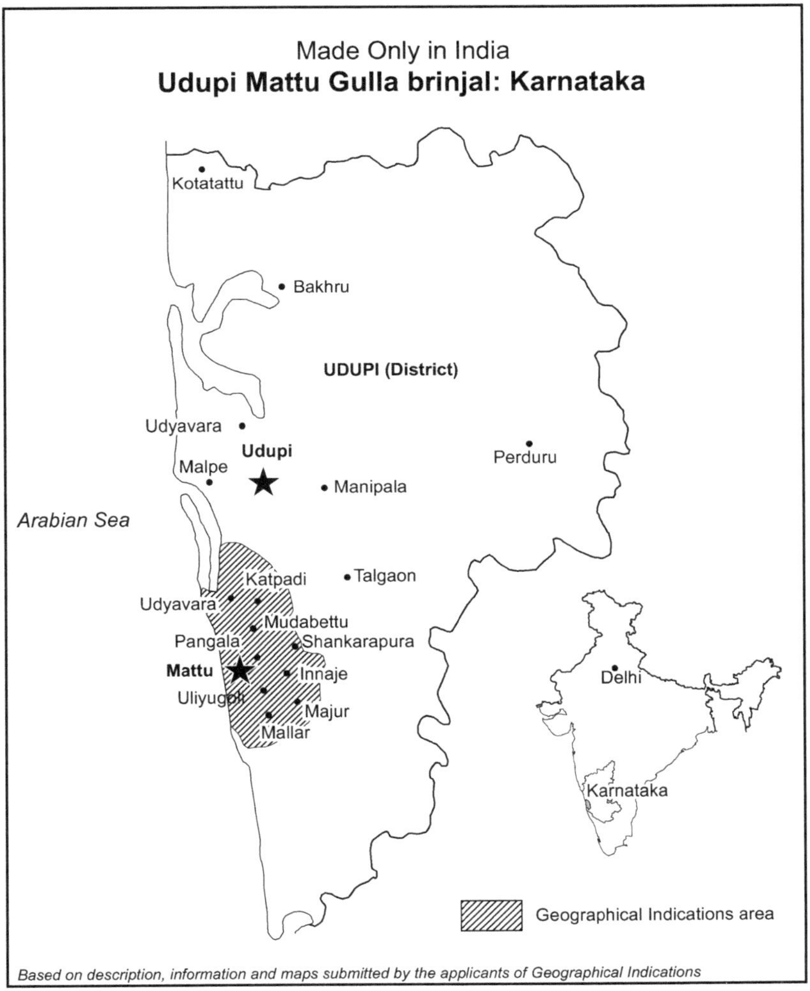

Figure 3.2 Udupi Mattu Gulla brinjal: Karnataka

The temple of Lord Jagannath in Odisha is another case, which nourished the manufacture of various kinds of textiles which today carry Geographical Indications. The kings of Odisha patronised appliqué as an offering to the deity Lord Jagannath. Pipli has a group of artisans called *darjees* who specialise in tailoring. They were allotted the work of the temple as *sevakas* or servants of god for stitching decorative and ornamental clothes for Lord Jagannath. In exchange, the *sevakas* were given some land that belonged to the temple to earn their livelihood. Another silk fabric woven is Khandua in Nuapatna since the sixteenth century for idols of Lord Jagannath. Calligraphic *ikat* is also closely associated with Lord Jagannath. It is believed that to script the lyrics of the *Gita-Govinda*, the twelfth-century poet Jaydev used tie-and-dye, a technique popular at his birthplace Kenduli in Odisha. The offering of the *Gita-Govinda* continues, and in 2006 Odisha Ikat found recognition with a Geographical Indications tag. While Pipli appliqué was added in 2008, the Geographical Indications of Khandua sarees and fabrics were recognised in 2010.

A temple dedicated to Lord Panakala Narasimha is situated on a hillock in the heart of Mangalagiri town. The saree produced here has a border of intricate checks with minute dots in between. As a custom all pilgrims on their way back purchase a saree from a local weaver before leaving the place. The tradition gave impetus to its weaving industry. The Mangalagiri saree was registered in 2012.

Hindus glorify their gods by adorning them with jewellery. 'Nagracot', writes Sir Thomas Roe, an English diplomat, in 1615, 'has a temple as richly set out with all sorts of ornaments as any in India. The ceiling and pavements are both of the purest silver and the embossing and engraving about the whole is almost endless' (Foster, 1899). Jewellery made in gold and encrusted with rubies, uncut diamonds and emeralds is crafted from Nagercoil, the capital of Kanyakumari, a district in the southernmost part of Tamil Nadu (Figure 3.3). Nagercoil derives its name from the Nagaraj temple. Early in the seventeenth century, kings and chieftains from Chettinad came to Nagercoil and purchased jewellery for offering to the temples across the region.

Since the offerings, be they headgear, coronets and special ornaments, were for the deities, these ornaments became popular as temple jewellery. Nagercoil temple jewellery received the status of Geographical Indications in 2007.

A temple sustains place goods in other myriad ways. Hindus believe that a particular type of cosmic sound purifies space, protects followers and draws the attention of the gods to listening. It is in the ambit of the temple that evolved the classical music and dance of India. Indian classical music is believed to be a divine art form whose origin is seen to stem from the Hindu

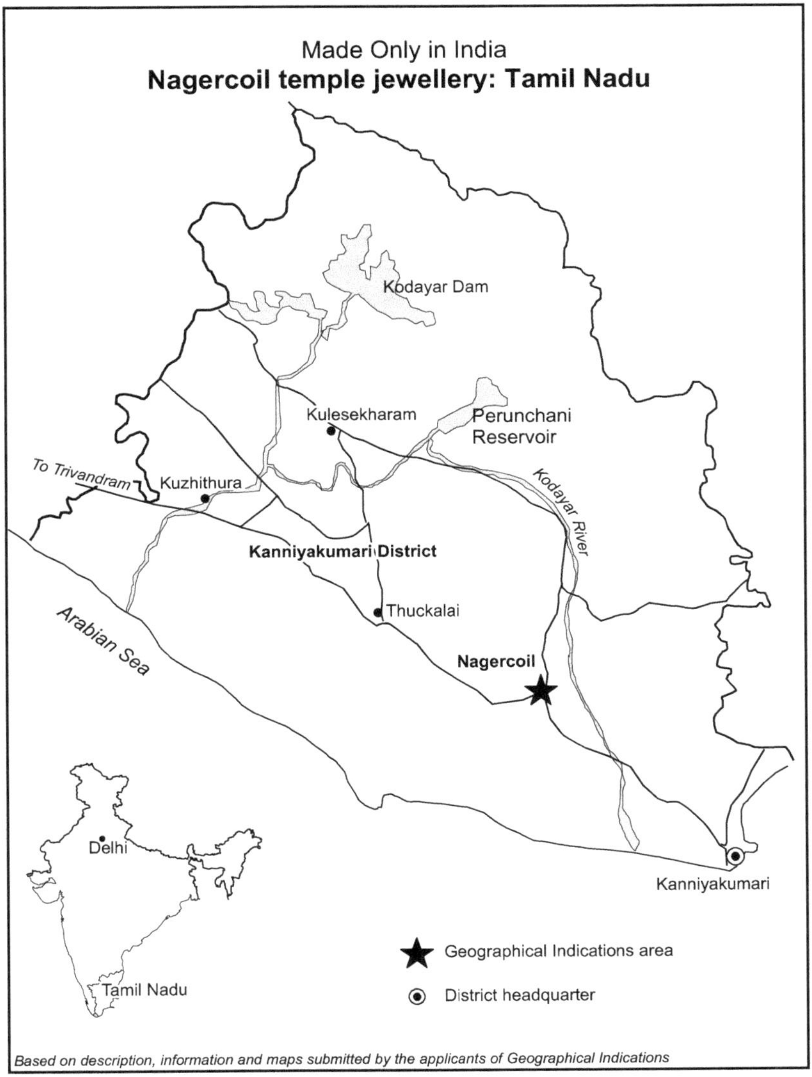

Figure 3.3 Nagercoil temple jewellery: Tamil Nadu

gods and goddesses. Percussion instruments like the maddalam, a kind of barrel-shaped drum made of leather and the veena, a string instrument, are considered to be *deva vadhya* or divine instruments because they are a major accompaniment in the dance of Shiva. Maddalam is one of the ensemble of five percussion instruments, traditionally and culturally associated with temple festivals in Kerala. The maddalam of Palakkad earned the Geographical Indications tag in 2008. In the Vedas the stringed instrument *veena* is referred to as one of the three celestial musical instruments, along with flute and *mridangam*. Saraswati, the Goddess of learning, is always identified with her playing the veena. Among the many varieties of *veena*, the one manufactured in Thanjavur, a city on the south-east coast of Tamil Nadu, is known for its special mellow tonal quality which is capable of evoking a meditative atmosphere. Therefore just as the violins from Cremona became celebrated in Europe for the 'warmth' of their sound, so the maddalam of Palakkad along with Bobbili Veena and Thanjavur Veenai gained the tag of Geographical Indications in 2008, 2011 and 2012 respectively.

The temples also generate a demand for goods that are needed to serve the devotees. The twin towns of Bhavani and Kumarapalayam, situated on the confluence of River Cauvery and its tributary Bhavani, have a sizeable population of *dhurrie* weavers. The origin of the multicoloured, striped cotton flat-weave *dhurrie* called *jamakkalam* is linked to temples, as the latter require floor spreads to seat the devotees.

A visit to a Hindu temple is incomplete without *prasad*, a 'return gift', which is special because it carries the divine blessings. A classic example is the Thirupati *Laddu*. Weighing 100 grams each, the *laddu* is cooked by hereditary priests, known as *archakas*, in the temple kitchen. With a daily sale of 150,000 *laddus*, and an annual revenue which runs over Rs. 11 million, the origin of this place good which gained a Geographical Indications tag in 2009 is solely because of the temple of Lord Venkateswara at Tirumala.

Role of religion beyond temple on place goods: Religion is not just confined to a visit to the temple but manifests in the everyday lives of the people of India. Its impact is evident in the symbols and motifs which are used on many of the goods produced in different places. Thanjavur art plates are round or oval in shape and decorated with figures embossed in silver and copper foils (Figure 3.4). The designs depict the *Dasavarataram* or the ten incarnations of Lord Vishnu, miracles of Shiva and the eight forms of goddess Lakshmi (Registered in 2007).

As part of its religious and cultural heritage Mithila, in Bihar, is known for the production of distinctive paintings. The inspiration for these paintings illustrates folklore from the Ramayana, local epics and ritual activities in the vicinity.

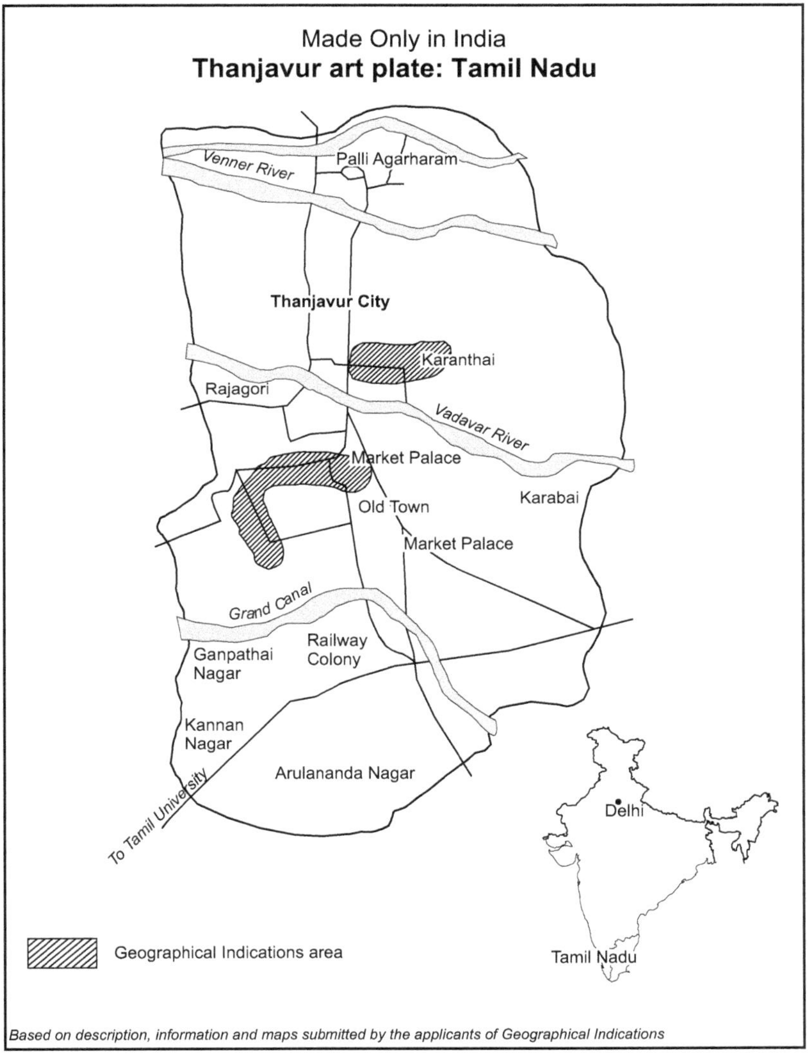

Figure 3.4 Thanjavur art plate: Tamil Nadu

Madhubani paintings carry the images of Krishna, Ram, Shiva, Durga and other gods and goddesses. As Madhubani brings fame to Bihar, Thanjavur paintings of Tamil Nadu, with their surface richness, vivid colours and dense compositions, also serve as devotional icons. A typical painting consists of one main figure which is the childlike Lord Krishna in his various pranks. The child is plump and thus exudes well-being.

Pichwais are a form of traditional fabric painting rooted in Rajasthan which carry the theme of Hindu gods, goddesses and saints. These wall hangings are used as backdrops to idols in the temples of Krishna. The Odisha pattachitras illustrate the Jagannath Temple of Puri. The craftsmen of Molela make votive plaques with images of male and female deities in anthropomorphic forms for worship.

Religion finds expression in the selection of motifs which are considered sacred. In the Kasuti embroidery of Karnataka, the repertoire of motifs includes *gopurams*, chariots, palanquins, lamps, conchshells, birds, animals, fruits and flowers. The Chamba *rumal* or kerchief (Registered in 2008) is a speciality of the Chamba district, which was once a princely state in Himachal Pradesh. The *rumal* which is approximately a two-square-foot cloth usually depicts scenes of Radha-Krishna, Shiva-Parvati, Ganesha and *Nayak-Nayika* among others. The most popular subject in the *rumals* is *rasamandala*, the dance of Lord Krishna with the *gopis* or the cowherd girls. Bengal's *namavali* cloth is adorned with icons of Radha-Krishna and Ram-Sita. The *Vrindavani vastra*, named after the childhood home of Krishna, depicts scenes of Krishna's life at Vrindavan. Reinforcing the creative and destructive principle of the cosmic energy of the Mother Goddess are hand-painted shrine cloth hangings called *Mata-ni-Pachedi*. The art of miniature painting which was practised and developed in the erstwhile princely states of Rajasthan flourished from the sixteenth century to the seventeenth century. Thus many goods including a range of textiles that feature in the Registry at Chennai today are associated with Hindu religion.

The omnipresent stamp of religious belief is universal to India. It is apparent in goods even when they are produced in places separated by thousands of kilometres, even when the goods are made of different mediums be it clay, silk or cotton and even if the goods are put to different uses be it as plaques, carpets or textiles.

Hindu religion consists of a pantheon of gods, numbering in hundreds, who supervise the universe and differ in function and importance. The imaginative interpretation and creative expression of these gods has resulted in a vast diversity of symbols and motifs. Therefore, from the crafts to the pots to the saree *pallus* all carry symbols venerating the gods. It is this that makes goods distinctive and as Birdwood remarked 'characteristically

Indian' too. It is within the Indian hallmark that the cultural influences of the region and its people are responsible for the distinctive characteristics of goods from different places of India. This illustrates to the best why they are the Made Only in India.

The association of a place good with the sacred enrolled the support of the people and thus allowed their continuity. This is akin to the concept of sacred forest or sacred grove where the latter are protected areas of forests because of the religious beliefs that the 'soul' of gods and goddesses resides within the trees. In a world gripped with deforestation, sacred forests have survived because they have a religious role protecting the community. As religion inspired the creation of many place goods, it is tradition which has kept them alive till today.

For most devout Hindus a visit to a temple on festive days is almost a need if not a compulsion. A temple till today remains a place of sanctity, religious presence, cultural production and a significant social centre for Hindus across all parts of India. It is this unfettered religious association which has continued without much change that has made possible the continuity of goods and preserved the knowledge of how the goods are to be produced, processed or manufactured. This association between religion, temple and the goods is what has given India a heritage of handicrafts and the list of goods with Geographical Indications.

It is hard to pin down the exact time of the origin of place goods, but it does seem that the windows of creativity and production may have waxed and waned along with the episodes of peace and war, nature's wrath and wealth, and the individual tastes of patrons and elite; but there is little to doubt that many of the goods which have gained a Geographical Indications tag today do have an origin that is associated with temples and date back into history. Enmeshed with stories, anchored with rituals and driven by religion, many place goods endured. As religion inspired the creation of many place goods, it is tradition which has kept them alive today. Interwoven with the ways of society and the mores of tradition a single good which shows continuity and is very much a product of the feel of a place is the saree.

Tradition endures place goods – a case of the saree: The word 'saree' is from the Sanskrit word *śāṭī*, meaning a strip of cloth, transformed into Prakrit *sadi* and was later anglicised into saree. Saree, a garment that represents the expression of Indian womanhood, has been in use for no less than 5,000 years and is one which has survived centuries of history, foreign influx and the dictates of contemporary fashion. It is worn across the length and breadth of the country, yet each area wears a different style and manufactures a specific type of saree. There are regional differences, and it is estimated that there are more than 800 ways of draping a saree! Different areas have their own loom, thread, colour, their own pattern, design and expression. Exemplifying a combination of features of the natural environment and traditional practices of the people, a saree carries a cultural flavour and thus is a place identifier (Figure 3.5).

A visit to a few handpicked saree-weaving centres of India is enough to gain a snapshot of the different types of sarees and the role of geography. Gadwal, a town in Telangana, is known for its cotton sarees with an

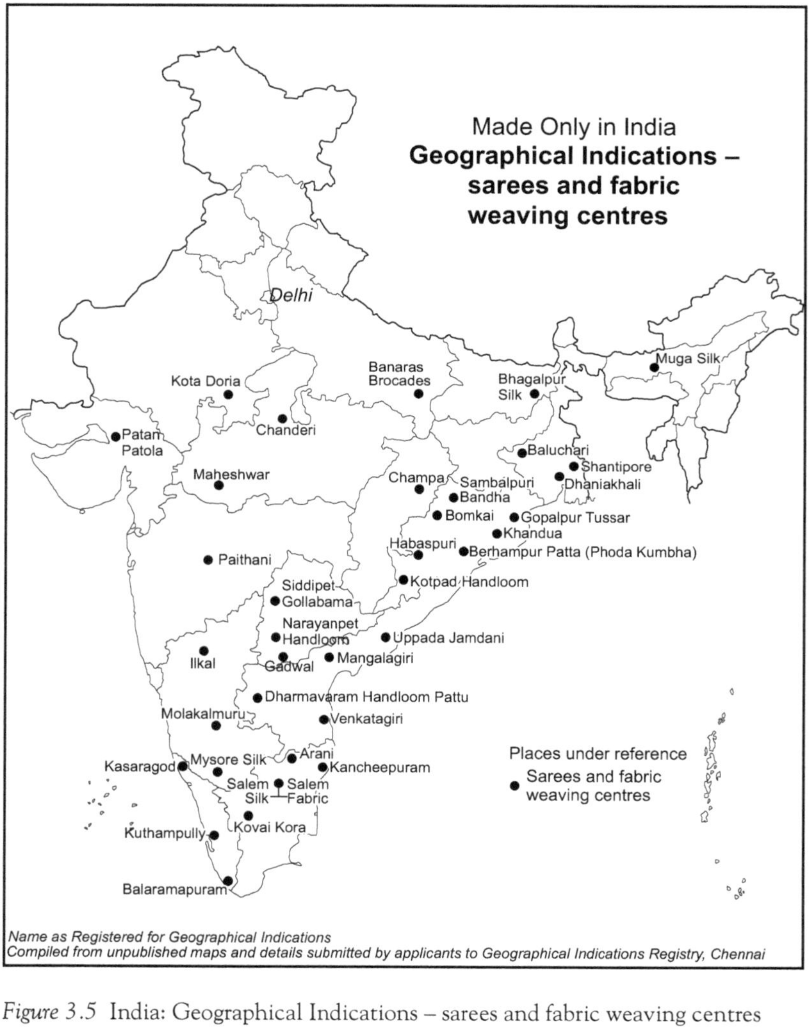

Figure 3.5 India: Geographical Indications – sarees and fabric weaving centres

attached silk border and *pallu*, the falling edge of the saree. The flora and fauna of the region so influenced the weavers that the dominant design of the body is usually of swans and peacocks. Within the district of Nellore, in the neighbouring state of Andhra Pradesh, are woven the Venkatagiri sarees of finely spun cotton with borders and *pallu* brocaded with motifs, worked in gold combined with thick coloured yarns. In Dharmavaram, a town in the Rayalaseema region of Andhra Pradesh are woven the sarees in pure silk with broad solid colour borders. Located on the banks of River Vaigai, Madurai in Tamil Nadu lends its name to the saree called Madurai Sungudi. A distinguishing feature of the sungudi saree is the pattern made with dots throughout the body.

After agriculture, weaving is the main occupation of the people of Molakalmuru taluk, in the Chitradurga district of Karnataka. Molakalmuru silk sarees are known for their sheer texture and have a border and *pallu*, which carry a contrasting colour from the main body. This is also true of the Kancheepuram sarees of Tamil Nadu. The designs in the body of the saree are woven with gold thread. Since Kancheepuram is a temple town, the *gopurams* or the ornate monumental towers constructed at the entrance of any temple, especially in South India, form a prominent feature of the design on the sarees. A silk saree which carries the religious motif of rudrakhsa is called the Narayan or Divine Peth saree. Rudraksha is a tree and a seed, and the scriptures state that Rudraksha evolved from the eyes of Lord Shiva, where Rudra means Shiva and Aksha means eyes. The motif of Rudraksha is adorned because of its religious value. The Narayanpeth saree is woven in Solapur town 400 kilometres south-east of Mumbai in Maharashtra. A few kilometres north-west of Solapur is Paithani. Here the influence of Buddhist paintings of the Ajanta caves can be seen in the Paithani motifs, many of which carry oblique square designs, with peacocks on the pallu. In the Vidarbha region of Maharashtra one encounters the Karvat Kati or saw-edged saree, so named after the design on the border which resembles the teeth of a saw. In the town of Chanderi, on Malwa plateau of Madhya Pradesh, is woven the gossamer thin saree, which carries traditional motifs and fragile pastel colours.

Many of the designs have been taken from the paintings on the wall, roof and pillars of the Lepakshi temple near Hindupur. The Maratha queen Ahilyabai Holkar, who ruled Malwa from 1767 to 1795, built a fort on the banks of the river Narmada, at her capital called Maheshwar. The borders and pallav of the Maheshwar sarees carry the design of the paintings, carvings and scriptures of this fort. The geometric patterns of woven mat, brick layout and the *chameli* flowers are a distinction of the Maheshwar sarees (Figure 3.6).

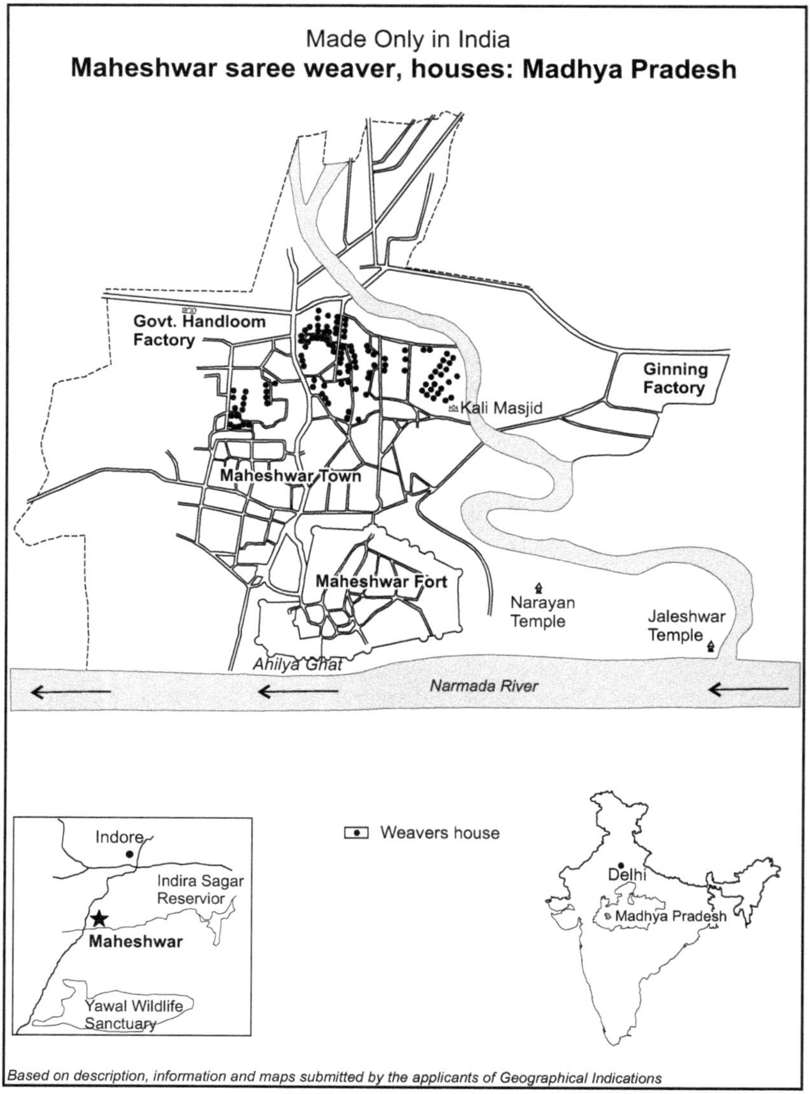

Figure 3.6 Maheshwar saree weaver, houses: Madhya Pradesh

The weavers in the Chicheguda village of Junagarh block of Kalahandi district weave sarees in cotton that carry traditional designs of the Kandha tribes, like fish and flowers. These Habaspuri sarees were registered in 2012. Berhampur in Ganjam district of Odisha weaves the saree the face and backside of which are alike. The uniqueness of the saree is the solid border designs with *kumbhas* or pillars, which is why they are known as Berhampuri phoda kumbha design.

In the Hooghly region of West Bengal and about 60 kilometres to the north-west of Kolkata are woven the Dhaniakhali sarees in off-white with contrasting coloured borders, which can be in stripes and checks. A short 100 kilometres to the north-east of Dhaniakhali is the town of Santipore. The Santipore sarees carry coloured strips, checks or spots on a grey or white bleached background.

The sample of sarees referred to here is a sliver, tiny piece of the large variety woven in India. A collector's wardrobe could also boast of a Patola from Gujarat, a Kosa from Bastar and a Champa from Chhattisgarh, Kasaragod from Kerala, a Kovai Kora from Tamil Nadu and many more. This short tour of the sareescape brings out the astonishing variety of sarees, produced only in India.

What has maintained the unique quality and character of each saree? It could be said that the physical geography of India comprises of high mountains, dense forests, vast deserts, numerous rivers and many wetlands and marshes. All such features acted as barriers and so kept a distance between places, which thus encouraged individualised local styles. It could well also be said that because of this isolation imposed by natural barriers the sarees woven in different parts of India reflect the geography of the place be it in the form of the available resources of cotton or silk, or influence of a temple or a fort; or the impact of the physical, human and divine environment on the motifs and weaves. The uniqueness of sarees has resulted from the long occupation of the same area and represent the interplay of human ingenuity and curiosity with the ecological givens of place. Moreover the demand for sarees was high. This is because the saree is a ready to use garment, it does not need to be stitched, it is easy to wrap around one's body and is all weather, as it covers the entire body as per personal needs and comforts. Given these advantages, it endured as a national dress. Since local demand was high the need to mix and match designs to align and attract tastes of other regions did not arise. Moreover, the design of the saree was expressive of the local identity. It would not be wrong to add that the prolific variety in sarees is also the result of the creativity of each region and subregion asserting its own identity and holding on to its unique culture and expression. There was no attempt at imitation but a conscious effort to be distinctive.

Generations of weavers have adhered to the traditional style and patterns. For a traditional saree weaver, a sense of belonging to his place so imbued his whole existence that he strongly held on and maintained his identity and did not copy or change his design.

Therefore, when the Indian woman drapes a saree she in fact preserves and flags a creative ensemble of the weaver, dyer, printer and embroiderer of a particular place. In the saree she represents her domicile. Preserving individuality, may it be of the *pallu* or a motif or the type of embroidery, has its merits. One look at the backlash of monoculture or homogeneity and it would be enough to convince that the weavers were aware that following tradition is a secure way to ensure a niche in the market and thus a source of livelihood. It is this tradition and rootedness to place which today has given the saree a dominant share of 37 out of the 199 Geographical Indications goods registered at Chennai.

The tending of goods amidst an exceptional ecology of place be it for the temple or through tradition has meant that India was able to garner a front rank among the trading partners of the world. Trade nurtured demand.

Trade nurtures India's place goods: India's dominance in proffering high-value goods for trade is evident from different quarters. It was through the discovery of the monsoons by Hippalus, a Greek navigator and merchant who lived in the first century BCE, that a direct route from the Red Sea to India over the Indian Ocean was discovered. With this discovery the Egyptian merchants fixed the departure of their ships: 'They sailed confidently across the "black waters" of the Arabian Sea and reached the Malabar coast in 30 or 40 days' (Thomson, 1948: 46).

The seasonal dance of the monsoons is the reason why they were known by the name *vyapari ware* – winds useful for sea trade. But it must be reiterated that while the metronome of the winds moved the trade, it is the goods made only in India that were responsible for the type and volume of trade. The fact that many goods from India were moving along that route was perhaps why the ocean came to be named Indian Ocean. No other ocean in the world is named after a single country! A sure trade between India and Egypt in the ancient times was the fine Indian cotton which wrapped the mummies of Egypt. Bengal has been known for its fine cotton from ancient times. *Malmal*, referred to as Gangetic muslin, in Greek and Roman records was described as being transparent and light, *mehula venit* meaning woven winds. Foreign trade was considerably high under the Mauryas, and guilds of textile workers were prominent during those years (323–185 CE). The *Arthashastra* mentions places specialising in certain textiles. 'Of cotton fabrics, those of Madhura, of Aparánta, western parts, of Kálinga, of Kási, of Vanga, of Vatsa, and of Mahisha are the best' (Shamasastry, 1909: 68). The

Gupta period saw a significant expansion of trade activity, and the Jatakas mention the merchandise for which certain centres were famous, such as Varanasi for silk and fine muslin, Gandharam for red blankets and Punjab for woollen textiles (Singh, 2008).

An item much in demand was pepper. It was traded in bulk to flavour the otherwise bland wheat and barley of the Mediterranean cuisine. The only surviving cookbook of the era, written by Apicius, included pepper in 349 of its 468 recipes! The Romans poured pepper not just into their main courses but also into their sweets, wines and medicines (Apicius cited in Bernstein, 2008). Persius captures this in his poem: 'The greedy merchants led by lucre, run / To the parched *Indies* and the rising sun; / From thence hot pepper and rich drugs they bear, / Bartering for spices their Italian ware' (Persius cied in Bernstein, 2008: 41).

Pliny calculates that in exchange for Chinese and Indian goods sold among the countries of the Mediterranean, Egypt sends to India every year gold and silver worth over 400,000 pounds sterling: '. . . in no year does India drain our empire of less than five hundred and fifty millions of sesterces, giving back her own wares in exchange, which are sold among us at fully one hundred times their prime cost'. Pliny the Elder, a naval and army commander of the early Roman Empire, growls 'so much our luxury and women cost us' (Pliny cited in Kulke and Rothermund, 2009).

Marco Polo and his crew of 300 men halted at the Coromandel Coast of India on their return from China in 1292 CE. Arriving at the kingdom of the Tamil Pandyas, near modern-day Thanjavur, Marco Polo called this 'the richest and most splendid province in the world. . . . Further north workshops make cotton and leather goods shiploads of which go west every year' (Almeida and Gilpin, 2006: 89). About Gujarat, Marco wrote, 'They also work here beautiful mats in red and blue leather, exquisitely inlaid with figures of bird and beasts and skilfully embroidered with gold and silver ware. They are marvellously beautiful things; they are used by the Saracens to sleep upon' (Yule, 1920: 393–394). This was written 700 years ago and refers to none other than the Kutch embroidery which found entry in the Registry of Chennai in 2008.

The temples, tradition and trade all played a critical role in fostering place goods. While the origin, diversity and reason for many of the goods can be attributed to availability of resources and the generous patrons who supported the construction and looked after temples and tradition which reinforced the continuity of distinctive cultures at a particular place, a question that needs to be resolved is what made these place goods be it the making of idols or the weaving of sarees distinctive such that centuries later today they find an entry into the Registry of Geographical Indications?

While it is hard to draw a decisive conclusion yet an overarching factor that strings through most of the place goods which belong to this time period is their connection with the gods. The fact that every good was to be offered to the Divine means that perfection was to be a way of being and thus doing. Goods or objects produced were thus imbued with value and spirit. Attached to major temples were centres or places of production, be it Kancheepuram, Thanjavur, Nagercoil, Konark or Banaras. In other cases, again it was the deep religious sentiment that manifested as a collective symbol and motif into the goods and gave the distinctive features, be it to the Mithila paintings, Molela plaques or Chamba rumal. Sustained by the patrons of temples, more often than not, goods were seen as offering to the Divine and not mere 'products' or items of utility, be it the case of casting the idol or crafting the temple jewellery or fashioning the maddalam.

Excellence and striving for perfection earned merit, and merit by itself was a reward. Such a thinking and spiritual energy created goods that were distinctive and carried perfection. It was the perfection acquired in the making of goods for the gods that set a benchmark for the production of all other goods. People took pride in the goods they created and worked more like devotees rather than craftsmen, even less like workers and still lesser like labour as one today seems to judge of them. Such was the intention and attention of the devotees that rooted in place they created the finest of goods. This grounding helped shape the distinctive identity of place, which the goods carried on as hallmarks of Geographical Indications. The many goods which belong to this phase of history, registered today at Chennai, confirm why the age of the mighty Hindu kingdoms just before the onset of the Turko-Afghan invasions is often called the 'apogee, the highest point in the development of our culture'.

Since many a places produced the most enchanting and distinctive goods, it is no surprise that Basham calls the Pre-Muslim period 'the wonder that was India'. It is due to attraction to this 'wonder' that frequent invasions and conquests poured from the West into India. High on the list of plunder and loot were temples like Somnath, Mathura, Kannauj, Nagarkot and the riches of Thanesar's temples. Temples became targets because of the wealth of exceptional goods. The continuous warfare was a serious blow to the serenity so essential for creativity which had gathered around certain places. A clue to the role of the destruction is the absence of any place good in the Registry of Chennai from the Turko-Afghan invasion, right up to the Mughal period.

Early in the eighth century Arabs turned their attention towards India and conquered Sind. From the twelfth century onward many Muslim armies began to invade India. Since north-west India, at that time, consisted of a number of kingdoms ruled by the Rajputs, mostly preoccupied with fighting against each other, the situation provided an easy access for streams of invaders to gain a foothold. Chronologically, the Muslim presence can be seen in two phases: the first that of the Delhi Sultanate and their string of rulers from 712 to 1526 and the second that of the Mughals from 1526 to 1857.

The binding feature of both the Sultanate and the Mughals was Islam, a monotheistic religion, which, unlike Hinduism, does not believe in idols. Therefore, unlike the temple where the buzz of the deities and Brahmins kept the coterie of silks, flowers, perfumes, food and finery alive, the mosque does not generate a demand for a host of such goods. So with the new people and different religion the demand for goods like silk veils or temple jewellery would also take a new form. Devout Muslims observe a fast during Ramzan, the ninth month on the Islamic calendar. The fast is broken only after an evening prayer. In Hyderabad, a city in Deccan India, a way to break the fast is by eating Hyderabad haleem. This basically is a meat, usually mutton-based, stew with special ingredients which involve long hours of preparation and so is called 'haleem' which literally means patience. The origin of Hyderabad haleem is often traced to the Asaf Jahi Dynasty, which ruled the state of Hyderabad from 1724 to 1948. Hyderabad haleem found entry in the Geographical Indications list in 2010.

The multicoloured beads of agates are another place good which Islam valued as prayer beads. Agates occur in shades of white, green, grey, brown, red and black and are believed to bestow grace and luck on the wearer (Draco, 2012). Demand for them escalated when Cambay became a principal port for embarking on Haj to Mecca. The Agates of Cambay were registered with a Geographical Indications tag in 2008.

While there must be more distinctive place goods that were nurtured in India under the religion of Islam as of the present, the logs of the Registry at Chennai list only the above two; however, there are a cluster of goods with Geographical Indications that were patronised by the Mughal badshahs.

Nurturing of place goods by Mughal badshahs: In 1526, Babur, a descendant of the Mongol warriors Timur and Chengiz Khan, founded the Mughal Dynasty in India. By the beginning of the seventeenth century, the Mughals had established an extensive empire in North India and much of the Deccan. The patronage of Akbar and his successors created many place goods which today find a mention in the ledgers of Geographical Indications. How could a group of people coming from outside India get to nurture place goods which today are registered at Chennai with a Geographical Indications tag? The Mughals after all did not have a comprehensive know-how of the resources of India, neither did they have eons of observation and experience of the spatial differences of the country, nor a reverence to serve a multitude of gods, yet they were successful in nourishing some distinctive place goods. The reason for this ability seems to be fourfold: first, the Mughals were urban people; they not only lived in towns but they also established new towns; as a case, Akbar founded Fatehpur Sikri, while Shah Jahan built Shahjahanabad. In these urban centres were laid mosques, public buildings, forts, palaces and courts. It is in the latter that a demand for a variety of goods was generated.

Second, the Mughal badshahs were mobile kings, and their imperial court culture was rather peripatetic. Their travels were royal both in content and display. A European merchant described the ceremonious travel of a Mughal royal thus, 'All the face of the earth, so far as we could see, was covered with people. All this moving in one, on so many huge elephants, seemed like a fleet of ships with flags and streamers . . . so that all together it made a most majestically warlike and delightsome sight' (Balabanlilar, 2009). The tours and expeditions exposed the Mughals to the potential wealth and variety of goods in different places in India.

Third, the Mughals came with a lively intellectual and scientific curiosity and had a passion to enjoy the best of things in life. To address their taste, the producers were driven to collect, collate and experiment with new materials, designs and styles.

Fourth, the Mughals were keen patrons of arts and transferred many of the skills of their lands into India. The artistic and cultural influences however, had to adapt to local circumstances and were transformed by powerful indigenous traditions to produce goods that essentially were Indian.

Given these four characteristics first, the passion to build and construct, second, the bohemianism, third a deep desire to enjoy the best of things in life and fourth, the cross pollination of skills, the Mughals surely were in the right place at the right time: India having the requisite resources and the political state of disarray and declining wealth in temples meant that it had craftsmen in search of patrons. The Mughal nobility fitted this niche. To furnish the palaces and mobile courts and to satiate the ego of the self, the Mughal badshahs indulged in the best be it clothes, shawls, jewels, perfumes or even playing cards.

The desire to harness the finest raw material from different places is seen in the construction of the Taj Mahal at Agra, 1632–1653, a mausoleum built by Shah Jahan for his favourite wife, Mumtaz Mahal. Here are the details: white marble came from Jaipur, yellow marble from the banks of the Narbudda, black marble was brought from a place called Charkoh, crystal came from China, jasper from the Panjab, turquoise from Tibet, loadstone from Gwalior, onyx from Persia and sapphires from Ceylon (Wood,

1949: 9). To ensure that the exquisite glory of Taj Mahal can never be repeated in any other 'place' in the world the myth goes that Shah Jahan ordered the thumbs of the craftsmen who created this monument to be cut off. It remains till date one of the wonders of the world.

A very different yet equal reflection of the search for the finest is the painstaking gossamer quality chikan or jali work embroidery. Chikan was in demand not only in Delhi and Agra but also with the nawabs in Awadh and Lucknow, so much so that the latter established repute as the 'place' for production. The Lucknow Chikan gained the Geographical Indications tag in 2008.

Lucknow was a site also for the zardozi, a technique where a thick thread is worked to create the design and on this as a binding medium, a variety of metallic threads along with beads, stones and beetle leaves are used to create the details. The court costumes of Mughal emperors were made in zardozi which often used gold. Not only were the nobility dressed in embroidery and jewels, but their horses, camels and elephants too wore adorned with rich saddles. All these demands sustained the Lucknow zardozi works (Registered in 2012).

An item of acclaim was the shawl. The demand nurtured the looms of the Kashmir Valley. They were in general worn singly around the shoulders, but Akbar fancied them so much that he introduced the fashion of wearing two *do-shala* stitched back to back (Karpinski, 1963). Akbar's Toshikana, or the imperial wardrobe, had some of the finest shawls. Abul Fazl, in *Akbarnama*, mentions that Akbar was exceedingly fond of perfumes, and the court chamber was continuously scented with flowers and fumigated with incense sticks and aloes (to recall that *dhoop batti* were lit for 'gods' through the day in Hindu temples). Emperor Jahangir AD 1605–1625 mentions the discovery of rooah-e-gulab by Noorjehan in Tojak Jahangiri. Situated on the banks of the river Ganga the area around Kannauj was chosen as a site for cultivation and growing flowers and *khus* (commonly known as vetiver). Soon this place became famous for the manufacture of natural *attars* from sandal, musk, camphor, saffron and other such aroma-bearing substances. Kannauj perfumery gained a Geographical Indications tag in 2013.

Firozabad met the royal demand for *jhad* and *fanus* (types of chandeliers), and later on phials (kind of bottles) for itra or attar, scents and other cosmetic products. Glass was made long before the arrival of the Mughals, but was probably never a significant industry in Hindustan. Abul Fazl records that in Akbar's reign it was produced at Alwar and mentions in passing that Bihar produced glass. Akbar encouraged its production around the court of Agra and today 40 kilometres from this city, Firozabad has become an important centre for glassware. It acquired the Geographical Indications tag in 2013.

What lent an air of majestic leisure to the court was indulgence in fanfare and games. A special one among the many games was Ganjifa. *Ganj* in Persian means wealth. This is a card game in which the number of cards could range from 24 to as many as 600. Ganjifa cards are circular and carry exquisite motifs of birds, leaves, animals, kings, *vazirs* (ministers) and *gulams* (slaves). They are handmade, drawn and painted by special craftsmen. The Mughal emperor Babur in his memoirs wrote, 'the night we left Agra, Mir Ali was sent to Shah Hasan in Tatta to fetch for him playing cards (ganjifa) he much liked and had asked for' (Babur, 1921: 584). As this game spread from the royal court at Delhi to other parts of the country, the demand for painters or *chitrakars* grew in number. Ganjifa found its way into the list of Geographical Indications in 2007.

The lure for the Mughals of the different and distinctive from places far and wide is a well-established fact, and to ensure a steady supply of the best goods, the badshahs established ateliers or *karkhanas* in close proximity to the courts. Similar to places supported by temples these 'imperial centres' housed and supported some of the best weavers, designers, painters and other craftsmen of the times. The schools of miniature painting exemplify the role of the ateliers. This 'small-format' of painting can be traced to the Quran. Only a miniature or small style of painting could be used to decorate the margins and pages of this revered book. So popular was this style that soon India had different schools of miniature paintings.

Nurturing place goods: schools of miniature painting: The Mughal rule lasted in India for over 300 years. Babur reigned for four short years and he neither brought artists with him nor founded an atelier. He was succeeded by Humayun in AD 1530, but Humayun though fond of ornate books also had no court atelier of artists. It was Akbar who formed an atelier of at least 30 Indian artists and, Abul Fazl notes, more than 100 painters have become famous masters of the art. Further he adds, 'The number of master-pieces of painting increased with the encouragement given to the art. Persian books, both prose and poetry, were ornamented with pictures, and a very large number of paintings was thus collected' (Havell, 1928: 193). India had different schools of miniature paintings between the sixteenth and nineteenth centuries. The principal schools were at Rajasthan, Pahars, or Hill States, and the Deccan. Cradled within differing geographical ambit the schools display different styles and themes of painting. Rajasthani miniature paintings progressed rapidly under local painters and evolved varying regional styles and ethos of its own. Mewar, Bundi, Kota, Jaipur and Kishangarh in eastern Rajasthan and Jodhpur, Bikaner and Jaisalmer in the western region became important centres of painting. The Rajput paintings have the strong lines and colours and the same chivalric character as that of the land (Rajasthan) from which it comes. In winter, Rajasthan is full of colour, but in summer, before the rains the landscape is dry, parched and drab. Perhaps as an attempt to compensate for the bleached surroundings and as a reminder of the more colourful seasons, the artists in this area developed a special penchant for primary colours: reds, blues and yellows.

In the foothills of the Himalayas, or pahars, are the centres of painting like Kangra, Chamba, Kulu, Mandi, Guler and Jammu. Pahari is an adjective which means 'belonging to the hills'. Inspired by the natural scenery the illustrations of Pahari artists are filled with hills, shrubs and flowering trees of the region composed in forms according to their own choice. Absorbed with the environs the paintings 'adopt a cool soft colour, where the landscape is rich and varied, the women are numerous and love is recurrent theme' (Randhawa and Galbraith, 1968: 3). It reinforces how a place nurtures a style (Figure 3.7).

In contrast to the Rajasthani and Pahari schools the miniature paintings at Deccan are more Persianised. The Deccan sultans maintained close cultural ties with Persia rather than their religious rivals in Delhi. This is because the rulers of the Deccan states such as Golconda and Bijapur were Shias and the Safavid kings of Persia were also Shias. The Mughals on the other hand were orthodox Sunnis. The Persian influence, with the use of rich and luminous colours like blue and red and much use of gold and white, is the reason for how Deccan paintings retained an unmistakable individuality of their own in all the three main centres of Ahmednagar, Bijapur and Golconda.

The Persian influence in the Deccan is also evident in the origin of Bidriware. This is the art of encrusting one metal in another in the form of a wire, which undercuts and is hammered into the metal which it intends to ornament. Damascening in silver is called bidri. Abdullah-bin-Kaiser, a craftsman from Iran, was invited by Sultan Ahmad Shah Wali (1422–1436) to work on decorating the royal palaces and courts. According to some accounts, Kaiser joined hands with local craftsmen and gave birth to Bidriware (Desai, 2006). Bidriware was registered with a Geographical Indications tag in 2005.

Bidri, Kashmir shawls, miniatures and Lucknowi zardozi are only a few handpicked from a basket of goods in which the Mughals indulged. On their list are the likes of Golconda diamonds or the knives of Rampur and many more. With the Mughals a royal connect with place goods deepened.

A royal connect with place goods: The special kind of shawl woven, with the down hair of the *chiru* or Tibetan antelope, by the weavers of Kashmir

Figure 3.7 India: Geographical Indications – centres of painting and schools of miniature paintings

and claimed to be the world's finest and warmest woollen material is known as *shahtoosh*, a Persian word meaning 'pleasure of kings'. The heavy fabric with a floral or figured pattern known most for its woven *butis* and *jals*, with silk as the warp and *tilla* as the weft, is called Khinkhwab; *Khwab* in Urdu means 'a dream' and it is said that even with such a name 'Its beauty, splendour and elegance can be hardly dreamt of'.

Keen to impress their royal clients, the embroiderers of Kutch *arri* work quickly incorporated motifs like peacock, *butis* or flower and bud designs. When in keeping with the clients' preferences big-sized motifs dotted the garment, the butis were referred to as 'Nadir Shah buti'. Jamdani is a Persian word derived from *jaam-daar* meaning floral designs in cotton thread. Jamdani weaves formed part of the annual tribute paid by Dacca (a place now in Bangladesh) to Aurangzeb (1658–1707). To ensure complete allegiance Aurangzeb forbade the weaving of jamdani by any other than the court weavers. A sure case which would have gained the place good certificate was Dacca muslin. The fineness of it may be judged from an early nineteenth-century report where one-pound weight of cotton yarn was found to be 250 miles in length (Hankin. 2003). It was described in poetic terms such as *abrawan*, or running water; *bafthoioa*, or woven air, and *shubanam*, or evening dew.

The royal connect comes from other parts of India as well. Shaphee Lanphee is a type of hand-woven fabric shawl made by the Meetei women from Manipur and Nagaland. It carries stylised embroidered motifs such as the sun, stars, fish, spear, peacock, buffalo horn, horse and the elephant. Tribal people use it during burial or wedding ceremonies. Meetei Kings presented Shaphee Lanphee as rewards to the worthy Naga chiefs of Manipur (it gained a Geographical Indications tag in 2013).

The relationship of 'special connect' goes even further back in history. Just after AD 630 the Chinese pilgrim Hsuan Tsang arrived at the monastic university of Nalanda to perfect himself in the study of Sanskrit and Buddhism. The Chinese biographer reports of Hsuan Tsang's reception: 'He was lodged on the fourth storey of Buddhabhadra's house . . . every day he was provided with 120 *tambula* leaf-bunches, 20 areca nuts . . . and one *shang* measure of mahasala rice. This rice had grains larger than the black bean, and when it was cooked it had a fragrance which *no other kind* of rice possessed. It was produced only in Magadha and was not found elsewhere. As it was offered only to kings and well-learned monks of great virtue, it was called "mahasala" rice' (Kosambi, 1965: 176).

The royalty therefore watered many place goods. The skill, artistry and mastery which showed up in carpet, shawl, zardozi, chikan or paintings were the creation of the people of India. The weavers, embroiderers and carvers, among others, had practised to perfect their art for eons. A trained, skilled population does not find it difficult to adapt its competence to new demands. It was not difficult for the weavers of sarees to shift to the weaving of fabric, or the sculpturists to that of painting. While the skills were transferable, what had to be absorbed and transformed were the motifs and designs. Islam abhors the use of idols or humans or divinity in the pattern of their designs. Therefore in the design of goods in shawls, carpets or carvings, nature was imitated and flowers, ferns, trees and animals became a more evident form of the pattern. A new religion, new rulers, a new set of demands and patrons continued to add to India's directory of distinctive place goods.

Therefore, just as in the twenty-first-century cinema and software industries have crystallised around the technical expertise that accumulated in Bollywood, Hyderabad and Bengaluru, in the sixteenth century, centres such as Dhaka, Srinagar, Kasimbazar and Broach attracted spinners, weavers and finishers. Moreover, products of the likes of Bidri, Kannauj, Moradabad, Cashmere, Chikan, and Mughal paintings acquired worldwide fame. All are a compliment to none other but to the Made Only in India. The exotic goods gave India a lead in trade, which boosted demand and in return nurtured place goods.

Trade under the Mughals nurtures place goods: Tomé Pires, an apothecary from Lisbon who was in Malacca from 1512 to 1515, writes in the *Suma Oriental* that 'Four ships come every year from Gujarat to Malacca. The merchandise they bring is cloth of thirty kinds, which are of value in these parts' (Pires, 1515: 269–270). Most prized of the Indian commodities were cloth of which he documented 30 types! By corollary it would not be far from the truth to infer that 30 different places wove these specialised textiles. Linschoten, the young Portuguese who travelled to India and stayed in Goa for five years from 1583, says: 'There is great quantity of pepper, for that they are able every year to lade a shippe with 7000 or 8000 quintals of pepper, and it is the best and fullest berries in all Malabar or India' (Linschoten 1598: 21).

'At the end of the Kingdome of Orixa and the coast of Choramandel begin the River Ganges in the kingdom of Bengalen: Besides their Ryce, much Cotton linen is made there which is *very fine*, and much esteemed in India, and not only spread abroad and carried into India and al the East parts, but also into Portugal, and other places' (Linschoten, 1598). The quote (retained in its original English spelling) reinforces that places were known for their quality of goods be it the Malabar Coast for pepper or Bengal for cotton linen.

Travelogues of the period are replete with descriptions of bazaars and goods. When Father Monserrate with his fellow Jesuits visited the bazaar at Fatehpur Sikri, near Agra, in 1580, he observed 'the bazaar at Fatehpur extended for more than half a mile and had an astonishing quantity of every description of merchandise'. The Jesuit marvelled at the 'great number of artisans, iron workers and goldsmiths in Agra' (Monserrate, 1922: 31). Pyrard de Laval, the French traveller to India in the middle of the seventeenth century, notes, 'the principal riches consist chiefly of silk and cotton stuffs, wherewith everyone from the Cape of Good Hope to China, man and women is clothed from head to foot' (Pyrard cited in Gray, 1887: 247–248). Without taking Pyrard literally what seems clear is that he was struck by the popularity of Indian textiles abroad. Bernier, the French traveller in Akbar's court in 1670, had a theory that all 'gold and silver coinage after circulating elsewhere comes at last to be absorbed in India' (Bernier cited in Thomson, 1948: 301).

Even though Europe's reserve of silver had been greatly increased from Mexico and Peru, yet there was a drain of bullion for luxuries and it was grumbled that Europe 'bleedeth to enrich Asia' and 'all nations bring coin . . . and this coin is buried in India, and goeth not out' (Thomson, 1948: 301).

The high-quality goods that were exported from India to Portugal around 1600 CE is evident in the title of the exhibition 'Luxury for Export' curated at Boston in 2008. The call suggests that the objects exported to Europe were not mere ordinary products but rather sophisticated and special goods for those who could afford and appreciate 'luxury'. The Europeans cast their aspirations and sinuous intentions on the emporium of India's trade. The Portuguese, then the Dutch, the French, the British and other merchants all clamoured to gain a foothold and make a profit in the lucrative trade of India. Early in the sixteenth century, the Portuguese founded the first European trading stations and settlements. 'We seek Christians and spices' is the answer a sailor in Vasco da Gama's fleet gave when asked why the Portuguese had come to India. Vasco da Gama reached the port of Calicut, on the coast of Malabar on 22 May 1498. It would be no exaggeration to claim that when the British docked at the coast of India around 1600 CE, India was a land booming with place goods. There are many evidences which confirm that India was dotted with many places that produced exotic goods.

An undeniable inheritance of a rich legacy of crafts and goods was handed down to India. The synthesis of Hindu and Mughal cultures added to the list of goods. The motivations may have differed, one for the temples and the other for the court, yet both were endowed with a keenness for the aesthetic and the exotic. It is this inheritance of exceptional goods manufactured at key centres in India that were noticed, noted and documented by travellers. A proof of the many place goods nurtured in India is in the copious documentation by the British.

Evidence of innumerable place goods – early nineteenth century: To further the knowledge of the territories, the East India Company began to publish a series of gazetteers. In the *Imperial Gazetteer of India* (1909–1931), the British articulated a definite reference to the exceptional goods which carried a bond with place:

> A considerable industry in the manufacture of silk and cotton fabrics is carried on in Arani, a town situated in the Tiruvannamalai district, 142 kilometres to the south-west of present day Chennai.
>
> A more celebrated industry is the wood work of Saharanpur, this has long been established in the city, and has acquired a wide reputation.
>
> At Kondapalli there is a special industry, involved in the manufacture of small figures and toys from a light wood which grows on the hills.
>
> Among the muslins of Rajputana the foremost place is held by those of Kotah.
>
> The saffron of Kashmir is famous for its bouquet, and is in great request as a condiment and as a pigment for the sect-marks of Hindus.
>
> In India, fine colour is a splendid tradition. Champleve enamel soon attained a *remarkable perfection* of technique and purity and brilliance of colour almost unknown to the western nations. The Champleve enamel of Jaipur has most beautiful lustrous and transparent blues, greens and reds laid on a pure gold ground.

Other scholarly publications which detail on the place goods may be listed below:

> Sir George Watt in *1902–03* wrote, The art of enameling, to its highest perfection, is peculiar to the city of Jaipur.
>
> (Watt cited in Cole, 1874)

> The prolificacy of exceptional goods is evident. The best Hindu jewelry, is the beaten gold of Sawuntwari, Mysore, Vizianagram, and Vizagapatam. . . the old Delhi work in cut and gem encrusted jade is priceless, the pottery of Madura and the Punjab and Scinde can be classed of the highest excellence. . . . very good brass work is made at Ahmednagger and Ahmedabad in Western India, but that of Madura and Thanjavur in the Madras Presidency is superior to all. . . .
>
> (Birdwood, 1878)

> The Kinkhab of Benares is renowned and is equalled in quality only by that from Ahmedabad and Surat in the Bombay Presidency.
>
> (Colonial and Indian Exhibition, 1886)

> The Sanganer town of Jaipur State must, however, be regarded as the very metropolis of the calico-printing craft of India so far as art conception and technique are concerned.
>
> (Glazier, 1899)

> Fine cotton-painting comes mainly from the Palakollu area, at the delta of the Godavari, and Petaboli (Nizamapatam), where painters worked directly under merchants supervision.
>
> (Bowrey, 1903)

Daniell's work on the industrial competition of Asia confirms, 'trade . . . of India was available from no other quarter except India' (Shah, 1923). The phrase 'no other . . . but India' is a tribute to the Made Only in India.

As the British encountered the exotic and different goods a new set of place-related vocabulary rapidly found its way into the English lexicon. Between the seventeenth and twentieth centuries 1,079 Indian words entered the English dictionary (Table 3.1). The addition of 35 words per decade in the seventeenth century slackened to 16 in the eighteenth century, rising again to 32 words per decade in the nineteenth century and 25 words per decade in the twentieth century. When words related to place goods were searched for, on the list were the likes of Bengal, Bidri, Bombay duck, Calico, Cashmere and Golconda.

Therefore, when the British arrived there is little doubt that India was a country with innumerable distinctive goods that carried an association with a particular place. The British were quick to document and include them into their vocabulary. To the list of place goods the British made additions. Two main sets of consideration influenced their keenness to seed new place goods: The first focused on those places where goods for military supplies could be manufactured, and second, they looked out for those places which could grow or manufacture goods that assured a profit back in England. In the first category came the leather, silk and ceramic centres and in the latter group came tea and coffee plantations and cotton textiles of India.

Place goods for military supplies: India was a colony of the British when World War I (1914–1918) and World War II (1939–1945) broke out in Europe. Wartime created a spurt of demand for certain goods in Europe. To cater to these the British were alert to select those places in India which could swiftly meet the demand for those goods.

During World War II the countries of the world got organised into two groups, the Axis powers and the Allies. Among the Axis powers was Japan, which captured China, which was a main centre of silk production. This

Table 3.1 Place goods of India: a lexicon in the English dictionary

Word	*Year*[1]	*Description*	*Place*
Bengal	1678	Cotton cloth	Bengal (now state of West Bengal)
Bidri	n.d.	Alloy	Bidar, a city in north-eastern Karnataka
Bombay duck	1803	Bummalo, fish	Bombay (now Mumbai), capital of Maharashtra
Calico	1616	Cotton cloth	Cotton cloth, after Calicut, a city in Kerala
Cashmere	1822	Shawl	Northern most state of India
Chikan	1886	Embroidery	Lucknow, now capital of Uttar Pradesh
Golconda	1583	Source of riches[2]	Ruined city in Hyderabad district, Telangana
Jodhpur	1899	Horse-riding dress	Jodhpur, a city in Rajasthan
Madras	1654	Handkerchief[3]	Madras (now Chennai), capital of Tamil Nadu
Malabar leaf	n.d.	Cinnamon	Malabar is a district in Kerala
Pulicat	1793	Cotton cloth	Pulicat, seashore town in the state of Tamil Nadu
Surat	1643	Cotton cloth	Surat, seashore town in Gujarat
Trichy	1877	Trichinopoly cigar	City in the state of Tamil Nadu

n.d. – Not dated

[1] Year represents first known occurrence of the word in English.

[2] Golconda had the only known diamond mines in the world. By the 1880s, Golconda was being used generically by English speakers to refer to any particularly rich mine, and later to any source of great wealth.

[3] These are multicoloured check-patterned cloths woven out of yarn dyed in nonfast colours. On washing, the colours will bleed and give an effect which has an appeal of its own.

Based on: Rao (1954)

meant that the Allies (which included Britain) faced a severe shortage of silk to manufacture the much-needed parachutes in time of war. To bridge the gap, the British were quick to tap into the silk production at Mysore. The silk industry at Mysore owed its origin to Tipu Sultan who ruled Mysore from 1782 to 1799. A reflection of Tipu Sultan's interest in sericulture was that he sent for silk worms from Bengal and established 21 centres in his dominion to rear the silk worms. This established the foundation for sericulture in the region. The demand for silk to manufacture parachutes during the world wars ushered in the heydays of Mysore silk (Geographical Indications tag in 2005). It was during this war that a demand also arose for ceramic ware for hospitals which nursed wounded soldiers. To meet this requirement the entire production of ceramics at Khurja, a city situated around 85 kilometres south-east of Delhi, was diverted to war needs by the British. This brought Khurja into prominence. Today Khurja supplies a large portion of the ceramics and pottery used in the country.

Battles and fights between 'colonists and the natives' became frequent even on the turf of India especially since the uprising of 1857. The growing disturbances made the British realise that England was 'too distanced to ferry goods from there to India' and goods like leather ware could easily be manufactured in India.

The Mutiny of 1857 demonstrated the need to have supply centres for horseback saddles close to the army base. Kanpur housed a cantonment since 1801 and so was chosen as the site for a government harness and saddler factory in 1867. The effort to supply saddles to warring countries in Europe led to a spurt in the growth of Kanpur saddler products (Roy, 1999). Tanneries were set up additionally in Madras and other places such as Trichy and Dindigul and what got created was the famous East India Tanning Technology Institute in 1915 at Madras. Flagging colonial heritage in the name 'East India' these leathers received a Geographical Indications tag in 2008 (Figure 3.8).

Therefore supply to military garrisons was a factor that motivated the British to nurture a few place goods, but apart from the play of historical events like the world wars, the role of geography was far more pervasive as is brought out by the case of plantations.

England falls in the temperate latitude, whereas India is a tropical and subtropical country. This climatic contrast means that there are certain produce that cannot be raised in England. In colonial times the mode of transport was slow, refrigeration little known and so perishable goods could not be transported over long distances. British soldiers, administrators and their families stationed in India craved for temperate fruits in tropical India. The possibility of meeting this demand existed because India has mountains and hills. This means that inspite of the tropical latitude, the topography allows climatic zones to develop that grade from the tropical and subtropical, to the temperate and arctic. This geographical character paved the scope for the British to set up places that could grow fruits and beverage for the colony and for their home, England.

Plantations: Among the fruits and beverages registered at Chennai, a small number trace their inception to the colonial period. Mahabaleshwar was the perfect summer getaway for the administrators residing in the Bombay Province. Located in the Sahyadri mountain ranges on the Western Ghats this plateau is never too hot because of altitude and never too cold because of the tempering influence of the warm winds from the Arabian Sea. Inspired by the ecology, British officers introduced the cultivation of

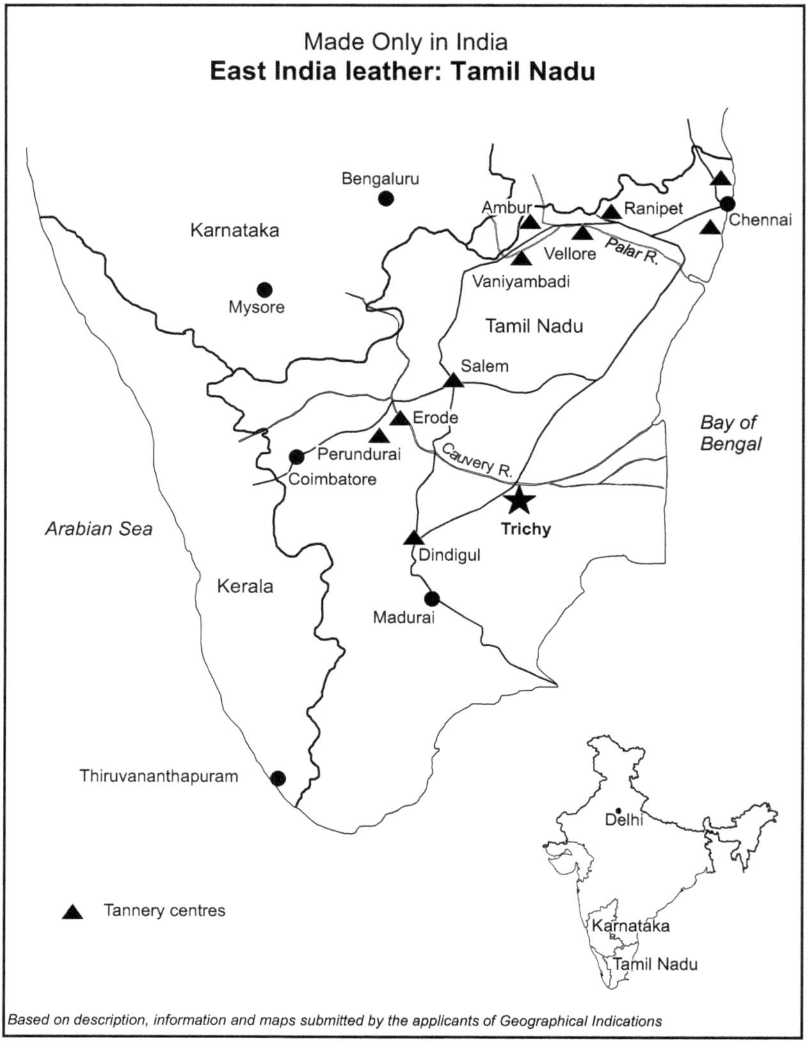

Figure 3.8 East India leather: Tamil Nadu

strawberry at Mahabaleshwar in 1920. Mahabaleshwar strawberries attained the status of Geographical Indications in 2010.

Inspired by the British, Shree Ramrao Jairamji Gaikwad almost ushered in a grape revolution in early 1925 at Ojhar, a small town lying 20 kilometres to the north-east of Nashik. The bunches of bold, fleshy and elongated berries of the Nashik grapes were labelled with the Geographical Indications tag in 2010. But the finest example of British investment with a place is in the plantations of coffee and tea.

Coffee it is said was introduced into India by a saint called Baba Budan in 1670 CE. On his pilgrimage to Mecca he travelled through the seaport of Mocha, Yemen, where he discovered coffee. To introduce its taste to India, he wrapped seven coffee beans around his belly and got them out of Arabia. He planted the beans in the hills of Chikmagalur located in the foothills of the Western Ghats, which in his honour are named Baba Budan Hills.

In the 1850s, the British decided to clear acres of forest in the Western Ghats and set up coffee plantations. A region specially suited was Malabar. Lying between the southern Western Ghats and the Arabian Sea, Malabar was a part of the British-controlled Madras Province. From this region, the ships on sail took six months for the unwashed cherry coffee to reach Europe. During this transit, the coffee in the damp hold of ships was exposed to sea winds saturated with high humidity. This exposure allowed the coffee to acquire a special vintage flavour which was liked by the consumers in Europe. When the Suez Canal was opened in 1869, the time taken to travel 7,000 kilometres from India to Europe was reduced from six months to a journey of one month. This shortened time of sea travel affected the taste of coffee. European consumers complained that they missed the distinctive flavour of musty age in the unwashed Indian coffee. To re-create the special taste, the producers and exporters of coffee in India invented the method wherein they spread the coffee beans out in open trays to allow the latter to absorb the moisture and thus 'monsoon' the coffee. The region thus became famous for the Monsooned Malabar Arabica Coffee and Monsooned Malabar Robusta Coffee, both of which earned the status of Geographical Indications in 2008. More than coffee, it was tea which held the imagination of the British.

The British East India Company was established in 1600, but the tea trade did not begin until the late 1670s. China is considered to be the country of origin of tea. It is said that Buddhist monks introduced it to Japan between AD 520 and 800. In the sixteenth century it was the Christian missionaries and sailors who carried the knowledge of the cultivation and beneficial effects of tea to Europe. The trade began with the shipping of tea to Amsterdam by Dutch merchants in 1610 (this explains the use of orange pecko, orange being a colour associated with the ruling family of the Netherlands) (Wachendorf, 2007). Tea culture was brought to England by the Dutch, where it eventually became the national drink. In 1699 the English entered the trade, and tea began to be imported by the English East India Company. The latter enjoyed a monopoly until 1833.

The popularity of tea in Europe is often attributed to the Portuguese Queen Catherine who married King Charles II of England. The poet and politician Edmund Waller (1606–1687) while writing a poem in honour of Queen Catherine on her birthday credits her for making tea a fashionable drink amongst courtiers: 'Tea both excels, which she vouchsafes to praise, / To best of Queens, and best of herbs, we owe / To that bold nation which the way did show / To the fair region where the sun doth rise / Whose rich productions we so justly prize./ The Muse's friend, tea does our fancy aid'.

By 1700, tea was on sale in more than 500 coffee houses in London. Tea drinking became even more popular when Queen Anne (1665–1714), the seventh Duchess of Bedford, introduced the idea of having tea in the late afternoon. During the Industrial Revolution, working families would return home tired and exhausted. The table would be set with any manner of meats, bread, butter, pickles, cheese and of course tea. Because it was eaten at a high dining table rather than the low tea tables, it was termed 'high' tea. Till date 'high tea' is inseparable from the English way of life. To back this demand, the British during the eighteenth and nineteenth centuries converted large acres of land in India for cultivating tea. Tea came to the official attention of the East India Company in 1834, and its potential for cultivation was submitted to the council by Lord Bentinck to lay tea gardens in Assam. The Tea Committee of 1834 set out the procedures. Today the plateau and the hill slopes on either side of the Brahmaputra river is the largest continuous tea-growing region in the world. The cultivation of tea in Darjeeling began in 1841 when one Dr Campbell stationed there as medical officer planted tea seeds in his garden. The first commercial plantation of tea in Darjeeling was established in 1852. By 1870, the number of plantations in Darjeeling had grown to 56 covering 4,400 hectares and producing 71,000 kilograms of tea. In 1834, experiments of cultivating tea were undertaken in Kangra in Himachal Pradesh and Sikkim, followed by efforts in the Nilgiri highlands of South India (Figure 3.9). The East India Company marketed the tea in a way that soon this hot drink brewed from dry leaves became a physiological necessity to millions in the world.

Soon the 'annual production of what may be called plantation products in India amounts in value to about 74 million sterling . . . entire districts have been occupied by European planters. There are the coffee plantations of Coorg and Mysore, the tea plantations of Assam and the Himalaya and the indigo estates of Tirhoot and the Gangetic Valley' (Watson, 1876: 23). The plantations laid by the British seeded the efforts to establish the tea industry. In the world tea is the second most consumed liquid after water. Today tea is the most popular and cheapest beverage in India. The industry employs over a million persons, half of whom are women. With over

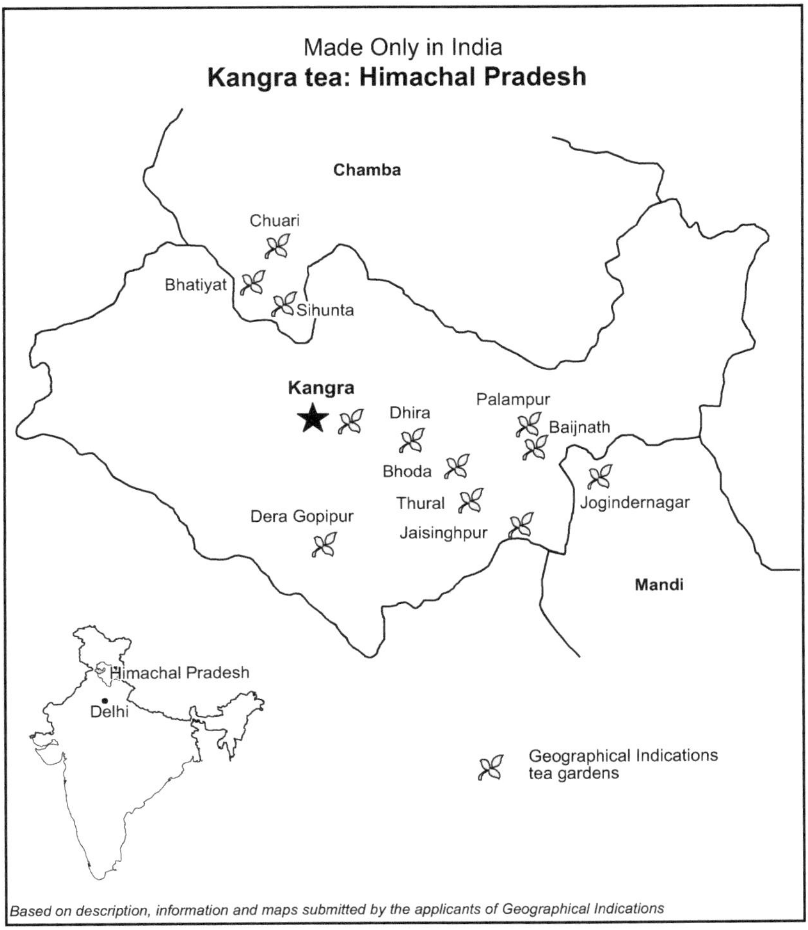

Figure 3.9 Kangra tea: Himachal Pradesh

one-third of the world tea production, India is the largest tea-producing country. There are over 13,900 tea estates large and small, spread over the north-east, south and north-west parts of India. Each place produces its own distinctive type of tea.

The delicate soft lemony aroma is that of Nilgiri tea, Tamil Nadu. It is crisp and clear, and as it does not cloud it is perfect for making iced tea. Tea from Kerala and Karnataka has more coppery overtones. The most famous of all is Darjeeling. Its leaves are generally very large and the liquor aromatic with hints of muscatel in the flavour. The mellow Darjeeling tea (2004), the brisk Nilgiri (2004), the aromatic Kangra (2005) and the malty Assam tea (2008) all have successively gained the tag of Geographical Indications.

Among the goods nurtured by the British was also sandalwood oil. Sandalwood is an evergreen tree almost entirely confined to the forests of Mysore and closely adjacent districts (Guenther, 1948). Sandalwood oil is distilled from the roots and heartwood of *Santalum album Linn*. The golden yellow oil of this tree differs in chemical composition and fragrance from other so-called sandalwood oils. That the East India Company carried a pride for place is apparent from the fact that to distinguish their products in trade, they called it the East India Sandalwood Oil. It recently was renamed as Mysore Sandalwood Oil. It gained a registration at Chennai in 2005. But more than feeding the military garrisons and laying the plantations, the trading activities of the British gave a sudden fillip to the export of cotton textiles and with it the many centres engaged in textile production.

Textiles: During the birth of the East India Company in 1600, India was a land of many places of cotton textile production. Cotton is easy to grow but requires an enormous amount of labour to produce. India has the ideal, black cotton soil of the northern Deccan and climatic conditions most suited for the cultivation. The Deccan Traps are one of the largest volcanic regions in the world. They consist of more than 2,000 meters of flat-lying basalt lava flows and cover an area of nearly 500,000 square kilometres in west-central India. The weathering of basalt builds a soil which has a high clay content, the latter characteristic allows soil to retain moisture which is favourable for the growth of cotton plants. In addition cotton requires mild, cool, dry climate with abundant sunshine and light to moderate rainfall distributed throughout the year.

India not only meets the physical conditions for the growth of cotton but also has a large and inexpensive workforce with centuries of expertise in weaving textiles. The variety and quality of textiles lured Europeans, be it the Dutch or the English, at first to use textiles as an item for barter in exchange for spices from the Malayan Archipelago. It was the cheaper and coarser grades of both plain and painted cotton cloth that were in demand. The weavers were scattered in villages around Golconda near Hyderabad and the trade was carried out mainly through the port at Masulipatnam (Figure 3.10).

The pattern of spice trade with the West involved a three-direction movement. Ships, crewed mostly by Arabs, left the Red Sea and Persian Gulf with bullion. This gold was first exchanged in India for textiles. Then the textiles were carried by the same ships to Malaya and there were bartered

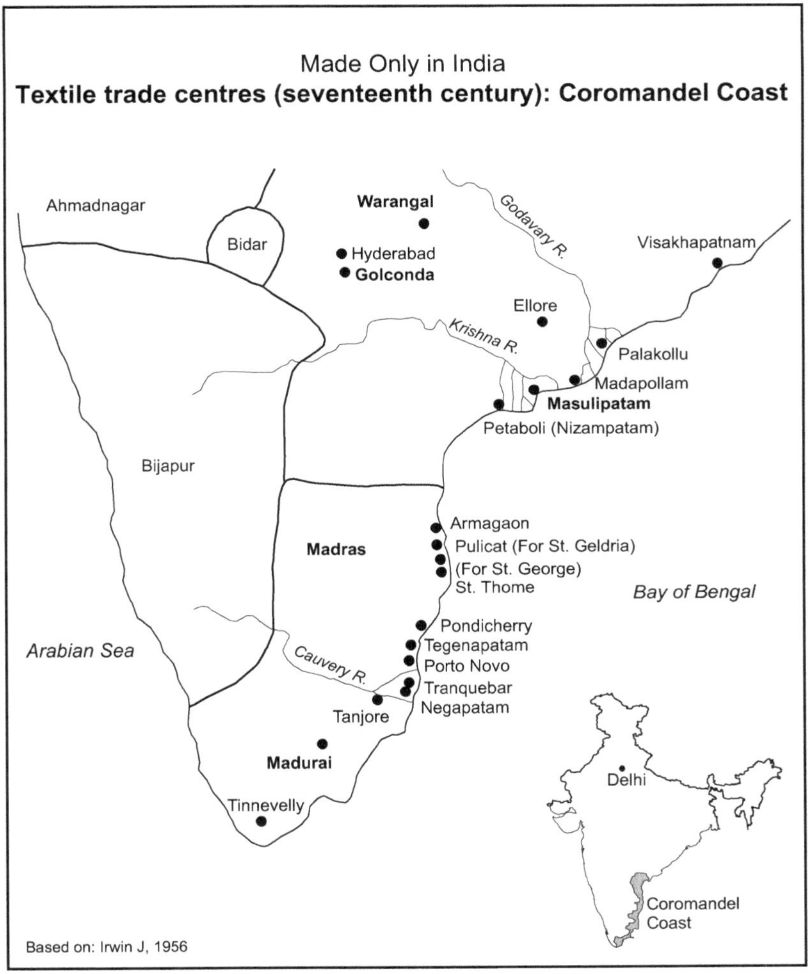

Figure 3.10 Textile trade centres (seventeenth century): Coromandel Coast

for spices. These ships then returned to the Arabian Peninsula, laden with spices which were then again exchanged for bullion. After this, the ships began their next round. The export of the textiles of India was used to fund the spice trade, and the English ships began calling at Masulipatnam in 1611 and four years later founded a factory there. It was not until 1649 that any English vessel returned direct to England from the Coromandel

Coast with textile goods. The records of the Dutch and English East India Companies show a pattern of rapid, almost explosive growth of demand for fine Indian textiles in Europe. In 1610, European- and Asian-owned ships were carrying about ten million yards of cloth to South-east and West Asia, plus a few yards of samples to Europe. By 1625, the volume within Asia had doubled. In the 1650s, the Asian trade had begun to level off at 25–30 million yards, but several million now went to Europe and Africa. In the late 1660s, European imports passed the 10 million mark and continued to rise sharply, reaching a yearly average between 35 and 40 million yards by the early 1680s. In the peak year of 1684, the English East India Company alone imported 45 million yards of Indian cloth, more than six yards for each man, woman, and child in Great Britain. 'If one adds in the exports carried by the Dutch and other Europeans and the native Indian and Arab traders in 1684, Indian exports to all points totalled more than 100 million yards' (Bronson, 1983: 18).

To boost trade, the East India Company in the mid-seventeenth century realised that if the fashion leaders wore Indian chintz and hung calico drapery, others would quickly follow. Enrolling the monarchy was an obvious choice. One courtier had observed in 1688 that the Queen of England's chamber had 'all Indian embroidery on white satin presented to her by the Company' (Bernstein, 2008: 255). This was true of other textiles like shawls.

By the eighteenth century, ornamented Kashmir Pashmina apparels had become fashionable in Europe. Historians credit the Emperor Napoleon Bonaparte's fashionable wife Josephine de Beauharnais for making shawls a European sensation. Her fascination with Kashmiri shawls grew after Napoleon's Egyptian campaign in 1798, when the French Army, returning from the Egyptian campaign, brought many items including a lot of shawls. Josephine, historians say, was the proud owner of 200 to 400 Kashmiri shawls. In a number of paintings depicting her, she can be seen wearing Kashmiri shawls (http://www.kashmirlife.net/opening-up-vistas-1456/).

The European market was almost inexhaustible, and the demand for textiles appeared to have no limits. Besides textiles many other place goods of India be it wooden crafts, metal crafts, jewellery and carpets all enjoyed great demand and growth in demand. But prosperity was short-lived. Ironically it was the British who had taken many place goods to great heights of production and fame, and it is they who plunged them into the worst of abysses. The destruction was neither innocent nor an accident. The colonists laid out a vicious path for the destruction of the Made Only in India.

4

DESTROYING

Place goods

By the nineteenth century the heyday of place goods of India was nearing an end. British rule in India was for less than 400 years. In this span a synergy of colonial policies and actions propelled an epidemic of demise. This is evident from a comparison of the number and variety of place goods that flourished at the time of British arrival and the status of these by the time British had to leave India. The destruction was not limited to one or two centres or to a few goods. The blue print of destruction was carefully planned and cleverly operationalised and therefore was successfully accomplished. The sudden and hurried style added to the crises. Different means were employed to ensure the destruction.

To gain an insight into the process of destruction, it is worth its while to focus on the traditional textile weaving industry. This industry as was seen had supported and created beautiful fabrics like the sarees, shawls or carpets of India. The demand by the upper echelons be it the patrons of temples, the nawabs of courts or the queen of England for the textiles was based on their excellent and exceptional quality. These goods were responsible for upholding India's lead in international trade. Besides being a hugely important sector that engaged a large section of the population of India, the textile weaving centres were niches which housed local resources, local cultures and local wisdom and carried the flavour of place. Moreover textiles constitute 44 per cent of the goods registered for Geographical Indications in Chennai. For reasons like this and more the textile weaving centres have rightly been called the backbone of India. When the British set out to calculate that manufacturing textile goods in England would skyrocket their profits, they unleashed a strategy to tear down India's manufacturing base bit by bit and piece by piece. Most if not all that were severely hit were place goods.

Strategy to destroy: The British set out a multipronged approach to destroy India's places of production. An important step towards this was the collection and documentation of the samples of goods and their process of manufacturing.

Document and research: Towards this end, many seemingly innocent travellers, who in reality were British agents, were commissioned to observe and file away information about the process of production of the goods. The agents incognito as travellers took detailed notes about the preparation of raw materials and about the techniques of spinning, weaving and setting the pattern. Special reports were prepared on themes like the dyes, threads, colours and styles of weaves in India. The *Journal of Indian Art* was launched in 1884 and it ran a series of articles covering textiles and other crafts of India. An enviable dimension of Indian textiles was the perfection in the art of dyes. The British were quick to compile information on the techniques in the publication titled *The Dyes and Tans of India* (1887), which carries copious notes of 3,500 dye samples produced from 181 varieties of Indian dye! The publication was nicknamed the Blue Book after Indigo the blue dye derived from the leaves of a leguminous plant which grew in India. John Forbes Watson (1827–1892) compiled a collection of 700 different textiles from various parts of India for the East India Company. This almost complete range of India's textile products was then arranged into 18 volumes, each dedicated to a different textile type. The volumes were accompanied by a lavishly illustrated edition titled *The Textile Manufacturers and Costumes of the People of India.* Twenty sets of this volume were prepared of which 13 were distributed in Great Britain and 7 in India. The idea of 'exact counterpart' was created to allow easy and quick references. Each sample of textile in these volumes was prepared in such a way as to indicate the character of the whole piece from which it was cut and thus enable the manufacturer to reproduce the article. The set of volumes may be regarded as '18 industrial museums, illustrating the textile manufactures of India' (Watson, 1876: 1). The importance of all this documentation to manufacturers in England hardly needs elaboration.

Exhibit to see and learn: A visual is more powerful than a written word. To take the best places of India back to their homeland, the British organised international trade exhibitions. Among the many, three exhibitions were large in scale: the Paris Universal Exposition of 1878, the Colonial and Indian Exhibition of 1886 and the Manchester Royal Jubilee Exhibition of 1887. Celebrating the recovery of France, following the 1870 Franco-Prussian War, was the Paris Universal Exposition of 1878. During the planning stages, the Prince of Wales sought from the French authorities the western half of the vestibule for India's displays. Over 12,000 specimens of objects were exhibited in the Grand Vestibule of the Palace of the Champ de Mars. Visited by an unprecedented 16 million people from all over the world, it was the distinctive quality of goods on display that allowed India to bag the position of honour among the foreign departments. Judges awarded the sections on India 11 gold, 15 silver and 21 bronze medals in addition to 10 diplomas of honour. To commemorate Queen Victoria's golden jubilee, South Kensington in London in 1886 held an exhibition titled the 'Colonial and Indian Exhibition'. A sure reflection of the importance of the Made Only in India was her name in the caption and in the quarter of the 22-acre space devoted to the displays of India. The bond with place was evident in the plan laid out for display at the Colonial and Indian Exhibition 1886. Here it was decided that the exhibit in the art ware court would be geographical, and goods would be displayed with reference to locality and place of manufacture. The reason given was that

> in India the art manufactures of any one place are, as a rule, so different in character from that of any other place that they ought not to be confounded by being brought under the same name. The geographical classification which has been followed in the art ware courts has the advantage of indicating, with considerable clearness, the changing complexion and character of art manufacturers as we pass from one part of India to another.

To bring to light the role of geographic origin the production, consumption and commercial distribution of art ware, 'would be shown by maps, and their prices, with their fluctuations and averages, will be recorded by maps and diagrams' (Colonial and Indian Exhibition, 1886).

The exhibition was inaugurated by Queen Victoria on 4 May where the Prince of Wales stated, 'the purpose of the exhibition is to stimulate commerce and strengthen the bonds of union now existing in every portion of her Majesty's Empire'. This was followed by the Royal Jubilee Exhibition of 1887 held in Manchester. The display remained open for 166 days, during which there were four and half million paying visitors, 74,600 in one day alone (Newton, 1998). The road show of the Manchester Exhibition travelled across to many art and technology colleges in England. The displays of Indian silks in London and Manchester were also exposing possibilities for English textile design education. Trade, not taste, was the main motive of the exhibitions (King, 2005). It is not a coincidence that the city of Manchester was soon to become the industrial hub of England.

Exhibitions are ephemeral and transient in nature. Because of this they do not allow a thorough examination of the goods. To render a more enduring and steady educational influence the idea of a museum was strongly mooted.

Museum for plagiarising: 'In the number of characteristic and valuable products, India surpasses every other country'. This is a sure true tribute to the Made in only in India.

> . . . considering the special interest attached to commercial information bearing on India . . . it is not surprising that the subject of the India Museum has of late attracted considerable attention on the part of the Chambers of Commerce of the United Kingdom. The India Museum . . . will hold . . . all facts and conclusions directly applicable to Indian trade, and render them universally available for the mercantile community.
>
> (Watson, 1876: 41–43)

The East India Company Museum was thus established at South Kensington. From 1858 it was known as the India Museum. Recently, its collections were absorbed into the Victoria and Albert Museum. In the museum were housed 'samples' of distinctive goods from different places of India, ready to copy and duplicate. In cases where the description, exhibition and museum failed, there was no hesitation in stealing designs through making detailed drawings and dispatching them to England.

Steal to copy: An example of how Indian designs came to be plagiarised can be seen from this particular incident. Moorcroft, a superintendent of the East India Company, was very keen to acquire the most 'perfect' sample of shawls. To this end, he commissioned a native painter to copy the characteristic cone motif from Kashmir shawls and sent 34 of these patterns to England. To glean the cunning here is the description:

'Painted on paper in brilliant coloured gouache, each design is over a foot long and about six inches across, and show a stylized cone set in a field'. In Kashmir, the preparatory drawings were usually in black and white outlines and rarely coloured (Karpinski, 1963: pp. 121–122). Moorcroft ensured that the designs were coloured and translated to graph paper for the guidance of the weaver.

To copy the creative genius of India 'agents were posted in London to trace the latest shawl designs as soon as they arrived from India . . . these tracings were dispatched at once to Paisley and within another eight days imitations were being sold in London' (Irwin, 1974). In terms of sheer numbers, the Scottish weaving town of Paisley copied and produced such high volumes of shawls at cheap rates that it totally crashed India's export.

The shrewdness to imitate was not unique to the British alone. The Portuguese had suggested such a scope nearly a hundred years earlier, as evident in a letter which states, 'I could submit on the way the Indians paint their clothes in Pondicherry, if you could consider them appropriate, they may help you in bringing to Europe the secret of the Indies' (Schwartz, 1956).

The intention was to 'mass copy' comes from all quarters. 'We might note in passing that the high quality of Indian designs is proved not just by the few cloths that have survived but by the reactions of European manufacturers . . . who were apparently in private making every effort to imitate them' (Bronson, 1983: 20). But where the book and look did not work, an effort was made to build an opportunity for a direct face-to-face contact of British entrepreneurs with the Indian craftsmen.

Invite craftsmen to learn by direct interaction: Master craftsmen were invited from India to England to display their work and were given special cubicles in the exhibitions. The highly skilled craftsmen along with their equipment, tools and traditional knowledge were thus readily available for manufacturers to learn and question. As the native and naïve craftsmen shared India with pride, little was he aware that his goods were being keenly observed, more for motives to copy and soon he would be robbed of his skill. So that it would not appear a callous and calculated move of exploitation, after the Colonial and Indian Exhibition, the Queen invited all the craftsmen in the exhibition for lunch at Windsor Castle. Thirty-four of them were from India.

Besides the effort to bring the craftsmen to England for a short duration via an exhibition, the more blatant attempt was to 'import' the supply of resources and craftsmen on a more permanent basis. Moorcroft again is an exemplary case.

Transfer resources and skill to produce the best: Moorcroft wanted to have a large-scale breeding of the peculiar *Capra hircus* (goat) from Tibet in Scotland. For this purpose he trekked from India through Nepal to Tibet, in 1812, in search of both Turkish horses and shawl goats.

While he could not find any horses, he managed to acquire 50 mountain goats. His herd of goats embarked for England, with the males on one ship and the females on another. This brilliant scheme, however, turned into a blunder, for the ship carrying the females was wrecked with no survivors! Similar was the outcome of the French experiment. While the French were successful in transporting 200 to 300 goats, all soon perished in the new environs (Karpinski, 1963).What the goats could and humans could not sense was the geographical difference between the Pyrenees and the Himalayas!

But failures were not a deterrent, and Moorcroft went so far as to campaign for the emigration of whole families of Kashmiri shawl manufacturers. In a letter, dated 21 May 1820, to C.T. Metcalfe of the East India Company, he writes:

> I must request the favour of your obtaining the sentiments of Mr Redding on the matter of inviting some Kashmiris to immigrate and if they be favourable that you will bring it under the notice of the government as expeditiously as possible in any shape you may think fit. Among the many thousands of individuals employed in the shawl trade in Kashmir, it would probably be no difficult task to induce two or three families in a noiseless way to leave that country. Nothing in the climate to Britain is likely to prove unfriendly to the constitution of Kashmiris for at this moment in Kashmir the thermometer out of doors stands at 24 degree (4 February).
>
> (Moorcroft in Irwin, 1974)

In a careful reading of this quotation one can see how the argument for migration is rooted in the concept of similarity of place: Kashmir vs. England.

Therefore in sum 'It cannot be denied that for centuries the West had assimilated Asia's materials, techniques and designs and the ancient textile traditions, particularly those of India, which were a major influence on the English weaving textile development' (King, 2005: 159).

The modus operandi for collecting samples, preparing documents, curating exhibitions, along with tracing and transferring details, was bound to deliver success. The manufacture of cotton textiles was started in Glasgow in Scotland in 1738. In Manchester, the manufacture of printed calicoes was established in 1764. After the invention of Arkwright's machine in 1769 the production of Manchester calicoes grew rapidly. This invention developed the frame for spinning thread or yarn from fibres such as wool or cotton in such a way that combined, power, machinery, semi-skilled labour and the new raw material to create mass-produced yarn. But in spite of the establishment of these centres in England, the British could not compete on fair free trade principles with the low-priced and superior manufacturing of textiles from different places in India. Colonists resorted to more lethal tactics.

Impose a legal embargo to protect self-interest: The British farmers and wool manufacturers were adversely affected by imports of Indian silk and cotton. They influenced the English parliament which gave a directive in

1678 that the people should wear only woollen apparel during winter. To make matters worse it was declared that all corpses had to be wrapped only in cotton cloth! In 1700, import of silk was banned. Despite these measures, many consumers still preferred to wear cotton. This led to the incidents of 'calico chasing', gangs of weavers roaming the streets of London, tearing cotton cloth off the backs of helpless female passers-by and triumphantly parading their captured trophies, around the streets on top of poles (Beattie, 2009).

At the heart of the issue lay the fact that the manufacturers in Britain persisted in lobbying hard for stringent controls on Indian imports. They coerced the British Government which passed the law, 'that from and after the 29th day of September, 1701, all wrought silks, Bengalis, and all calicoes, painted, dyed, printed or stained there, which are or shall be imported into this kingdom, shall not be worn or otherwise used in Great Britain; and all goods imported after that day, shall be warehoused or exported again' (Birdwood, 1878). With this law Britain was able to erect a 'wall of protection' which banned the import of painted and dyed calicos and silk from India into England. Unpainted fabrics were still permitted but they became subject to a 15 per cent import duty. Finally in 1721, the British Parliament banned the importation even of plain Indian cloth. As an extreme step wearing textiles from India was declared a crime and violators were fined £5. After the enactment of the law, only thread or raw cotton was imported. The fact that India was a colony made her impotent, as Britain could implement rules and regulations, at will, at both ends, in England and India.

There were other outcomes. When the manufacturers of England got the tariff protection they wanted, they did not relax into old and inefficient ways. Instead, they launched an aggressive long-term programme of research and development. They made intensive use of the copious notes, samples and descriptions they had accumulated on Indian weaving, cloth-printing, and dyeing methods. The innumerable ideas from India stored by the British in their official notes, books and museums were a handy source to learn and copy. By 1785, after two decades of innovation, Europe had made most of the key inventions of the Industrial Revolution and was in a position to sell textiles even more cheaply than that manufactured by India.

The Kashmir shawl was presumably introduced into England about the middle of the eighteenth century by Anglo-Indians returning from the East. Quickly becoming an article of high fashion, it remained prohibitively expensive until the English decided to produce a domestic copy. The decade 1850 to 1860 was the last years of prosperity for the Kashmir shawl industry. Thereafter, the European world began to copy it in great detail. Norwich in 1803 became the European centre of shawl-weaving which began imitating Kashmir shawl patterns. The early imitations of Kashmir shawls came also from Edinburgh, where the weavers sought to duplicate both the Kashmiri texture and style, employing a brocading method similar to the twill-tapestry technique. In terms of sheer numbers, Paisley, the town in Scotland, produced such high volumes of shawls at cheap rates that it crashed India's exports (Karpinski, 1963).

By 1800, Indian textile exports to Europe had fallen almost to zero and were dropping sharply in Africa and North America. Around the 1830s, the mills of Manchester shipped 40 million yards of cotton cloth to India. Ironical as it may seem the bulk of the coloured clothes produced by the power looms of Manchester in England were still called by Indian names such as ginghams, chintzes, and calicoes and were printed with flower designs nearly identical with those shipped from India to Europe 200 years before!

There were other ironies as well such as the reverse naming of a place. Kanpur, a city in Uttar Pradesh, at one time was a great textile production centre. It was given the epithet 'the Manchester of India'. Is it not a fact that considering who copied whom the reverse would be truer if Manchester had been called the 'Kanpur of England'? This reverse mirroring to reinforce the false 'colonial inventiveness and leadership' is also evident in the case of converting the name of the Scottish town of Passlet into Paisley. The name refers to the famous Indian Keri or mango-shaped floral motif which was curved into the more stylised paisley, by the embroiderers of Kashmiri shawls.

The Industrial Revolution was undoubtedly based on the invention of textiles, but its magnitude, scale and style damaged many good things and places along its way. Hand in glove with the commercial pulse of the colonists was the grand design to lay railways, dig canals and build ports in India. Aligned to a colonial self-serving force of trade these infrastructural projects cut through forests, jungles and tattooed the surface of the land. The first train in India steamed off from Bombay heading to Thane on 16 April 1853. Between 1853 and 2000, 63,000 kilometres of railway track had been laid in India. Eighty-two per cent of the railway network was constructed in the initial 60 years, while the remaining 18 per cent took 80 years after 1910 (Goel, 2005). I am, however, not going to dovetail into details of the impact of this, as much has already been written on the colonial impact on the environment (Grove, 1995; Gadgil and Guha, 1993; Kapur, 1995; MacKenzie, 1990; Rangarajan, 2007; Tucker, 2011). Moreover it was on these tracks that foreign machine manufactured goods flooded every part of India and what was siphoned for exports were natural resources.

Destruction of place goods: By the end of the eighteenth century the status of such distinctive goods had fallen into an eclipse, and the situation worsened in the decades to follow. Not only did the weavers suffer, but the East India Company also had a demoralizing effect on the majority of other artisans and crafts across many areas of India. There are many evidences of this:

> Baroach, a town in Gujarat, 36 miles north of Surat, was a great centre of cotton manufactures, from the stoutest canvas to the finest muslins; here the industry was ruined by the unrestrained Manchester imports, and of the 30 odd varieties of cloths enumerated in the factory diary for 1777, now only six are made. At Hoshungabad, in the Central Provinces, the weaving trade flourished until the enormous demand for cotton wool in 1863–64 raised the price of the raw material beyond the weavers' means. All the cotton wool in the district was exported, and since Manchester piece goods were imported, native looms and the local manufacture succumbed.
>
> (Birdwood, 1878: 96)

Likewise in the seventeenth century, the mercantile companies of England and France competed with each other to buy the products of Salem handloom weaving. But with the proliferation of textile manufacturing machines in England and the colonial policies of putting an embargo on the import of textiles from India, the production of Salem's handloom industry suffered a decline. In 1930, the price of the finished handloom goods dropped 50 per cent, throwing the 3,000 weavers in Gugai and Sevvoypettai into unemployment. In Salem city alone, at least 35,000 individuals depended on the looms. During World War II, the condition of weavers worsened due to the scarcity of yarn and other raw materials (Rajannan, 1992).

An avalanche of synthetics and cheap imitations: The introduction of crude colours and the fugitive tendencies of the synthetic dyes of Europe was another worry. When chemical dyes, like the Magenta series, were being 'pushed' on the *tussar* silk of India, the results were so obnoxious that the Maharajah of Cashmere adopted an effectual plan for the suppression of the chemical Magenta within his kingdom. First, a duty of 45 per cent was levied on it at the Frontier; and at a certain distance within the Frontier, it were confiscated and immediately destroyed (Birdwood, 1878).

Surat, a city situated on the left bank of the river Tapti in Gujarat, was popularly known till the Mughal period as the *zari* city. In 1614, the East

India Company established a factory at Surat because by this time it was an important business and industrial centre on the West coast of India. During the British period, two events ushered in a crisis for the *zari* industry. France established itself as the *zari* manufacturing country of the world, and the British shifted the seat of their operations to Bombay in 1686, causing Surat to fall from the pinnacle of its glory.

If import of cheap substitutes was the ruin of Surat *zari*, it was the cheap synthetic stones which knocked off the importance of the agates of Cambay. Cambay, also known as Khambhat, is a seaport in Gujarat situated at the head of the gulf named after it. Here, flourished the agate industry which attained prosperity during the sixteenth century and continued its importance till the eighteenth century. There were several reasons for the decline of the agate industry. The construction of the railway line between Ahmedabad and Bombay during the latter half of nineteenth century diminished the importance of Cambay as a centre of maritime trade, and moreover it severed its relationship with its hinterland. In addition the Cambay Port got silted, which made it impossible for a large vessel to reach the harbour, and as a result the port lost its former glory. Above all, as noted earlier, the import of cheap synthetic stones led to a sharp decline in the demand for the agates of Cambay. There were other losses, both Cambay and Surat artisans made 'little cabinets, coffers, and boxes of tortoise shell, which they polish so clear that nothing can have a prettier effect, the shell being patterned by nature'. Although many fine objects were produced in this early period, it seems that by the 19th century, the technique of working tortoise shell had been lost in India, surviving only in Sri Lanka (Pyrard, 1619).

Rayon, a cheap substitute for silk, flooded the markets; indigo gave way to chemicals; ivory to bone; sisham to tal; pure zari to metallic threads; brass and copper to porcelain; ruin had no end in sight.

Dismissal of the indigenous courts: In addition to the import of substitutes and cheap goods, the colonial rule subjugated and or dismissed the indigenous court and in many parts. 'The decline of much Indian decorative art is due to the fact that manufacturers have now to work for a class of purchasers far poor as well as less luxurious in habit than the wealthy nobles and princes of the courts of ancient time' (Colonial and Indian Exhibition, 1886: 11).

In India, shoes are valued not so much for the soundness of their leather but for the beauty of their ornamentation. Previously, a great industry of gold-embroidered shoes flourished at Lucknow. They were in demand all over India, for the kings of Oudh would not allow the shoemakers to use any but pure gold wire in their work. But, when the kingdom was annexed by the British, all such restrictions were removed, and the bazaars of Oudh were at once flooded with embroidered shoes of impure threads and metallic wires.

If cheap substitutes and lack of patrons sounded the death knell of some products, in others the unruly interference with the creative designs of the craftsmen were a blow to the quality of goods that were produced. It needs to be reiterated here that it was the 'distinctive character of goods' produced at certain places that had pushed India's graph of exports; imperfection thereafter became a reason for the declining position in trade.

Interference with traditional designs: The gold jewellery of Tiruchirappalli, celebrated among Anglo-Indians, had been corrupted to European taste. Furniture made of shisham or blackwood when elaborately carved in a Dutch style produced a style utterly inapplicable to chairs, couches and tables. The look turned hideous when French polish, an 'improvement' to suit European taste, was applied on the furniture.

The English and French design of representing huge nosegays, or bunches of fern leaves tied together by flowing pink ribbons, on carpets, to create the effect of full relief was also inappropriate. In such a case, it would be difficult to decide where to walk among them! The Masulipatnam carpets

> were formerly among the finest produced in India. . . . The English importers insisted on supplying the weavers with cheaper materials, and we now find that these carpets are invariably backed with English twine. The spell of the tradition thus broken, one change after another was introduced into the manufacture, and these carpets *cannot* now be classed among the better fabrics of India.
> (*Imperial Gazetteer of India* – Volume 3, 1908)

The worst example of degeneration can be seen in the case of the nineteenth-century textiles which depict rows of bicycles alternating with the tree of life and depiction of currency notes on an otherwise traditional design (Ramaswamy, 1985).

Evidence of demise: This I found literally 'written on the walls' of the India section of the Victoria and Albert Museum where I spent a fortnight in December 2013. Here are some of the notes I took:

> A title with a scarf of gold brocade on ground of silk, from Varanasi dated 1880 in the Museum, states, 'Through the second half of the 19 th century, many of the centres of traditional textile production declined as a result of competition from imported cloth and the drop in demand by the local elite'.
>
> A note clipped to a writing box, cabinet and water vessel dated 1850 in the Museum reads, '. . . decorative paper machie was a speciality of Kashmir and was made for both local and European

markets. Painted and varnished wood was often used in place of true paper machie from the later 19th century onwards. . . .'

Another detail of a handkerchief in white muslin with pink silk embroidery reads, 'The muslin industry of Dacca declined rapidly in the 19th century. Some Muslin embroiderers moved to Calcutta and produced items like the handkerchief for the British'.

Next to Kashmir shawls is the caption: 'these shawls became fashionable in Europe around 1770s. They were imitated in Britain and France from about 1800. But prosperity was short lived. As soon as the shawl was discarded as an item of fashion, a sharp decline was noticed in the Indian and European shawl industry from 1870 onwards'.

Interestingly, while the Museum preserves the vestiges of India's finest art and the demise is mentioned, the Museum authorities make no effort to own up to the fact that it was 'their' colonial strategy which systematically destroyed the place goods in India.

Decline in employment for craftsmen: Confirming the demise was the cry for livelihood which came from different quarters. The plight of the weavers of the Kashmir shawl is a case in sight. George Forester, visiting the valley just after the end of the Mughal rule, was told by the Kashmiris that there were 40,000 looms at that time, each giving employment to three men at a time. At the end of the eighteenth century, 24,000 looms operated in the Valley, giving employment to 72,000 weavers. According to Moorcroft, who travelled to Kashmir in 1821, the number of weavers had drastically come down to around 12,000–13,000. The 1901 census records only 5,037 shawl weavers.

In overall terms the British are responsible for reducing India from an artisan-driven industrial economy to a subsistence agricultural one. In the Imperial Census of 1891 and 1901 the population engaged in producing textiles, fabrics and dress declined by 11 per cent, industries and craft shared a loss of 13 per cent, matting of leaves 91 per cent, glass, earthen and stoneware another 9 per cent. In overall terms, nonagricultural workers with unspecified skills saw a drop from 23.82 million to 16.94 million from 1891 to 1901 (Sikdar, 1997). In the absence of any legal protection or efforts at conservation, crafts that relied on a combination of high skills and low wages lost any chance of maintaining the bond with a place. The lives of artisans no longer revolved around the temple, nor did they serve the royal courts. Most of them were forced to leave their homes and seek employment in European factories, the marker of black towns. A situation was reached when poor weavers 'could not even put the cloth on the loom without an advance', as the Agent of Fort St. George, Langhorne, commented in 1675. Lord Bentinck, the Governor General of India (1833–1835) observed, 'The bones of the cotton weavers are bleaching the plain of India' (Ramaswamy, 1985). As the 'fabric' of India's economy was torn, many place-based centres either perished or were taken to the verge of extinction. The trend could neither be reversed nor arrested. The decline was so widespread that at the national level the share of textiles in exports dropped from 70 per cent in 1926 to 20 per cent in 1946. The damage was long term. In monetary terms, textiles which contributed 58 per cent of the exports in 1916–1917 dropped to less than 12 per cent in 2008–2009 (Table 4.1).

Thus place goods were destroyed because of a variety of reasons: machine-made goods and demand for handcrafted goods declined; the royal patronage which protected the goods was withdrawn, cheap substitutes flooded the market, the wages of the *karigar* or *artisans* became so low that they were forced to abandon this work, and but most important no one cared to understand that these were not mere products or objects for sale but the life

Table 4.1 India's composition of exports 1916–2008

Categories	*Percentage of total exports*	
	*1916–1917**	*2008–2009*
Mineral products	0.4	18.77
Pearls, stones/metals and articles thereof; jewellery and coin	0	15.32
Textile and textile articles	57.9	11.73
Base metals and articles	13.6	9.54
Products of the chemical or allied industries	3.5	9.47
Transport equipment	0	6.10
Vegetable products	20	5.31
Instruments and apparatus; clocks and watches	0	5.22
Others	0.06	18.54
Total	100	100

Based on categories defined by the World Trade Organization

* Pertains to the export commodities and values of the Calcutta and Bombay ports and not for the whole of India

Data for 1916–1917: Superintendent, 1918

Data for 2008–2009: Department of Commerce, 2009

and soul of the people in different places of India. They created the Made Only in India.

A brief stock taken of the history of place goods registered at Chennai reveals that many trace their inception to the phase when they serviced the Hindu temples, while some like the saree have an antiquity and have endured because of tradition. The number of goods that belong to this phase is difficult to estimate, though their scale can be gleaned on the basis of three facts: first, the plentiful number of temples across India must have generated a demand for goods; second, India was able to capture a large trading compass on the shoulders of its characteristic goods and third, the reference to these goods by different travellers, administrators in gazetteers and other official documents means they were in abundance and could not go away unnoticed. And fourth, it is about the people of India, 'We cannot overlook the serenity and dignity of this life if we would rightly understand the Indian handicrafts man's work. He has his assured place . . . contentment of bind and leisure, and pride and pleasure in it for its own sake, which are essential to all artistic skill' (Birdwood, 1880). 'Assured place' played a sure role in the things that were grown, produced and hand-created.

The Mughals especially were keen patrons of distinct goods. But the craftsmen made 'patterns and designs' that were copies of the natural world be it flowers, trees or fruits. This is apparent in the shawls, carpets, silks or even the paintings. These copies were not poor in quality; in fact, since the craftsmen had earlier been superbly trained they also copied the details to perfection. The difference was, however, in the fact that the pre-Muslim craftsmen created from an imagination of the celestial and divine realm, while the inspiration of the craftsmen of the medieval phase relied on the terrestrial and material realms. Perhaps in this shift came the decline of the originality of the goods, for is there not a limit to copy while the imagined is unlimited in its hold and behold?

During the phase of servicing temples the 'doers' were called *silpkars*, a word which is difficult to translate but could mean 'multifaceted', and comprised art, skill, craft, labour, ingenuity, rite and ritual, form and creation. Neither the word artist, nor artisan, nor craftsman is an adequate translation of *silpin*. During the medieval phase, the 'doers' were akin to craftsmen whose skill was valued according to their level of perfection. But in the colonial period, the producers were categorised as workers. *The Census of India* defines a worker as one engaged in 'work' defined as participation in any economically productive activity with or without compensation, wages or profit.

When kings were patrons of temples, the former believed that offering the best of goods and produce is one way to serve, please and reach divinity. The destination and destiny of place goods was thus engaged with the Divine, and the temple was a driving force. In contrast, the *darbar* or the court was the chosen site of production in Mughal times. To keep vigil on the production, *karkhanas* or ateliers were attached to the royal palace. Here goods were produced not for divinity but for nobility. During this period, the demand was ushered by the urban-based nobility, and distinct goods were produced with a motive to gain patronage and other favours from the court. During the colonial period, except for the plantations that were nurtured that too for the pure motive of commercial profit, most existing place goods were systematically destroyed. With the temples and tradition there was a sense of reverence when creating a good; this gave way in the medieval phase to a sense of personal pride when producing goods; but under colonial rule the overriding motive was that of monetary price and soon what followed and mattered was only a cheap price.

This change from the temple, to the court, to the market, to the port or industrial site altered the status of place goods. Inspiration was no longer drawn from experience or attachment to a temple, tradition, community or nobility anchored in a specific place but came from a far-off market and an anonymous customer. What shifted with all of this is the concept of place. In the phase of temples and tradition, a place was to be revered and moreover transcended. During the medieval phase, there was a gradual shift when the physical details of a place were studied and copied. In the colonial phase, place became a lifeless entity that was either to be controlled or exploited for commercial use. It seems that whereas a deep consciousness of divinity influenced creativity in the temple phase, what operated in the Mughal phase was a sense of consciousness of beauty and perfection to please a few individuals, such as the *badshahs*. The colonial rule it seems, however, is marked by a 'collective unconsciousness'. This is why the degradation, defacement and the degeneration of goods with all their imitations, cheap substitutes and uncalled-for-designs happened during this period. Most significant was the disruption of the connect between a good and the place. With profits as the sole purpose and motive of the colonists, the destruction or bulldozing of years of expertise accumulated in different locales of India did not figure in the scheme of things or the thinking.

From bonding, nurturing, to near destruction, place goods have taken a long and torturous walk. From goods for the gods, to those for the durbar and royal court, for a short while place goods embellished the Crown of England. But soon they were degenerated and destroyed. In this trajectory, just as the arriving fleets and warehouses dumped machine-made goods from the West, many of which had been plagiarised from India, the beauty of India, shahtoosh shawls, agate beads, champlevés jewellery, Mughal miniatures, Kashmir silk, India ink, Dacca muslin and Jamdanis disappeared from the world's wharves.

When a large species becomes extinct many smaller, unknown, unrecorded yet important ones are killed along the way. Lost in the pages of time would be many other goods that carried within themselves the smell and sense of the place.

India – loss of place and place goods: In 1947 the subcontinent of India was partitioned. A new country Pakistan and later Bangladesh on its fragmentation was culled. With the loss of territory what also was lost was several places that produced orign based goods. Among others, since the town of Chiniot located in the hills 160 kilometres to the north-west of Lahore went to Pakistan, the Chiniot woodwork was also lost to that country. The pottery and tiles handicraft at Hala in Sind and the soft saponaceous earth Multani mitti, found near Multan on the banks of River Chenab, also went to Pakistan. Similarly to East Pakistan (Bangladesh since 1971) went the famous weaves of Dhaka Jamdani, the Hilsa fish in the Meghna and Padma rivers and the Fazle Mango from Chapainawabganj, an area about 300 kilometres north-west of Dhaka.

In the post-independence years the status of place goods did not improve. Similar to the conditions in the colonial phase the loss was not just one place, one good or one product; but the entire ecology that built a distinctiveness, as emerging from a sense of place, was under stress. Some efforts of revival were there. By the end of the nineteenth century, a new generation began to realise that Hindu culture had much of permanent value, and that the slavish importation and imitation of the West was adding to India's problems. At this juncture many organisations such as the Arya Samaj, Ramakrishna Mission or even the Theosophical Society began to rediscover and bring to light what was 'good' in Hindu society. The Indian National Congress, in the early twentieth century, began to endorse a policy of *swadeshi* (of our own country), which called for the boycott of imported British goods and the promotion of Made in India. Shops selling foreign goods were picketed, and the boycott developed into a nationwide movement for not using English cloth and other products.

The mood was set for an Independent India, and it was during this time that nationalism spurred recognition for regional identity and alongside was created a window for the revival of some place goods.

In an effort of revival of the indigenous, Rabindranath Tagore, in 1932, developed Santiniketan Leather Goods in the Birbhum district of West Bengal. The 'Shanti leather products' have beautiful coloured graphic designs with embossed and batik prints made from vegetable-tanned skins called East India tanning. The production and manufacture of these goods was subsequently supported by stalwart artists like Nandalal Bose, Suren Kar and Ram Kinkar Baij who provided their innovative ideas and designs. It was registered with a Geographical Indications tag in 2008. The Puneri Pagadi, registered at Chennai in 2009, was a symbol of pride and prestige for the city of Pune, and this pagadi or turban gained much reputation and recognition during the time of Lokmanya Bal Gangadhar Tilak, India's popular leader who spurred the Indian independence movement. The pagadi thus became an essential especially for the elite in the legal profession as it represented intellect and tradition.

While these efforts were made, yet they were too few, too small and too isolated to make a marked difference at India's national level. To rejuvenate the 'life of a place' what was needed was a national level 'movement for place', much more than a piecemeal attention to one or two individual items at a few places. The approach that should have been adopted and followed should have been to counter and learn from the many steps and policies the British had deployed to destroy India's place goods. The task was conceivable and achievable but remained unheeded. The one sole leader who abjured the West and believed strongly in the fundamentals of the revival of the village where a good bonds with place was Mahatma Gandhi.

Gandhi: a plea for revival of place: Mahatma Gandhi propagated the idea of village revival based on khadi, which included other traditional village industries as well. For Gandhi, khadi was not merely a piece of cloth, but the emblem of a whole programme of rejuvenation of the villages. Writing for *Young India*, Gandhi, in 1920, stated, 'I feel convinced that the revival of hand spinning and hand weaving will make the largest contribution to the economic and moral regeneration of India. . . . Spinning was a cottage industry years ago, and if the millions are to be saved from starvation they must be enabled to introduce spinning in their homes, and every village must repossess its own weaver' (Singh, 2010: 13).

Swadeshi was defined by him as 'that spirit in us which restricts us to the use and service of our *immediate surroundings* to the exclusion of the more remote'. The immediate surroundings are a sure reference to place be it first and foremost at a local level. But Gandhi's idea of bond with place was not given enough credence.

The original national flag of India patterned against British imperialism had carried the symbol of the charkha or the spinning wheel. But on the eve of Independence this was replaced with the Ashoka Chakra, the wheel of law. Small as this gesture may, yet the change is symbolic of the fact that priority and incentives to indigenous craft and manufacturing handloom textiles was not given! Gandhi's sage advice was ignored.

When India gained independence, the model of self-reliance and development that was adopted was one where investment was made in infrastructure for modern large-scale industries. Self-reliance was sought, but not the Gandhian way. This being the approach in 1947, the scope of revalorizing the value of 'place' inherent in Gandhi's philosophy of revival of life in millions of villages of India was pushed to the back seat. A politically freed India failed to establish and nourish the reciprocity to build sustainable places, where the government was a patron and the public its keen appreciator and consumer of its craft, industry and produce.

In the post-independence years, India could not revive the Made Only in India label, which had once been a feather in its cap and had given it a definite lead in world trade. Embarking on a period of industrialisation, India not only chose to neglect its rich heritage but also failed to perfect the goods it manufactured in the modern large-scale industries. Therefore, as Swiss watches and chocolates, German cars, Japanese electronics and French wine dictated and filled the ledgers of trade, India stood watching and wasted.

In the twentieth century, India is no longer a country which moves large cargoes of trade. As per the World Trade Organization, India's share in global exports in 2011 was a paltry 1.7 per cent of the total exports in monetary terms. The loss of India's precious culture, craft and goods with Geographical Indications is apparent from the fact that in its nearly 70 years post-independence, the country has not nurtured a single 'new' place good worth its mention. Moreover by Independence the 'people in places which produced the place goods' had become too poor and ill-equipped to handle the range from procurement of raw material to the marketing of finished goods. The ecology had been ruined. This was the case be it for the carpets, sarees or silks across the works and regions of India. To nourish their morale, boost their creativity and promise them a future was a work that India chose to ignore. With the result, production of all kinds across different places in India languished. After lack of recognition for years, a hope for their rejuvenation seems to have arrived. This optimism has come not from local or national initiative, but this time round from a global platform. Ironical as it may seem, it is the Europeans who are responsible for the resurrection and protection of goods that carry a special bond with their place of origin.

5

RESURRECTING

Place goods

The winds of recent globalisation which began to blow near the end of the twentieth century resurrected the value of place goods. How could this be possible since a claim often made is that globalisation denied, if not obliterated, the role and presence of the local and the different? To draw a conclusion one needs to see the two-way impact of globalisation.

On the one hand, globalisation involves an unrestricted flow of goods, capital and people across the world. It channels and sustains itself through trade, finance and communication. The impact of this unhindered flow has been the possibility of propagating and implementing a similar set of dominant ideas across the globe. Take the case of architecture. The world over, the design and material for construction of buildings especially in leading urban centres is acquiring a similar kind of look. The Marriot Hotel in India, Los Angles or London is no different from the other. Shopping malls, airport or and even residential apartments carry features that starkly are 'look alikes'. The type of clothes people wear, food they consume or their style of life carry many common features and characteristics. In the sphere of agriculture too one can see extensive areas of row after row of the same crop. Monoculture is the rule for agricultural production. Through these examples it may seem that the forces of globalisation have come close to creating a world where variety and diversity are becoming irrelevant and insignificant. Here one is reminded of Norberg-Schulz's 1969 terse phrase 'flat scape', a world where heterogeneity and spatial variations are lost and forever gone (Relph, 1976). Some of the forces encouraging this 'flattening' are technological innovations like the World Wide Web permitting uploading and downloading of data and software from anywhere in the world, and processes such as outsourcing, offshoring, supply chaining or even online shopping through eBay or the Amazon website (Friedman, 2005). Therefore as identical goods, services and messages are being circulated all over the world, differences it seems are being washed over. Seen in this context the outcome of globalisation is a world in which the sense of placelessness is augmented and the particularity of places is reduced.

Therefore one could conclude that globalisation dilutes, if not denies, the presence and role of the local, the different, which is at the heart of place goods. But this is far from a complete picture. On the flip side, the context of globalisation has in fact helped enhance and recover the value of place and with it place goods. There are many evidences in support of the fact that with globalisation spatial variations emerge strong and have not been ironed out.

The ruin wrought by the practice of monoculture is an example. The wholesale dominance of one high-bred crop and its demands of water and chemicals has led to the decline in the level of ground water and increased chemical pollution which has poisoned food chains and led to the proliferation of pests along with the declining indicators of human and environmental health. In continuation of these problems, came the need to 'listen and reverberate, in harmony with the ecology' a realisation which fuelled the rising tide of environmental movement. Embedded within the environmental movement were issues of 'place keeping and place making' because the latter at its core is about the ways and means used by people to relate with their environment. This became a reason of hope for place. It is within a globalising world that the concern about the meaning and significance of place for its inhabitants and users ossified into areas like the search for place-based identity. The latter revolves around the idea that the feelings of identity are clued within the features and characteristics of a geographical locale. A community therefore values a river, a monument or even the name of a place because they serve as icons with which it identifies. It is because of this place-based identity that people strongly take on initiatives to rejuvenate a river, preserve monuments or wage a conflict even over the name of a place. Similarly, though on the one hand globalisation has seen an increase in the movements and migration of people within and across borders, on the other hand, it has also fostered an intensified sense of attachment to 'homelands' among the diasporic communities (Benedict, 1983) The rise of ethnic and cultural consciousness which reasserts the importance of being rooted in place has also been magnified within a globalised world. This is manifest through ethnic wars and protests and resistance movements of indigenous people against exploitation of environmental resources by multinational companies, such as Chipko or Narmada Valley in India. The emotional belonging to territories and birth of regionalism and emergence of new states in India like Telangana, Jharkhand and Uttarakhand are all indicative of the role of the local and a sense of belonging to a place. Even cyberspace which is a product of globalisation reinstates the value of place; there are many social networking clusters or forums for interaction within people belong to the same place, speaking the same language. The people in these forums may live physically across opposite ends of the world, but through the medium of these sites, they share a sense of rootedness and bonding with the people and the place. The uprooting and disconnect of people from and with their place is also said to be responsible for the rapid erosion of traditional culture, rising rates of crime and other social problems like alienation, depression and conflicts. It is also an age of identity, gender identity, self-identity and cultural identity among others. A thought which is aired is that the economy is globalising, politics is moving towards regionalism and society is localising. This trend enlarges the scope and importance of place. Within these larger trends and forces for the local is situated a fight for goods with place-bound identity linked to the origin and thus Geographical Indications. With these evidences of the way globalisation affirms the value of place, one can now move on to how the global has created a 'new market' for the re-emergence of the value of place goods.

Global new market – a place for place goods: A distinguishing feature of the global new market, because of an unhindered and rapid transport and transactions in trade, is that consumers are provided and promised a dazzling variety of food stuff, clothes, shoes, accessories and other goods and produce. Within this crucible the importance of place and goods has emerged in three different ways:

1) One good is now made in different places
2) goods are made to suit the specifications of different places
3) prominence and acknowledgment is given to goods from a particular place of origin.

Illustrating the first case is the fact that many labels of goods read products of more than one country. This happens because manufacturers take advantage of the range of resources, skills and policies across the world. Since these are distributed unevenly and the aim is to make profit, manufacturers assemble their goods with 'parts, ingredients and skills' from across the world. This reaffirms that each place has a different and valuable role in the production of the good. The inclusion of many 'countries' within a single label is basically a route through which manufacturers harness greater profits.

A second confirmation of the importance of place is seen from the fact of how global companies are 'tailor fitting – local suiting' their products to make a profit in different countries. Thus the creation of products or services is intended for the global market, but customised to suit the local cultures. Subway, the chain of sandwiches and other foodstuffs, is conscious of local religious sentiments of Hindus, and their outlets in India do not sell beef. Bottega Veneta, an Italian men's fashion brand, launched a limited edition of the closed-neck jacket (*bandhgala* worn by men) specifically for the Indian market. The American coffee chain Starbucks inaugurated their first shop in India in 2012. While setting out their menu they removed beef or pork from their seller's list and included the likes of Chai, Konkani twist and the *Chatpata parantha* wrap! It would not be too farfetched to suggest that had the multinational brands not kept the local place in their arena of planning, their markets would have faced far more difficult and different challenges.

The third arena of the role of globalisation is seen in the value to place goods. This has emerged because the new global market has made it possible for consumers to have a choice of many 'countries'. This is evident from the large variety of the similar type of goods but with different places of origin that are up for display within a single sales counter. It suddenly is possible to buy mangoes from many countries be it India, China, Thailand, Pakistan or Mexico. Tea from producers like India, China, Japan and Sri Lanka is found in the same basket. Wine from France, Germany, United Kingdom and Australia is on the same counter and coffee from Brazil, Vietnam, Colombia, Indonesia, India, Ethiopia, Honduras, Peru, Guatemala and Mexico is displayed neck to neck with each other. This is the case for a host of other products be it shawls, soaps, carpets or perfumes. Within a global new market the orbits of different countries intersect over 'similar but not same' type of goods. Not only has the scale and size of shopping plazas and chain stores become large and widespread, but it is within the time spent here, that people began to see, learn and get a 'look, feel or taste' of goods from the wide world.

In order for products to compete in this display of variety there arose the increasing need to differentiate between products on the basis of a number of criteria: goods could be environmental friendly, those which are ranked on line of being health friendly, or ones that are ethically produced, for example goods produced without engaging child or forced labour and also goods that support the cause of the underprivileged and many other such issues. One marker for purchase that emerged was the connect to place, that is goods which establish their credentials on the basis of their place of origin. To strengthen the importance of this relationship it was decided that the packaging, labels and advertisement of the products are to carry a certificate of authenticity on the criteria of their bond with place. Adopting this train of thought, traders began to propagate, negotiate and reinforce the idea of a reunion between a good and the place of its origin. Sensing the opportune time international organisations sought and fought to make room, for valuing place as the marker of distinctive goods, this time around on a legal platform. The leaders to spearhead this were the manufacturers and traders in Europe. The latter got together to seek a legislation which could protect the commercial reputation and interests of their goods, in reference to their separate geographical localities. The idea of Geographical Indications was introduced to carry forward the case of origin of goods. Though the trajectory of place goods reveals that India had irrigated and supported the cause of the distinctive goods from different places all through historical times, as evident in the case of the textiles, rice, saree or paintings, yet the term Geographical Indications as a concrete expression has emerged from the West. The idea of giving 'indications' to place of origin a legal status was that of the West, more specifically the European world, and not India. Since Europe blew the trumpet for the need for a Geographical Indications tag, it would be in order to trace the evolution of the idea of the 'law for place' within their philosophical strands.

Antecedents to the idea of law for place: The genesis of an idea for a law for place can be traced to the fundamentals of moral law for intellectual property rights. The concept of moral right emphasises the way an author projects his/her personality onto his/her work which makes their work theirs alone. Among the many philosophers who have expressed their thoughts on the ethical issue of moral rights, two views emerge most significant: one the natural rights theory and the second the utilitarian theory. In the context of natural rights, John Locke writes:

> in the state of nature, every person has . . . a property in his own person, nobody has any right but to himself. The labour of his body and the work of his hands we may say are properly his. Whatsoever then he removes out of the state that nature provided and left it in, he hath mixed with his labour and joined to it something that is his own, and thereby makes it his property.
>
> (Locke, 1690: 354)

A natural right not only justifies the existence of property but also defines the rights that should be attached to it. No one has the right to take another person's property. Property therefore is an immediate consequence of the law of the natural. For a natural rights theorist, intellectual property should have the same legal protection as tangible property. This obviously includes the rights of possessing it, enjoying its services, licensing it and transferring it to others.

Jeremy Bentham, in his utilitarian theory, states that every right is created by law and thus by a government. Whereas the natural theory does not provide any directive to the government to increase social welfare, the utilitarian theory claims that since the ultimate objective is to maximise general utility of a property, it is the utilisation of a property that should decide the action to be taken. In this context, let us argue that since the cost of imitation is always lower than the cost for development, imitators can successfully drive inventors out from the market, if inventions are not protected in some form or the other (Bentham, 1789). Being aware of the damage that imitators would cause, the inventors could well decide against investing in innovations and could divert their attention and resources in other directions and avenues. This deflection would be very dangerous because inventions provide new products and processes which are critical to the welfare that accrues to society. While almost all inventions are spontaneous outcomes of individual creativity, yet if the government does not intervene, the number of innovations in the face of mushrooming imitators is bound to decrease. The need to bestow a right on 'innovative ideas and designs' is also rooted in the realisation that there are very few 'innovators' and they and their products therefore need to be protected.

Though different in approach, the natural rights theory and the utilitarian theory both identify the right and need to protect intellectual property. Here it would not be out of line to mention that it is the fear of 'imitation' which led manufacturers and producers of unique goods in India to guard their processes and methods within a place. To safeguard the 'skills' perfected over lifelong learning some communities kept the know-how to manufacture a 'craft' or 'produce' a secret.

Secrecy is a way and indeed an ethical one, to prevent a distinctive feature of a good from being lost or imitated. The Chhipas guard the preparation of the dye which provides the special colours to the Sanganeri block printing. The making of the Pavithramothiram rings in their traditional originality is the exclusive privilege of the craftsmen of the Chovatta Valappd family who reside in the town of Payyanur in north Malabar, Kerala. In Sankheda, the art of the unique ruby lacquer coating remains within a few families engaged in this craft. The reputation of the Dharwad pedha was built with a missionary zeal by Ram Ratan Singh Thakur's grandson, Babu Singh Thakur. In order to preserve its authentic taste, only the family members are involved in making the Dharwad pedha. The family which crafts Aranmula mirrors do not disclose the secret of moulding and casting (Gopalakrishnan, Nair and Babu, 2007). The Muslim weavers at Navalgund in Karnataka produce the vibrant durries known as *jamkhans*. It is the only place where cotton weft-faced durries are woven on vertical looms. The weavers are possessive and impart their skill to no one other than their family members. The daughters are never taught the technique because it is feared that they would reveal the secret to their husbands' families. In contrast, weaving is taught to the daughters-in-law when they arrive in their new homes after marriage (Bheda, 1986).

The law for Geographical Indications is rooted in the need to safeguard the distinctiveness that accrues to a good from a place. So that others do not and cannot usurp the special identity of bond with place there is need to protect 'origin'. This is an important caveat for the continuity and right of the Made Only in India.

Though a law for place is important the formalisation of this law did not happen quickly or smoothly. It had to wait and wade its way for other concerns and events to take shape before it could gain attention. The forerunner of Geographical Indications lay in the recognition of the right of intellectual property. In line with the need to 'cultivate and nurture' innovations, the recognition of 'intellectual property' as a distinctive feature perhaps first came to the forefront when special prizes and awards were bestowed on individuals for creating distinct and different goods. The grant of privileges to exclusively trade in certain goods and services was another form of recognition. Privileges such as financial aid, tax reduction and protection from foreign persecutors were other methods employed to encourage innovations. The system of awards, rewards and privileges are predecessors to the idea of patents.

Patents: The word 'patent' is derived from the Latin term *literae patentes*, which means letters that lie open. So the exclusive rights of a person are written and 'lay open' for others to read and thus know and act accordingly. Later the word 'letter' was dropped and a patent was defined as an exclusive right or title for a fixed period to exclude others from making, using or selling an invention. Letter Patents are first known to have been issued by the British Crown, which gave select persons the monopoly to produce particular goods or services. The only requirement for it to be recognised as a patent was that the device or process under consideration should not have been known or used before.

Since exclusivity gave enormous monetary benefits to the owners, Letter Patents were granted at great cost. The British Crown, which was perpetually short of supply of money, used patents as a means to raise revenues. With the passage of time the Crown began to grant patents for a large assortment of goods many of which lacked the clause of distinctiveness. Thus the link between a privilege and some aspect of novelty of the product was abandoned, and privileges were often granted to persons who enjoyed the sovereigns' favour. This practice eventually became detrimental for commerce and after a public outcry all existing monopolies were revoked, and it was declared that the letters of patent were only to be used for 'projects of new invention'. Eventually, this led to the Statute of Monopolies in England in 1623, in which the Parliament restricted the Crown's power considerably. The Crown could now only issue Letter Patents and that also to inventors or introducers of original inventions for a fixed number of years.

The first-known patent was issued in 1421 by the city of Florence to Fillippo Brunelleschi for inventing a new type of ship. Venice was a hub of inventions, and the system of patents was perfected in Italy, mainly in Venice, during the fifteenth century. It was then adopted, between 1500 and 1550, in practically the same form in Germany, France, Netherlands and England. This widespread reception of the idea of patent within a short duration indicates that there was a driving force to monopolise design or goods. Moreover, historically it was a time of scientific and industrial revolution in the Western world. Ideas, innovations and design were at the core of this revolution. To spearhead progress in arenas of industry, trade and commerce protection of innovations was essential. Rooted in the right of intellectual property was also the concept of trademark.

Trademark: With the development of large-scale industrial production came the desire of individual producers to identify themselves as the originator and creator of goods. Trademark is a symbol that is capable of differentiating the goods or services of one person from that of others. A trademark can be created by a unique style of packaging, a graphic visual or a distinctive shape of the good or an aesthetic combination of colours. Trademark not only differentiates but is also a warranty for the quality of those goods. The registered trademarks system was thus developed to permit individual traders to enforce their marks as private proprietary rights (Prager, 1950; Weiss, 2010).

Britain saw the emergence of the modern trademark post–Industrial Revolution in the eighteenth century. Since India was a British colony the Protection of Inventions Act introduced in India was based on the model of the British Patent Law of 1852. The law gave manufacturers certain privileges for a period of 14 years. The period was fixed to grant a monopoly to the right holder and thus generate more revenue for the Crown (as such there seems to be no valid justification for the duration 14 years). The first patent granted in India was given to Alfred de Penning of Calcutta, who sought exclusive privileges under this Act for his invention which he called 'an efficient *punkha* pulling machine'. The invention was an imitation of the action of the hand (which was the conventional method to 'fan') by means of a lever that worked horizontally or vertically, the whole machine being fitted in a box. The legislation came on 28 February 1856 and De Penning was granted a patent on 3 March 1856 (Malavika, 2006).

The Indian patent regime has seen a torrent of amendments since the first filing of the patent by De Penning. In 1859, there was a modification of the Act. Its scope was widened where making, selling and using inventions in India and authorising others to do so for a period of 14 years from the date of filing specifications were allowed. Notwithstanding all these measures, there was no law for place goods.

Inventions and Design Act: Meanwhile in Europe the need for a more stringent patent and design protection act was felt when an international exhibition of inventions was planned in 1873 at Vienna, Austria. The need arose when several foreign exhibitors refused to attend the exhibition because they were afraid that their ideas would be stolen and exploited commercially in other countries. Ironically this was close to the years that the Colonial and Indian Exhibition was held in Kensington in England (1886), followed by one in Paris (1878). Since India was a colony, the producers of India's distinctive place goods had neither the freedom nor the knowledge nor the power to refuse to exhibit their goods. They perhaps were very naïve, and so did not even carry any fear that at these Exhibitions their creative genius would be copied or imitated. In fact taking pride in their ingenuity they so willingly shared the details of manufacturing, knowing little that they were being robbed!

In contrast to protect their inventions, the European nations passed the Designs and Protection Act in 1872. The first international patent treaty was mooted on the occasion of the exhibition at Austria. After Vienna, it was in the Paris Convention of 1883 that the first major international treaty called the Protection of Industrial Property was passed. The treaty was designed to help people of one country obtain protection for their intellectual creations in other countries, in the form of industrial property rights known as inventions, trademarks and industrial designs. The treaty was consolidated under the Protection of Inventions Act which later matured into the Inventions and Design Act in 1888.

Introduction of the term Geographical Indications in legal parlance: It was the treaty of Paris Convention of 1883 which for the first time made a reference to Geographical Indications under the term 'indication of source' and called on member countries to 'seize on importations' goods bearing 'direct or indirect false indications of source of the goods'. In this treaty each member country is responsible for adopting necessary measures to ensure compliance with the treaty. However, the Paris Treaty was not firm on its definition of indications of source or appellations of origin and unclear about the measures of enforcement. Among the European countries, France and England proposed amendments to the Paris Treaty to allow for more protection on Geographical Indications. These proposals finally resulted in a draft agreement submitted at the diplomatic conference in Madrid, Spain, in 1890. The Madrid Agreement confers additional powers on three points. First, Article 1(1) grants protection against 'deceptively similar' Geographical Indications. A deceptive mark is one that deceives or misleads. In a trademark, deception can be created by introducing a minor change which makes it appear like the original mark. Second, Article 3 prohibits false and deceptively similar Geographical Indications in advertising and in other forms of commercial communication like advertisements in print media, signage or hoarding (later this covered electronic media, promotional calls and even short message service (sms) over the phone). This expanded the protection to cover goods across all channels of commerce. Third, and most important, Article 4 prohibits member countries from faking 'regional' identities, particularly in the case of wines like Champagne or Scotch as generic terms. The Treaty of Madrid, 1891, was initially signed by 8 countries and currently has 34 member countries. Because of the limited number of countries that signed up for this and the restricted protection it afforded, the Treaty of Madrid could not make any real impact on the global protection of these appellations.

The next hope was pinned on the General Agreement on Tariffs and Trade (GATT), which was created in 1947 for the economic recovery, mainly of Europe, in the post–world war phase. The main objective of GATT was to reduce the barriers of international trade through the reduction of tariffs, quotas and subsidies. It was signed by 33 nations including India. The issue of Geographical Indications did not receive a serious hearing.

Even after the signing of the GATT, the attempts to strengthen the protection of Geographical Indications remained weak. A proposal mooted in Portugal was to secure protection of Geographical Indications on a new basis under the term 'appellation of origin', which not only designates the origin of a product like indication of source, but also requires certain essential qualities pertaining to that origin. The Lisbon Agreement of 1958 included the adoption of a registration system, but it could net only 25 member countries. Therefore in real terms since the Paris Convention in 1883 the case of protection for indications made little progress in trade agreements. It was only after a few critical international agreements were reached regarding the entire issue of intellectual property that the case of Geographical Indications attracted attention. This happened when the need for the protection of intellectual property was made out by an organisation called the United International Bureaux for the Protection of Intellectual Property, best known by the acronym BIRPI. Initially BIRPI was based in Berne, Switzerland, but shifted its base to Geneva in 1960. Finally BIRPI became part of the United Nations Organization and thereafter came to be known as the World Intellectual Property Organization (WIPO). WIPO was established in 1967 and is dedicated to developing a balanced and accessible international intellectual property regime. India has been a member of the WIPO since its inception.

In spite of the importance of these international institutions, the recognition of place goods had to wait another 28 years; the first significant milestone for the international protection of Geographical Indications was taken in 1995. This was the year that the agreement on Trade-Related Aspects of Intellectual Property Rights (TRIPS) was signed under the auspices of the Asia Pacific Economic Committee for Trade. TRIPS has been described as the 'most influential international agreement ever subscribed to intellectual property rights'. Its range extended from copyrights, patents, undisclosed information, trademarks, industrial designs, integrated circuits and Geographical Indications.

Alongside of the TRIPS came the World Trade Organization (WTO). In 1996, the World Intellectual Property Organization entered into cooperation with the WTO. With the WTO as a cover advantage, TRIPS gained immediate recognition and this added muscle to the cause of Geographical Indications for place goods. The strength came from two reasons: first, TRIPS provided the 'minimum' standards of protection for the Geographical Indications which as many as 153 member countries of the WTO were bound to comply with in their respective national legislations. Second, the members of WTO entered into an understanding of the procedures for a settlement of disputes. By announcing a mechanism in the form of settlement of dispute, the issue of Geographical Indications was clinched. Given the range of applicability and enforceability, TRIPS did herald a significant upgrading for Geographical Indications. India is a signatory to the TRIPS Agreement. It is in this context that India passed the Geographical Indications Act in 1999 and set up the Registry at Chennai to deal with the legal procedures.

The protection provided under the TRIPS Agreement can be divided into two categories. First, Article 22 requires members to adopt measures for protection of the Geographical Indications. Article 23 requires members to adopt measures with respect to protection of Geographical Indications related to wines and spirits. The clear level of protection given in particular to wine and spirits through Article 23 is an outcome of the fierce battle which the European Union put up for its products. The European Union, a club of 28 European countries, not only holds a bigger economy than the United States of America, but it also carries a powerful whine.

Whining for wine: The strongest *avatar* for the protection of Geographical Indications are the countries of the European Union, especially France, who claim that the wine produced in certain pockets of their territory can never be manufactured elsewhere bearing the same taste. The argument goes like this: the names Champagne and Burgundy cannot be used by companies and manufacturers elsewhere in the world. This is because wine from other manufacturers has not been produced and brewed at Champagne and Burgundy! Champagne is a sparkling wine produced exclusively within the Champagne region of France, from which it takes its name. The wine produced in France is exclusive and just cannot be produced anywhere else in the world.

To support their argument the French introduced the concept of terrior. Terrior is often italicised in English writing to show that it is a word borrowed from the French. The French word *terrior* has no equivalence or counterpart in English vocabulary. The concept of *terroir* is at the base of the French wine *Appellation d'origine contrôlée* system that has been the model for appellation and wine laws across the globe. At its core, *terrior* carries the assumption that the land from where the grapes are grown imparts a unique quality that is specific to that region. Terrior is thus a term signifying a set of physical and geographic conditions of a place to which an agricultural plant responds to produce a distinctive flavour. Terrior is the idea of an 'essential land-quality nexus', where the product qualities 'come with the territory'.

The idea of terrior is very likely to have been fuelled from the regional school as espoused by the French geographers Vidal De La Blache, Jean Brunhes and Fredric Play. Regional geography is ideographic, concerned with the unique and revels in the particular. Play developed a geographical account of France around the categories of place-work-folk and so created the concept of cultural homeland as an area of axe and plough, which belongs to the people who have carved it out. The French tradition of *la geographie humaine* associated with Vidal De La Blache, at the end of the nineteenth and beginning of the twentieth centuries, was an influential tradition in human geography. Although the word 'place' was not its central object, its focus was on *gere de vie* – ways of life – which is the belief that the lifestyle of a particular region reflects the economic, social, ideological and psychological identities imprinted on the landscape. This *gere de vie* captured the complicated interplay of the natural and cultural worlds in particular parts of France. Blache and his followers asserted the importance of culture in transforming the natural environment. 'Culture' they argued sprouts within a geographical basis in that 'habitual and shared communication is likely to occur only among those who occupy a common area' (Wagner and Mikesell, 1962). Extending a similar grain of argument, the producers of goods claim that the uniqueness in the place good does not and cannot occur in any other part of the world. Goods from 'a particular area . . . their area' will always be unique.

Tomer Broude, an academic of law, observed that '*terroir or terrior* is the epitomic opposite of globalization: an exemplary reflection of place and people' (Broude, 2005: 651–652). He insightfully elaborates on the argument, 'As such terroir arguably deserves protection, even enhanced protection, from commercial forces that threaten to compel homogenisation and obliterate local cultures of production. Geographical Indications are ostensibly a targeted way of achieving this, since each terroir, as officially defined and delimited, is granted a separate legal source of protection' (Broude, 2005: 652). Taking another case, Feta is a curd cheese produced from the milk of sheep in a traditional way. Only cheese made in some areas of Greece and the island of Lesvos can use the name Feta.

The Europeans go to the extent to insist that whereas Europe has traditional agricultural practices, North America, Australia and other New World countries work with an 'industrial' type of agriculture. The large-scale commercial farming in the case of these countries, it is argued, is conceptually not very different from big industrial enterprises. The land is ploughed with machines, water is drawn and distributed with heavy dependence on electricity, the crop is grown with the nutrients that are enhanced by chemical fertiliser, pests are controlled by insecticides and fungicides and weeds controlled by herbicides. Surviving on a series of industrial inputs such an 'assembly line agriculture' bulldozes spatial nuances and erases out areal variations. Professor Norbert Olszak, one of the few French legal academics to write at length about Geographical Indications, characterises new world agriculture as, 'The vast spaces and the recourse to technology permitted the development of very large enterprises producing standard wines for the consumption of the masses'.

In contrast to the regional and ideographic, the proponents in North America, Australia and New Zealand retaliated by arguing that 'similar' places exist all over the world. The Mediterranean climate may be typical of the Mediterranean Basin, but essentially it is a particular variety of subtropical climate and its characteristics prevail in much of California, in parts of Western and South Australia, south-western South Africa, sections of Central Asia and central Chile. There could be other such similar associations of soil terrain and human elements. So the opponents of Geographical Indications assert that goods produced in different parts of the world but within similar environs, be it that of soil, climate or terrain, carry the same taste and properties. They go as far as to claim that majority of the consumers would not even know the subtle differences in the taste of wine from one place to another. The war is about wine and spirits. Of the 9,926 goods protected with Geographical Indications across the world 8,106 or 81.66 per cent have taken a registration of wines and spirits. That the warriors are the Europeans is apparent from the fact that of the 9,926 Geographical Indications that are registered worldwide, 60.66 per cent belong to the 28 member states of the European Union (Table 5.1).

Table 5.1 Number and type of protected Geographical Indications in the world

Nations	*Total*	*Percentage of*	
		Wines – Spirits	*Other products*
European Union (28 member states)	6021	86.36	13.64
United States of America	910	80.22	19.78
Switzerland	682	96.77	3.23
New Zealand	600	91.67	8.33
Australia	427	100.00	0.00
China	403	5.71	94.29
Russian Federation	223	0.00	100.00
South Africa	174	100.00	0.00
Canada	109	54.13	45.87
Turkey	107	49.53	50.47
Chile	82	97.56	2.44
India	**45**	0.00	100.00
Cambodia	36	0.00	100.00
The former Yugoslav Republic of Macedonia	25	100.00	0.00
Cuba	19	0.00	100.00
Japan	16	31.25	68.75
Morocco	16	100.00	0.00
Mexico	11	45.45	54.55
Thailand	10	0.00	100.00
Georgia (country in Caucasus Region of Eurasia)	10	80.00	20.00
Total	**9926**	**80.75**	**19.25**

Based on data from Giovannucci, Josling, Kerr, O'Connor and Yeung (2009).

The virtually endless battle between Europe (the old world) and North America (the new world) is well documented (Dominique, 2000; Mahert, 2001). The slow pace of success met by the European countries meant that they had to garner more countries into their cause. They found their allies in the developing countries of the world.

As representatives of the countries of Africa and Asia sat in the discussion forums of the WTO, they too were enrolled into the merit of recognising and protecting their place goods with Geographical Indications. The decision-making body in the WTO is the ministerial conference, which meets at least once every two years. In its third meeting at Seattle, it received the following communication, dated 2 July 1999, from the Permanent Mission of India: 'In the light of the provisions contained in Article 23 and 24 of the TRIPS Agreement, additional protection for Geographical Indications must be extended for products other than wines and spirits'. In 2001, in its Doha round of negotiations, there was a further commitment to extend the system of internationally recognised Geographic Indications to products other than wine. In subsequent meetings it was agreed that the scope of protection would be widened (Giovannucci *et al.*, 2009).

Place in the lexicon of trade and commerce: While a formalised evolution of Geographical Indications is rooted within the European world, it would not be out of context to state that as an 'idea' it existed and was reinforced in India since long when goods were referred to not only in accordance with the place that they came from but also by their distinctiveness as seen in the case of sarees and other products, which was recognised and maintained. The trajectory of place goods of India has shown that many gained name and fame for the place they hailed from. It was because of their bond with place that they became part and parcel of world trade during ancient, medieval and colonial times. The movement and demand through historical times confirms that place goods are not a recent sprout in the parlance of trade.

Cutting to modern times, on 1 January 1988 the World Customs Organization introduced the Harmonized Commodity Description and Coding as the basis for custom tariff and compilation of trade statistics all over the world. The inventory was structured to monitor the contribution of each country to international trade. The data on trade is organised into 22 sections and 99 chapters, with a total 11,578 commodities. Of the 11,578 commodities, only 57 items carry the name of good with a reference to place, and it is an interesting fact that 15 among these belonged to India. The goods from India include the likes of the Bleeding Madras fabric and small Alleppey green cardamoms and Madhubani paintings (Table 5.2).

Table 5.2 Number of items in international trade that carry 'place' in their name

Place	*No.*	*Items of trade*
India	15	Indian Kaltha (1), Indian Lead Seals (1), Madhubani Paintings (1), Rajasthani Paintings (1), Bleeding Madras (7), Dried Bombay Duck (1), Bombay Duck (1), Cardamoms Small Alleppey Green (1), Cardamoms Small Coorg Green (1)
China	11	China Clay Crude (1), Sanitary Fixtures of Porcelain/China (10)
Yemen	8	Coffee Arabica Plantation A' (1), 'B' (1), 'C' (1), Coffee Arabica Cherry 'AB' (1), PB'(1) Coffee Arabica Cherry 'C' (1) other grade (1)
England	5	Portland Cement Dry (1), Coloured (1), Pozzolana Cement (1), Slag (1), Other Portland Cement (1)
USA	5	Kentucky Blue Grass (1), Flue Cured Virginia Tobacco (1), Sun Cured Virginia Tobacco (1)
Australia	2	Australian Lupin seeds (2)
Brazil	2	Brazil nuts fresh/dried in shell (2)
Tripoli	1	Tripoli earth
Ocean	1	Pacific Salmon Atlantic Salmon (1)
Niger	1	Niger Seed
Jamaica	1	Pepper Jamaica
Germany	1	German Silver Jewellery
Austria	1	Venetian/Austrian Blinds
Asia	1	Asian Gum
Yemen	1	Gum Arabic
Africa	1	African Gum
Total	57	

Calculated from data of India's trade in the world from http://commerce.nic.in/tradestats/indiatrade.asp. Brackets refer to the number of items of trade.

The criterion adopted for creating a new code into the harmonised system is a minimum trade volume of US$20 million. However, this criterion of a minimum trade volume has been amended in the case of goods of environmental and social concern. Such goods are controlled by international conventions like the Basel Convention on the Control of Transboundary Movements of Hazardous Wastes and Their Disposal (signed 1989 and effective 1992); CITES, the Convention on International Trade in Endangered Species of Wild Fauna and Flora (signed 1973 and effective 1975), the Montreal Protocol on Substances that Deplete the Ozone Layer, a protocol to the Vienna Convention for the Protection of the Ozone Layer (signed 1987 and effective 1989) among other such agreements.

In the scheme of things, the day is not far when place goods with Geographical Indications will also be recognised as a class apart in world trade statistics. This is because these goods share a bond with unique places, the goods are distinctive and a certification tag confirms that they need to be given a special status worldwide. This would especially be beneficial for developing countries like India where many place goods, especially those belonging to the category of textiles and handicrafts, are suffering and struggling to 'stay alive'.

In support and aligned with the international laws, there has been the birth of the International Geographical Indications Network, which is engaged in policy, research and awareness activities. Established in 2003, the International Geographical Indications Network – oriGIn – is a not-for-profit nongovernmental organisation based in Geneva. It represents today some 350 associations of producers and other Geographical Indications–related institutions from some 40 countries.

Similarly, recent years have seen many national, regional and international conferences as well as an increase in the capacity building and technical assistance activities on Geographical Indications. The International Symposium on Geographical Indications is organised every two years by WIPO. This is organised in cooperation with an interested member state drawing together international experts, academia, administrators of member states, producers of Geographical Indications and nongovernmental organisations. Such a symposium was held in San Francisco (2003), Parma (2005), Beijing (2007), Sofia (2009), Lima (2011) and Bangkok in 2013.

Over the last 50 years the importance of Geographical Indications has grown from a relatively obscure clause in the Paris Convention of 1883 and GATT in 1947 to the forefront of world trade negotiations with TRIPS 1994. The concept of place has been incorporated into the lexicon in trade and intellectual property rights through the route of Geographical Indications, slowly yet surely. The reasons for the acceptance and recognition are many and varied. A confluence of forces worked to make room for Geographical Indications. Most germane is the changing nature of international trade.

Changing structure of international trade: For many years the composition of international trade consisted of products which involved goods that are different from each other. What was exchanged via ocean liners were goods that the countries did not possess or could not produce and manufacture. This was largely because the cost of transporting goods was high, and so only essential items were selected for trade. But today, technological improvements have opened the gates for trade over long distances at strikingly low cost. The most significant has been the use of container vessels, which are designed to hold cargo in prepacked units and transfer them to and from trains, trucks or trailers. Containerisation has reduced the shipping time of moving cargoes by 84 per cent and that of costs by 35 per cent, and this has in turn helped the growth of international trade. Today, almost one quarter of the world's cargo is shipped by container (Talley, 2000). The improvement in containers in ships and transcontinental aircrafts along with a series of trade negotiations means that goods of all kinds can quickly and cheaply be carried across the world. To this can be added the role of online or e-shopping. This electronic commerce allows consumers to directly buy goods or services from a seller over the Internet using a web browser, such as that of eBay or Amazon. Business organisations offer online shopping not only because it is of much lower cost compared to brick and mortar stores, but also because it offers access to a worldwide market, increases customer satisfaction and builds sustainable capabilities. Today a host of items including Appemidi mango pickle, Darjeeling tea, Kangra tea, Niligiri tea and Naga jalokia are available online. The trade agreements and technology therefore have been able to create a global market out of what earlier was regional, or local.

The market of some of India's 'locally' produced place goods is worldwide. Here are some statistics: The total turnover of Firozabad glassware is around Rs 800 crore of which Rs 62 crore comes from exports. With an annual turnover of Rs 360 crore the saddler industry of Kanpur is a 100 per cent export-oriented industry. Moradabad exports metal goods worth Rs 2,200 crore every year. The woodcraft industry of Saharanpur generates a turnover of Rs 1,000 crore of which Rs 750 crore comes from exports. Of the Rs 325-crore production of Pashmina Shawls in 2010–2011, Rs 142 crore or nearly half came from exports (Yasmin and Bhat, 2013).

In a globalising world, express transport and electronic transfers have created a new market where 'similar' goods but from different countries are pitched into direct competition with each other. Goods from different geographical locations are collected and displayed at the supermarkets, malls and duty-free halls of airports. It is at swanky malls and shopping plazas like those at Harrow, Sainsbury or Ambience that a cross-section of people including the rich and not-so-wealthy participate, observe and buy products from around the world.

In this age of global reach, there is a tendency of the people to be always on the lookout for things, experiences, goods and services that are different and unique. Difference has its own charm; it is in the search of this feature that place goods found a market.

Consumers are attracted to special and exceptional goods. The yardstick to measure distinctiveness could range from taste, aroma and weight to strength or design of the good in question. The applicants for Geographical Indications make it a point to mention 'unique' features their goods acquire because of their rootedness to place. Here follow a series of samples:

Unique fragrance: High on the search of consumers is fragrance and aroma. There are more than eight varieties of jasmine grown in Karnataka; however, because of its unique moderate fragrance and the fact that the buds have a shelf-life of 3–4 days Udupi jasmine dominates all other varieties. Kalanamak is the finest scented rice that grows in the north-east plains of Uttar Pradesh. The outer layer of the grain is black and hence the name *kala*, but the aroma is stronger than that of any rice cultivated in India. The exclusive feature of the Alleppey Green grade of cardamom is its size. It stands apart from others in length (21 mm) and also in size (5–8 mm in diameter). This increases its chance of holding more oil and imparting a stronger fragrance.

Unique fineness: The mountain goat *Capra hircus* has hair of a fineness of 12–16 microns! See this in contrast to the finest of sheep's wool which is 23 microns thick and human hair whose thickness ranges up to 200 microns. Pashmina shawls are woven from such fine hair, and this is what makes them ever so light to drape and wear. Their sheer weightlessness is what creates demand for them. Made from Korai grass which grows on the banks of River Thamirabarani, Pattamadai mats have such a supple and lustrous fineness that the mat is called *pattu pai* or silk mat! As for 'the transparent Chanderi . . . it would be any bride's dream of a wedding dress material'.

Unique weight: In the Molela village in Madhya Pradesh plaques are very light in weight when compared with other terracotta products. The reason being that flat slabs of clay are handmoulded to give a raised form and the area underneath is kept hollow. The dimensions given to images through the raised work gives a lifelike impression which is unique. The producers claim that the qualities that make Moradabad metal craft unique are many, but one criterion is that the goods manufactured at Moradabad have lighter weight in comparison to the metal goods manufactured elsewhere. The lightweight is achieved by peeling off the extra metal from the inside of the good.

Unique designs: The distinguishing characteristic of the Kota Doria is the square locally known as the '*khat*' that is woven to make the base fabric. The *khats* are woven so skilfully that it makes the fabric transparent, and this is what adds to its beauty and hence the demand. About 80 kilometres west of Madurai and same distance south of Thanjavur is Chettinad. Here the basket called Chettinad Kottan is woven using an exclusive technique called *Sohi*, where an extra strip of palm leaf is drawn through the weave of the completed basket to create a surface decoration, much like embroidery, in different patterns and contrasting colours. Belonging to the group of hand-block printing are those from Farrukhabad in Uttar Pradesh. Farrukhabad is a veritable storehouse of designs of which the most distinctive is the design of the Tree of Life, a mystical concept, and the design consists of branches of the tree which reach high into the heavens, while the roots dig deeply into the earth. Patan is located in the district of the same name in north Gujarat , which is located between Aravalli Range and Gulf of Khambat. Patan patolas are double ikat silken fabrics where both the warp and weft threads are tied and dyed before weaving. The rareness of Patan patolas is that unlike the usual practice of dyeing the thread in one uniform colour, the warp and weft are both dyed in a variegated range of shades along the whole length of each single thread. Patan patola is such a fine piece of handwork that it requires a special tape that can measure hundredth of an inch. To retain their exclusivity they are not sold through retail outlets but interested customers are shown albums and on this basis the price is fixed and then on completion Patan patola after inspection is delivered to the customer!

A special relief work called *gesso* is done on Mysore paintings to enhance the visual impact of the jewellery and other embellishments. The *gesso* is later covered with 24-carat gold leaf just before the painting is given the finishing touches. Pure gold leaf not only enhances the lustre of Mysore paintings but also makes the *gesso* work look exceptionally attractive and last longer. Thewa is a traditional craft of fusing a 23-carat handcarved gold foil on coloured glass sheet. The union of the gold foil with the glass sheet is done without using any kind of glue or pasting material. The exceptional beauty of Thewa is what has added to its demand. Santiniketan leather is made from the skin of sheep and goat and is vegetable dyed. This gives an exclusive appearance of shine and gloss to the dyed products. The products have got a singular property of retaining their embossed imprint permanently, and their grainy surface turns glossy when rubbed with glass or cotton.

Thus place is factored in as the dominant reason to explain the distinctive properties of the goods. Otherwise how would one bid for the most precious cargo when textiles or shawls, fruits such as bananas and oranges, or rice, chillies and jasmine and other items of different countries are together put up for display on the same table? It is as an arsenal to battle with the trading authorities to gain a distinct shelf space in the market that the idea of Geographical Indications was invented. It is in this context that the treaties for Geographical Indications gained significance. It is through this mechanism that each producer and country can try to claim superiority of their good over the myriad number of similar goods up for sale in the world. Backing this demand for the distinctive that is available because of geographical differences, the well-informed consumer is also looking for and supporting a product that is traditional and ecologically sustainable. Many of the Made Only in India match this description.

Search for ecologically friendly goods: A hallmark of most of India's place goods is that they are low on energy consumption, intensive on labour and high on the use of recycled materials or minor forest produce which are locally available. Goods that carry Geographical Indications harness bio-resources from catchments which are dominantly rural. Take the use of colour. The colours used in *Bagru* printing are black, red and maroon. These three colours are extracted from naturally occurring sources: black is derived from worn-out iron horse or camel shoes soaked in water, red comes from gum paste and *phitkari* and maroon is a result of mixing the above two colours. The colours used on the Molela terracotta are made from natural stone and minerals. Palewa is the clay slip and forms different colours when mixed with other elements. For instance the reddish colour is made when *geru* (red soil) is added to the mixture of palewa and water. As the binder, they use a vegetable gum collected from the trees.

The fact that 137 of the 199 Geographical Indications of India are registered under the category of handicraft goes to confirm the role of simple technology which is employed for their production. This makes the goods environmentally friendly. The notion of handwork is carried by the goods, '*Kasuti*' – '*Kai*' hand, '*Suti*' cotton – means handwork done in cotton; or *Kalamkari* means work done with nib of a pen! The material base of all the handicrafts goods registered at Chennai reveals that they are either made of wood, stone, metal or fibres, parched leather, coconut shell, clay, brass or woollen and cotton yarn. All these are biodegradable and recyclable.

The wise ecological use of raw materials also contributes towards making them exclusive in some ways. Thanjavur dolls registered in 2008 are made with plaster of Paris, wood pulp and clay obtained from the banks of the river Kaveri. Sujuni is a term for straight running-stitch embroidery on layered cotton. Women quilt together old sarees and other pieces of cloth with tiny running stitches and embroider these beautifully. The sewing together and embroidering of pieces of cloth, salvaged perhaps from worn-out saris, forms the basis of Kantha, a living testimony of the thrifty nature of the Bengali housewife. Even the highly patterned Navalgund durries of Karnataka use recycled yarn purchased from the nearby industrial city of Hubli.

Hand in hand with demand for the 'handmade and ecologically friendly' is the rapidly rising trend in favour of the organic. Most of the rich, elite and educated have come to realise the dangers to health from chemically pumped fast and durable foods grown in monoculture. The people, especially those with privileged incomes, are now demanding 'designer' foods that are not only exotic and different but also most importantly 'green'. It is now rapidly being proved that for healthy food, agriculture has to be rooted in local economies and be distinctly place bound. In fact food items maintain their taste, aroma and nutrition, only and only if they are grown in a chemical-free environment, because it is their harmony with the ecological givens that the best of these distinct properties are gathered and sustained.

Pokkali is an organically cultivated rice of Kerala. The daily tidal inflow and outflow of backwaters, the luxuriant growth of microflora and fauna, the natural deposits of decomposed floating aquatic weed mass and left over biomass of rice plant after harvest make the Pokkali fields nutrient rich. Neither chemical fertilisers nor plant protection chemicals are applied to the crop. It is the mix of such factors which gives the Pokkali rice a good cooking quality and a special taste.

What adds value to organic products is their promise of medicinal properties.

Pokkali rice and other rice products have medicinal properties. The bran is believed to be good for soothing the problems associated with piles. Broken Pokkali rice is considered best for the preparation of starter food to be taken after recovery from diseases like cholera and typhoid. Gruel water from Pokkali rice is also rated as a highly suitable drink for patients suffering from cholera (*Geographical Indications Journal* – Supplementary 2, 2008). Navara, the 'pious grain', is valued for its curative properties in circulatory, respiratory, digestive and rheumatic complaints. The 'Navara Kizhi', the cooked navara rice tied in a cloth, is widely used in Ayurvedic massage *panchakarma* treatment for nerve and spine disorders and paralysis. The Naga King Chilli is believed to prevent and cure gastritis and is also used as a painkiller, pest repellent and *antivenom*. It is also a toxic and stimulant. The cashew Feni of Goa is used for treating sickness, low blood pressure, loss of sleep for aged people and diarrhoea.

Flavour and fragrance, the key ingredients for taste, 'evaporate' at the slightest spray of chemicals be it in the case of aromatic rice, tea, coffee, mangoes or jasmine. The new age consumer searches for the eco-friendly. These are just a few illustrations which confirm the value of looking after and certifying place goods.

Not just a tag but a certificate: While the search for the ecological has led to a demand for the handmade and the green, consumers nowadays are in search for the authentic and are weary and unsure of the fake and look alike. This has created a new breed of 'label readers', who carefully read the fine print about the composition of the product, its date of manufacture and also place of birth. The demand is now for goods which are what they claim to be and are also legally certified because this is a way to differentiate the authentic from the inauthentic. What has also helped boost the demand for origin tags is the emergence of a market for other certifications such as organic and fair trade, along with preferences for environmentally sound and socially responsible products.

An 'eco-label' certifies the proven environmental credentials of a product or service within a specific product category. In the heartland of Vazhakulam, farmers are following the cultivation practices standardised by the Fair Trade Labelling Organization. Fairtrade Labelling Organizations International was established in Bonn, Germany, and it launched the international Fairtrade Certification Mark. It is an organisation that aspires to reach the highest standards for defining ethical trade. The organisation certifies goods which do not use chemical pesticides banned by the World Health Organization. The label indicates that the Vazhakulam pineapples are free from hazardous chemicals (Figure 5.1).

Darjeeling tea gardens are certified as organic by the Institut für Market Ecologie, Switzerland, and Naturland-Verband, Germany, which carry out periodic inspections. Some estates have become bio-dynamic, a kind of superorganic farming developed first in Germany based on the concept of harnessing cosmic energy. The biodynamic approach is heavily dependent on traditional methods and has much in common with other organic approaches; it emphasises the use of manures and composts and excludes the use of artificial chemicals on soil and plants. Moreover it makes use of traditional and local breeds and varieties, and in addition emphasises the use of an astrological sowing and planting calendar (Tate, 1994 in Lotter, 2003).

Such inspections and certifications raise the status of the product in the eyes of those users who are quality and health conscious and moreover have the capacity to pay for such dividends. Place goods which have been given a label or the ones which are in pursuit of the tag are not ordinary goods from any and sundry places. They represent both a superlative skill and a mastery of material which is only possible within the ecology of special places. Geographical Indications are for goods which are genuinely rooted 'indications' of a place. A 'place label' which certifies the authentic details of origin of the good, therefore, gains importance.

The buyers of place goods with Geographical Indications today are the wealthy, connoisseurs of taste and seekers of health and pursuers of quality. Historically, the wealthy temples, the Mughal courts and the elite have indulged in and were patrons of these goods. The Mughal emperor Akbar

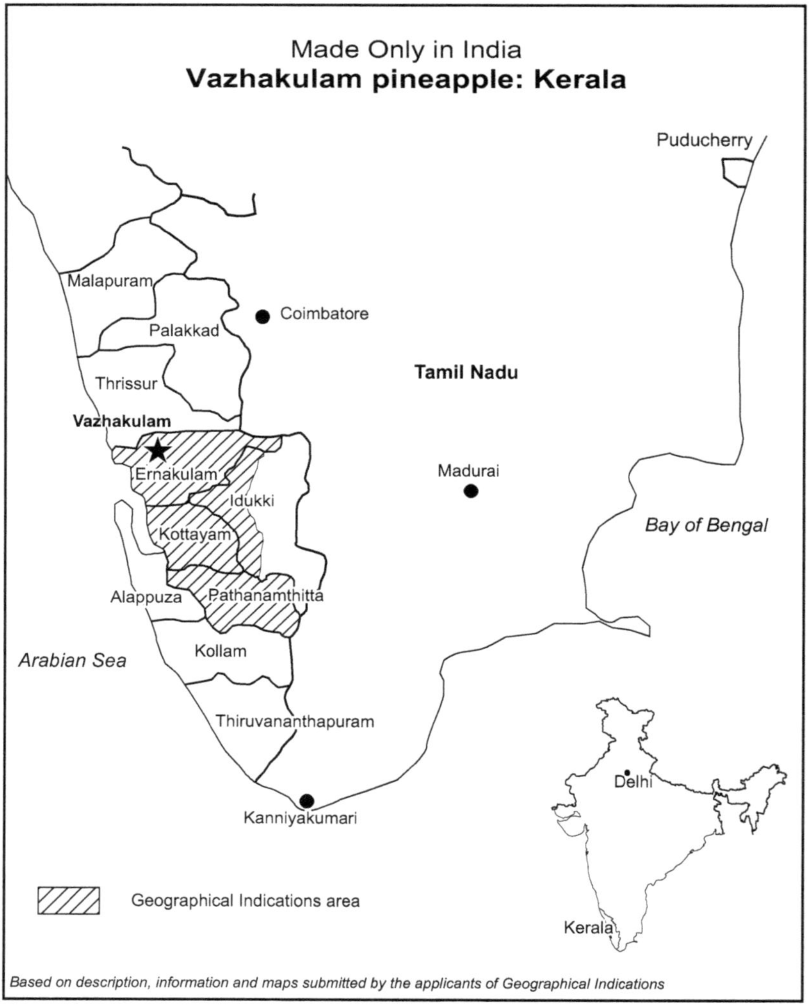

Figure 5.1 Vazhakulam pineapple: Kerala

supported the makers of shawls, the Nizams of Hyderabad patronised the wooden engravings and craftsmanship of Nirmal, the nawabs of Lucknow had adorned chikan! It has always been the upper echelons of society that have the surplus disposable income to pay for the exotic, the novel and the different. Today they are the ones who can pay for and promote the handcrafted over the machine made, the organic over the chemical and the style with the substance. Their numbers and demand are growing.

Backed by media campaigns and a dramatic rise in the power and reach of international intellectual property rights, both the producers and consumers want to give, get and gain the best. Ultimately, the gains for place good are not just about conserving ecology, traditional knowledge or heritage but are equally, if not more, about making profits and accruing financial gains. A legal certification tag of origin of place adds to recognition, boosts sale and fetches a profit.

Promising profit: Goods with a Geographical Indications tag fetch a premium price. A survey conducted by the European Union in 1999 found that 40 per cent of consumers would pay a 10 per cent premium for goods which carried a guarantee about its place of origin (World Trade Organization, 2004). In some cases the dividends scale higher.

> Unlike common table salt, which is mined from the land and then refined, the best specialty salts are 'harvested' from seawater that is allowed to evaporate in the sun. The process preserves the minerals that lend each its distinguishing appearance and flavour. Among the salts which carry these characteristics are the Portuguese Algarve salts, Australian Murray River Pink Flake salt and the shimmering Indian Black salt. Gourmet cooks pay as much as US$80 per pound for such varieties as opposed to 30 cents per pound for common table salt.
>
> (Agarwal and Barone, 2005: 2)

Indian pepper has a rich taste that makes it superior to rivals such as the Indonesian or the Vietnamese pepper. It, therefore, fetches a better price in the world market. Garbled bold pepper berries are usually referred to as Tellicherry pepper. Today Malabar and Tellicherry pepper constitute 90 per cent of the country's total black pepper production and 80 per cent of the exports. Usually, the flavoured superior grade Malabar and Tellicherry pepper with high pungency commands US$200–300 premium over fair average quality grade pepper in the world market (Ganguli, 2007).

Central Travancore jaggery is sold at a premium price of Rs 3–4 per kilogram higher than jaggery from other places. It is said that a quarter of a million flowers are required to make just one pound of Kashmir saffron. With a flowering period of two weeks in autumn, this deep yellow powder used for flavouring and colouring foodstuff is an expensive spice with a retail sale price in Delhi of Rs 2.5 lakh for one kilogram (2013). Sandalwood is the costliest of all the woods and is widely known for its special fragrance. Insects do not infest this wood, and valuable articles can therefore be stored in sandalwood receptacles with a certain amount of safety. The carvers consider only a 100-year-old tree fit for carving. Mysore is the world's foremost sandalwood producer. At present the Government of Karnataka distils over 75 per cent of the world's output of oil. Sandal is also the traditional wood used on the cremation pyre of the wealthy, but this extravagance must be rare when even the retail price for low-grade wood is about Rs 60 per kilogram. Nevertheless, token pieces are often used. High-quality wood suitable for carving is sold at approximately Rs 500 per kilogram. A comparative study shows that a 24-inch figure in sandalwood sells at Rs 12,000–15,000 whereas a figure in the same size but made of cedar wood retails at Rs 2,500 (Ranjan and Ranjan, 2007).

Place goods thus fetch many gains. Irrespective of the fact that India has been one country rich in place products of great merit and many communities and industries have been surviving on them, a legal protection of Geographical Indications has never been on the agenda of Indian lawmakers. The TRIPS Agreement knee jerked policymakers in India to explore the scope and potential of protection of Geographical Indications. It was under the umbrella of TRIPS that India enacted its first-ever Geographical Indication of Goods Act in 1999.

India surely would have saved and reaped more if such a protection had been implemented in the nineteenth century, a time when the colonists were systematically plagiarising and destroying its many place goods. History would have charted an entirely different route had India invented a way to vigilantly guard the secrets of its place goods be it the shawls, silks or handicrafts, and kept the wisdom of caring for 'place' be it in the rice fields, vegetable plots or aromatic fruits intact. But this was not to be. While the colonial rule exploited and destroyed each and every mode and method of India's creative genius, the post-independence years of rushing to adopt a developmental model of growth that bulldozed 'place' has left India bankrupt on the score of Geographical Indications.

The scope to resurrect place goods became possible when India became a signatory of TRIPS. But even with this treaty, India has enrolled a measly 199. The small number is evident from the perspective of the total of 10,000 protected Geographical Indications in the world, with an estimated total trade value of more than US$50 billion (Giovannucci *et al.*, 2009). The European Union has a sizeable share of 66 per cent of the total. Today it is 20 years to the decision made at TRIPS. India enacted the Act in 1999, and it came into force with effect from 15 September 2003, yet India has only 199 registrations on its rolls. Those seeking and awaiting registration are 243. Of these 125, nearly half are foreign applicants, with countries like

France 36, Spain 28, Italy 23, Greece 13 and Germany 11 taking a lead (Appendix 4). With this slow pace it should not happen that in years to come India is forced to accept the Geographical Indications protection for foreign goods and is left far behind in looking after its very own which are made only in India. This raises the curiosity to search for more goods that can make a claim of origin only in India.

6

SEARCHING

Place goods

India is a land of astonishing diversity. In the north, the Himalayas string and stretch like a sweeping arc, while a long indented coastline is what binds India's southern half. The upper portion, the Gangetic plain is a basin filled by alluvium; the southern part, the Deccan is raised like a tableland. In climate, India offers the full range: perpetual snows in the Himalayas, hot deserts in Rajasthan, tropical heat in the southern part and lashing monsoons drenching the north-east. The bio-geographical landscape of conifers, teak and palm builds the forest, the jungle and the grasslands. India is the only country in the world where tiger and the lion coexist. Contained within its binds is Ladakh, the highest cold desert in the world which carries an environment as stark as the prisoner's cell; and the Silent Valley of Kerala, a hub of tropical rainforest as dense in species as are the specimens in a collector's shop. Wide cultural diversity exists between Indians of the same region, state, district or city. India speaks many languages, harbours many races and endless are the gods that its citizens worship. North India carries the impress of Mughal and Islamic courtly life; South India is replete with temples, parts like north-east India and central India are more tribal. This multiplicity is the basis for the hope to find many more place goods.

Diversity gives scope to search for place goods: A textile line can be drawn between the South where the weave is an integral part of the woven fabric, and the North where there is an extra weft in its weaving. Embroidery abounds in the North and of it there are different types. A rather continuous belt of embroidery emerges in the states of Gujarat and Rajasthan. There is diversity within diversity. Embroidery worked with the help of an aar or a holed needle where the thread is introduced from below known as *mochi bharat* is carried out in Gujarat. Within short distances it has its versions. The women of the Rabri nomadic community of Kutch create a type of embroidery using mirrors of various triangular, round, square and almond shapes. This embellishment in aari is called *rabri bharat*. Slightly different is the embroidery that is worked in Banni, the semi-desert area of Kutch; here the women create minute designs in the embroidery. In the Himalayan belt, there is a difference between the sozani and kashida of Kashmir and the rumals of Chamba in Himachal Pradesh. Whereas the Kashida may employ a range of stitches from the stem stitch to the herringbone, a feature unique to Sozani is that it is done so skilfully that the motif appears on both sides of the fabric, with each side having a different colour. Consequently, there is no wrong side. In contrast the Chambal rumal carries an expression of embroidery which is done on handspun cotton with unfinished, home-dyed silk floss. It is a blend of the design from the miniature paintings into the form of embroidery (Figure 6.1). In Punjab is the phulkari, bagh and chope, and further in Uttar Pradesh is the chikan of Lucknow. Towards the east, there is the Bengal kantha and the Pipli appliqué of Odisha. South India stands different from the North. Except for the work of the Toda tribe and wandering banjaras, virtually no indigenous embroidery comes from South India (Dhamija and Jain, 1989).

India offers a plethora of ways to colour the fabric. Tie and dye refers to the technique of producing a pattern in a fabric by partly dyeing the threads before weaving. Tie and dye is also known as ikat, a word derived from the Malayan Indonesian language word *Mangikat*, meaning to bind knot or wind around. There are many ways to do this. If in a fabric the longitudinal warp and weft both are dyed with predetermined design and woven to meet each other in a weaving process, it is called double ikat. In the case where a single yarn either warp or weft is tied to form a specific design during weaving, it is termed as single ikat. India offers an assortment from the single ikat of Rajkot, to the double ikat of Patan and the highly complex patola from Gujarat, bandhani of Saurashtra, Kutch; tie-and-dye of Shekhawati, Jhunjhunu and Sikar in Rajasthan; or lehariya and mothra of Udaipur, Jaipur and Jodhpur, again in Rajasthan. All these are different types of tie-and-dye work where the cloth is tied in a variety of patterns. The difference in the way the fabric is tied influences the design. In lehariya or waves, the cloth is rolled edge to edge diagonally and bound in selected areas; whereas in bandhini the cloth is tied in small knots. Mothra is an extension of lehariya in which diagonal lines cross each other in opposite directions, at 45°, giving rise to small diamond shapes.

To visualise how the form and patterns that emanate at each place differ, compare Sanganer and Bagru in Rajasthan. The two settlements are located towards the south-east of Jaipur. Sanganer is 8 kilometres south of Jaipur, Bagru is 30 kilometres to the south-east. Sanganer print is usually done on a white background, whereas Bagru prints are on an indigo or a dyed background. Traditionally, motifs printed in Bagru are large, with bold lines as compared to Sanganer, where intricate detailing is practised using sombre colours and fine lines. The motifs of both are inspired

Figure 6.1 India: Geographical Indications – embroidery and dyeing and printing centres

from local sources. Bagru motifs are more geometric than the Sanganeri. What makes these unique is the geography of the area. Apart from the creative skills of the communities a fact also is that the water in Sanganer comes out best in its dark shade, while in Bagru it takes on a reddish tinge (Figure 6.2). To this can be added the likes of Baltora, a city in Barmer

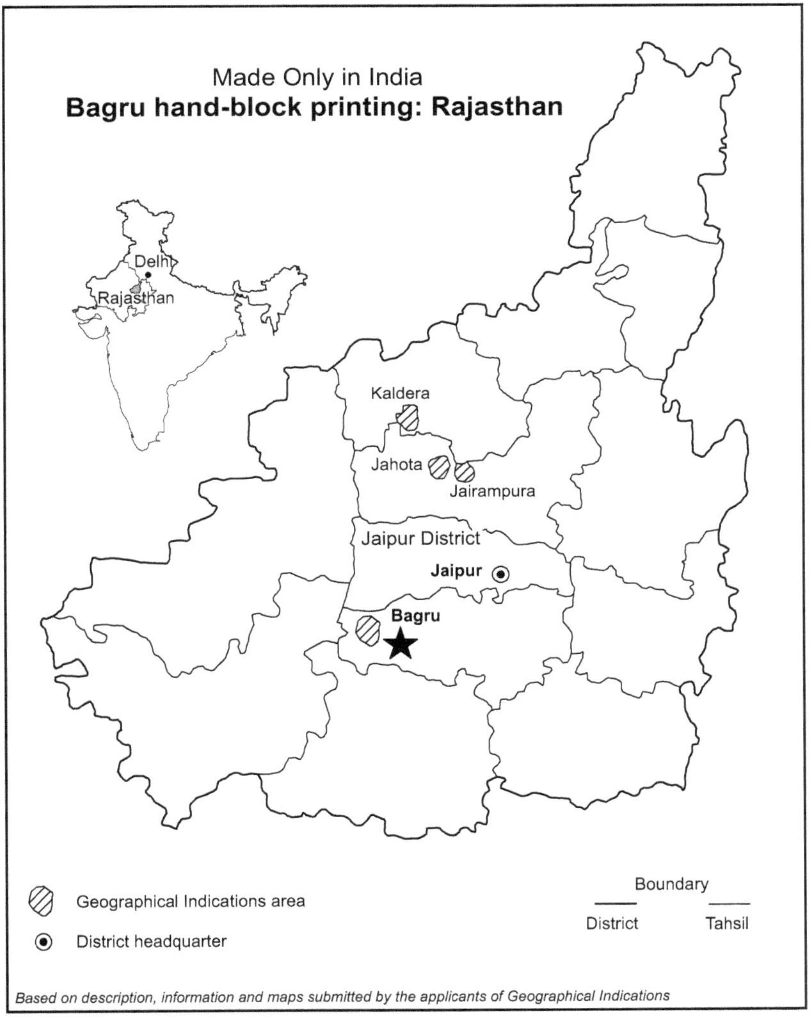

Figure 6.2 Bagru hand-block printing: Rajasthan

district of Rajasthan about 100 kilometres south-west from Jodhpur, where traditional block printing on the lines of Ajrakh has attained excellence. The speciality of the block printing of Balotra is that it is done on both sides of the cloth. The reverse side hand-block printing is done simultaneously even when the other side of the design print is wet. The hand-block printed fabric from Balotra is exclusive and could be considered for Geographical Indications.

Capturing the palette of variety, Pupul Jayakar, an authority on Indian textiles, eloquently observes that the textile colours in India coincide with the dyeing and printing belt, which extends from the interior of Sind through the deserts of Kutch, Kathiawar and Rajasthan to the borders of Gujarat.

> . . . It is as if the fierce sun and bare bleak stretches of sand have demanded compensation in the deep brilliant colours worn by the women of these areas . . . Colours appear here to be roasted and matured by the sun . . . As we go further south, colours lose their brilliance, they become darker and more subdued till at last they seem to quench themselves in the lush green vegetation of the backwaters of Malabar.
>
> (Saraf, 1982: 4)

India carries many symbols of diversity. The geographical differences of India can be read in the weaves of a simple basket. There are three divisions of the single state of Jammu and Kashmir. In the high-altitude desert of Ladakh, long conical-shaped backpack baskets are woven out of willow called *malchang*. In the Jammu region of Kishtwar and Bhardarwah a local strain of willow is used to make sturdy baskets called *kiltu* to carry fruits and vegetables to the market. The *kangri*, a willow basket with a handle, containing an earthenware pot, is the most typical and indispensable part of a Kashmiri's belongings. A sample handpicked from other parts of the country brings in more types. The women of the Mithila-Madhubani region in Bihar, apart from making paintings, are adept basketmakers. Every young girl is taught to make baskets with the locally available golden-coloured *sikki* grass. Extremely delicate, indeed the finest mats are those knit in the *kora* grass made in a place called Pattamadai in Tirunelveli . In contrast, the *thazhapaya* or screw pine mat of Kerala uses the sword-shaped thorny screw-pine plant. The process is tough as the leaf has sharp thorns growing in both directions. The finer varieties of mats need narrower splits, and to ensure they are extra soft they are boiled in pure milk. The weaving is done crosswise, and the edges are hemmed with narrow screw pine strips. Decorative embroidery adds to the beauty of the products (http://www.craftandartisans.com/screw-pine-thazhapaya-mats.html).

Recognising the bond with place, different types of sarees have been registered with Geographical Indications. Alongside the saree traditional Indian dresses according to the climate, natural resources, culture and skills that are readily available. The threat of modernity has impacted forms of dress, yet a must in the wardrobe of the people of India are clothes which are a traditional hallmark of 'their place'. This is true across the length and breadth of the country. Somewhere between a coat and a cloak is the *pheran* of Kashmir, a loose garment worn by the people in Kashmir to provide warmth and comfort while going about their daily chores. The 'free flowing loose cut of the garment' gives the space for holding the 'kangri' a small earthenware bowl filled with charcoal and embers, enclosed within a wicker basket to provide warmth in the winter. In Kerala, there is the Mundum Neriyathum, traditional clothing for women, which helps in beating the heat. This two-piece set of flowing fabric, one to drape the upper part and the other the lower, is unstitched and traditionally white or cream in colour, ideal for the hot humid weather. In contrast to the two-piece is the Mekhla Chadar, the traditional attire of Assamese women made up of three pieces, a skirt like a sarong, a blouse and an additional piece of cloth draped over the shoulder. The mekhla skirt is a thicker garment whereas to allow ease of drape the *chadar* is lighter. The mekhla or the skirt is known for its shine that comes from the Muga silk unique to Assam. As is the environment so is the variety of dress. Endless is the diversity of goods, types and produce of different places in India. The difference nurtured the differences and thus were born the place-based identities.

The areal variations both among the land and people of India is enough to convince that there is scope to 'find' a variety of goods and produce which could be couriers of geographical hallmarks. Why then has India registered such a small number (199) of place goods at Chennai compared with other regions of similar size and perhaps lesser diversity than her in the world? India is almost as large as the continent of Europe, and it perhaps has a broader spectrum of environmental habitats than Europe. If this truism were extended, then since the European Union has close to 6,000 protected Geographical Indications (O'Connor, 2004), India should at least have a similar number, if not more, of 'place protected geographical indication' goods in its pool. Where more could India search for these?

When an effort was made to plough through publications which could give a clue to India's place goods, a valuable source was the 2007 work authored by husband and wife Ranjan and Ranjan titled *Crafts of India: Handmade in India*. This document states that India's 'creative history is decipherable from the metal, pottery, textiles, wood, paintings, jewellery, grassmat, clay, stone crafts, which are prevalent in different regions of the country'. There are more than 23 million craftsmen engaged in different crafts sectors and it is estimated that there are over 360 crafts clusters in India. These clusters are grouped into 106 metaclusters. 'The basis of demarcating meta-clusters was either geographical or in some cases cultural proximity of districts. Some meta-clusters have emerged from a concentration of crafts in a region' (Figure 6.3).

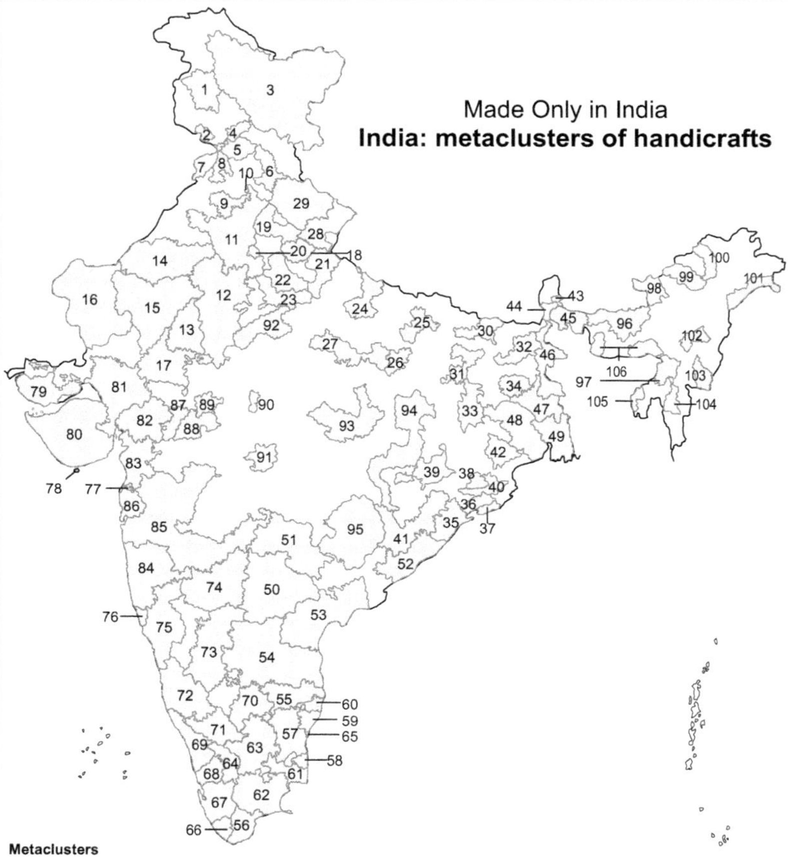

Metaclusters

1. Kashmir
2. Jammu
3. Ladakh
4. Chamba
5. Kangra
6. Kullu
7. Amritsar
8. Hoshiarpur
9. Patiala
10. Chandigarh
11. Haryana
12. Jaipur
13. Ajmer
14. Bikaner
15. Jodhpur
16. Jaisalmer
17. Udaipur
18. Delhi
19. Saharanpur
20. Moradabad
21. Bareilly
22. Aligarh
23. Agra
24. Lucknow
25. Gorakhpur
26. Varanasi
27. Allahabad
28. Almora
29. Dehradun
30. Madhubani
31. Patna
32. Bhagalpur
33. Ranchi
34. Dumka
35. Ganjam
36. Bhubaneshwar
37. Puri
38. Dhenkanal
39. Sambalpur
40. Cuttack
41. Koraput
42. Mayurbhanj
43. Sikkim
44. Darjeeling
45. Cooch Behar
46. Murshidabad
47. Birbhum
48. Bankura
49. Kolkata
50. Hyderabad
51. Warangal
52. Visakhapatnam
53. Machilipatnam
54. Cuddapah
55. Chittoor
56. Kanniyakumari
57. Cuddalore
58. Auroville
59. Kanchipuram
60. Chennai
61. Tiruchirappalli
62. Madurai
63. Salem
64. Coimbatore
65. Pondicherry
66. Thiruvananthapuram
67. Ernakulam
68. Thrissur
69. Kannur
70. Bangalore
71. Mysore
72. Mangalore
73. Bellary
74. Bijapur
75. Belgaum
76. Goa
77. Dadra & Nagar Haveli
78. Daman & Diu
79. Kachchh
80. Rajkot
81. Ahmedabad
82. Vadodara
83. Surat
84. Kolhapur
85. Pune
86. Mumbai
87. Jhabua
88. Indore
89. Ujjain
90. Bhopal
91. Betul
92. Gwalior
93. Mandla
94. Sarguja & Raigarh
95. Bastar
96. Nalbari
97. Silchar
98. Bomdila
99. Ziro
100. Along
101. Khonsa
102. Khomia
103. Imphal
104. Aizawl
105. Agartala
106. Meghalaya

Source: Ranjan and Ranjan (2007)

Figure 6.3 India: metaclusters of handicrafts

When crafts in these 360 clusters were studied two facts emerged: first, all clusters carried distinctive crafts and second, most clusters boast of more than one handicraft. Kashmir, for example, has the weaving of carpets and shawls, the carving of walnut wood and the manufacturing of *gabba* and *namdas*. It is also famous for copper work, papier mache and wicker work. Similarly, the cluster of Lucknow has zardozi, chikankari, tharu appliqué, clay toys and silver work. Chamba in Himachal Pradesh has jewellery, Chamba rumal, Chamba painting and Chamba embroidery on leather. Bankura, a cluster in West Bengal, is famous for terracotta (incidentally the Central Cottage Industries Corporation of India has the bankura as its emblem), Pattachitra paintings, Ganjifa cards, Coonch shell, stone and wood carving, along with weaving Maslond mats and creating lac-coated toys. The district of Kachchh records as many as 13 different crafts ranging from painted terracotta, Kachchi embroidery, Rogan paintings, bandhani dyeing to Ajrakh printing to silver work and bell making. If this and other such sources are searched one could safely add more place goods to the rolls of India's Geographical Indications.

What is evident in the case of toys was that the Jhabua dolls of Madhya Pradesh represent tribal men and women in colourful traditional dresses and enjoy national fame. There also are the Tirupathi dolls especially the *dampati* (man-woman) dolls; earlier these were made of clay and then changed to lightwood, locally known as *Poniki*: native artists exhibit an unusual facility in the way in which they are able to model in clay. The small toys and models of the different classes of natives are as rule well made. Models of natives made on a small scale are made in Bengal at Kishnughar and at Calcutta, at Poonah, in the Bombay Presidency, Lucknow models are made of figures, but the best are those representing different kinds of fruit. The models of fruit made at Gokak, near Belgaum, Karnataka, are celebrated throughout India (Cole, 1874). Gokak is on the rolls at Chennai, but others are yet to enrol.

Similarly, since the Bobbili veena has an origin tag then why are other musical instruments like the Miraj sitars from Kolhapur district or Tanjore Tanpura used widely by Carnatic music performers not on the list?

Mangoes account for nearly one-third of the total fruit export from India, yet the corky dotted Alampur Baneshan mango of Mahabubnagar, Andhra Pradesh; or the juicy and tangy Langra Benarasi, Lucknow; Safeda and Bangalora Safeda have still not processed their applications for the Registry at Chennai. The Nanjanagud banana is on the list, but the Mysore Poovan banana or the flavoured Nendran bananas are still missing. The Allahabad Surkha guava is registered while Banarsi Surkha, Madhopur guava, Mirzapuri seedless or the Navalur guavas from Dharwad are possible candidates for enrollement. A fruit from the pulp of which sherbet and syrup is made is bael; the famous Ayodhya bael can be a candidate for a Geographical Indications tag.

The Mysore betel leaf was registered in 2006 (Figure 6.4). The Magadhi variety from the Magadh region near Patna in Bihar, the famous variety of betel leaf from Venmony near Chengannur, Kerala, called Venmony Vettila and the one from Dhar in Madhya Pradesh all carry a distinct flavour and have the scope for a Geographical Indications recognition.

The only few food preparations which have been registered are Hyderabad haleem, Dharwad pedha, Tirupathi laddu and Bikaneri bhujia. Sharing many place-specific features if Bikaneri is registered, then Lonavala *chikki* from Pune, and Agra Petha, Kaman of Ahmedabad, Karadantu of Gokak, Khirmohana of Puri, Odisha, and Kundha of Belgaum and other sweet meats with a special taste could be pulled in too.

Stone is another unchallenged product where the desirable product qualities are intrinsically linked to a single area of geographic production. Stone does not reflect place but is the site and situation of the good. Quarried from different parts, India is a storehouse of a variety of stone. The pure white crystalline marble comes from Makrana, a town about 100 kilometres to the west of Jaipur, Rajasthan; and green marble comes from Rikhabdeo-Kesariaji area, 60 kilometres to the south of Udaipur, another famous city of Rajasthan. While Makrana is certified, the only calcite black marble available in the world from near the city of Abu in Rajasthan also has a scope of being recognised. Situated close to the famous Mount Abu, the calcite content of Abu Black marble makes it highly durable in various polishes. All these are yet to seek registration.

Widen the search to include different types of goods: India has two broad zones of staple food. Close to the state of Maharashtra one can almost draw a line, a hazy one, that divides the wheat-eating North (Kashmir is an exception) from the rice-eating South. Within the North, the eastern half eats rice, and within the South, millets are eaten in the dry interior areas. Within these broad belts India tables an amazing feast of all types of food. The diverse culinary heritage holds a promise of addition to the list of place goods.

To gain insight about distinctive foods a research was conducted of a stock 60 books on Indian cookery. Of the 11,166 recipes listed in these 60 books, 25 per cent mentioned a specific administrative state of India, among which Jammu and Kashmir, Punjab, Goa, West Bengal and Rajasthan took the sizeable share. Nearly 335 recipes carried the local ingredients and a specific place in their name.

Most if not all of the best foods of India hail from a specific place be it the aromatic rice called *Hyderabadi biryani*; chickpeas filled with masala called

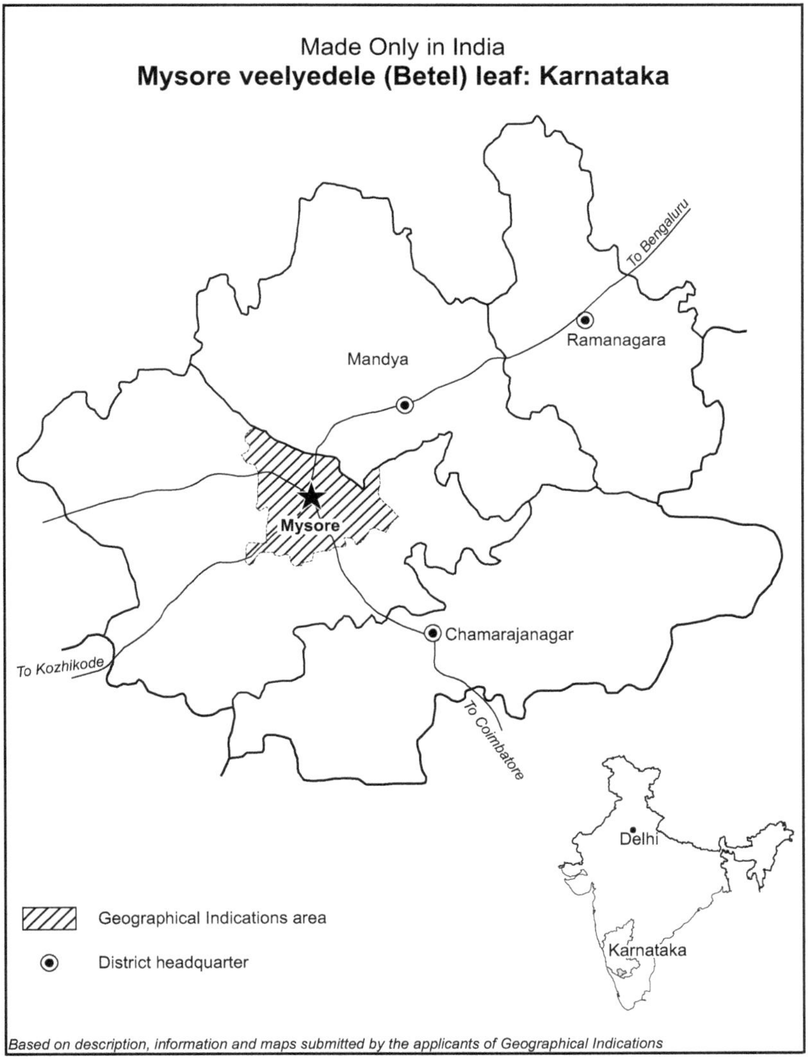

Figure 6.4 Mysore veelyedele (Betel) leaf: Karnataka

Amritsari chole; Kashmiri Rogan Josh, mutton marinated in yogurt and saffron; Kancheepuram idli, a savoury cake of rice; and *moong dal*, flavoured with cumin, coarsely crushed peppercorn and dried ginger all belong to a specific place.

Epitomising the feast of India is *wazhawan*. Comprising of no less than a 36-course delicious cuisine, the trend of which started with the *wazas*, the master chefs of Kashmir, *wazhawan* is not a simple meal but a ceremony. Hours of cooking and days of planning go into the making and serving of a *wazhawan*. Choicest delicacies such as *Tabakmaaz* or the Kashmiri red fried lamb ribs, *Rista* or the meat balls in red gravy, and a variety of kababs and vegetable preparations are a culinary delight. All the major ingredients needed to prepare the cuisine belong to Kashmir. The preparation of *Rogan Josh*, a kind of mutton dish (*rogan* means colour and *josh* passion), which is cooked on low-to-moderate heat, draws heavily on locally grown produce. Kashmiri chillies along with the extract from dried flowers, locally known as '*muawal*', provide the red colour and flavour. Classically, garlic and a paste of a local variety of shallots fried before grinding locally called 'prawn' in Kashmir are typically as essential as is saffron that grows on the Karewas. In Kashmir, *kaveh* is tea, often of the green variety flavoured with cardamom and served with almonds and saffron. All these go into the making of this delicacy of Kashmir. *Wazhawan* is a place package.

The town of Udupi on the west coast of the south Kanara districts in Karnataka whose cooks, trained in the kitchens of the great Krishna temple of the Udupi Sri Krishna Matha, are said to excel in their craft. An establishment named Udupi Hotel in 1975, while advertising a claim to provide high-quality South Indian vegetarian food, states, 'it is their place of production which gives them the art of this specialty cooking'.

When savouring 'local food' one is actually buying and consuming the flavour of the area. Research in the way consumers buy products in supermarkets also confirms a growing interest in place-identified or regional foods since the 1990s (Shaw and Carter, 1993). Confirming and cashing in on this is a popular slogan used by the tourism industry: 'A Taste of India'. The slogan seems to draw from the Scottish Tourist Board drive in 1972 which launched the tag line 'Taste of Scotland' as a catering initiative to valorise tourism by confirming the experiential connect between food and a place. Many of India's tourism websites of state governments carry a note on regional food specialities. Establishing the link between the 'preparation of food items and place' India could add a list of food items for Geographical Indications and why should this not be used as cachet after all if wine is a drink item that features so prominently so can preparations of food; the condition however has to be that it is distinctive and cannot be prepared such in any other place.

Food in all likelihood would fetch higher premium over handicraft, since the former is about health and carries the promise of enjoying quality of life. This could well be a fertile area for India to invest its search for Geographical Indications.

India is a vast country with heterogeneity of resources, people and goods. There are many items, goods and produce which can be searched on the basis of Geographical Indications and a case put forward for consideration by the Registry. The purpose here has been not so much to take a magnifying glass and look out to list the place goods, but the intention is to provide a clue into the enormity of diversity of all kinds that is India. Here it must be reiterated that if it is difficult to create place goods, they need more to be identified, recognised and nurtured. This is what the Mughal badshahs did. The current global interest in the label of origin gives a chance to do exactly this. It is an opportune time to search for the local and build global connections. India offers a vast scope to net goods with Geographical Indications, but hunting for the place goods or chasing a mere registration is not the end; the more serious question is to maintain the distinctive quality, build a market for the goods and protect the goods. The concerns that need care are many and deep.

7

CONCERNS FOR PLACE GOODS

Place goods are a spatial experience, and Geographical Indications are an acknowledgment of spatial distinctiveness which gives birth to unique products and goods. The continuity and durability of place goods depends upon patrons, traders, market and customers. Place goods cannot and do not sell themselves. To develop consumer perception about the quality, value and the place–product link requires sensitive rearing, upholding of standards by producers of goods and effective marketing.

In India many goods with a registered Geographical Indications tag were once patronised by the rulers and carried a name in world trade. But in the last 100 years or so these handicrafts and handlooms and foods and fruits have been nudged, pushed and dumped so much so that India will now have to make great efforts to revive their production and bring them into the mainstream by rerecognising their place-based identity.

Some beginnings are being made in this direction. The campaign 'Incredible India' was launched by the Ministry of Tourism in 2002. Its intention was to promote India as a destination choice for the discerning traveller. India was projected as an attractive tourist destination site by showcasing different aspects of her culture and history, including yoga and spirituality. The Incredible India campaign also included a component of rural India and carried descriptions of some Geographical Indications goods such as Chanderi and Pochampally.

Place-specific goods are a part of the package that brands India as incredible for these goods cannot now by law be produced or manufactured anywhere else in the world. That is why they are tagged as the Made Only in India. To build awareness of the role and importance of Geographical Indications, the Registry at Chennai organises workshops all over the country to enrol more goods. So that cost is not a deterrent the fees for registration has been kept as low as Rs 5,000 only. The tools of marketing, backed by strong media campaign, are essential for the sustenance of place goods.

After all, a product stamped with a certification of Geographical Indications does not automatically generate a comparative advantage if consumers do not recognise what the indication stands for.

While few goods such as Darjeeling tea, Kashmir pashmina, Alleppey cardamom and Basmati rice enjoy a global cachet many still have a long way to rebuild a name and lay a claim to fame. There is need to autonourish the bond of the good with place with due support, recognition and appreciation. The market I envision is not the common bazaar or the type of a shopping mall; it is more like that of 'collectors shops' where goods are valued beyond just cheapest cost. In this sense it is the connoisseurs that have the 'eye and taste' to appreciate such goods who would be the patrons of these goods.

The building of this connect is not difficult; if the good in question is exceptional, buyers are drawn to it like flies to honey. What is required is a serious commitment and movement to reclaim the value of place, on the lines of the Gandhian way where rural areas and village industries are given due cognisance and support. Along with the work to build and sustain goods and their market, an equally worrisome concern is the need to protect Geographical Indications from threats such as homonyms, generics, imitations and other such troublemakers.

Homonyms: Place names are the most common way to identify geographic features. But the problem with place names is that they often are not unique; some places may have many names and many different places may have the same name. Therefore, names exist which are spelt and pronounced the same, but refer to different geographical locations. When identical names refer to many different places they are called toponymic homonyms. Homonyms confuse customers about the geography-based reputation of goods. After all, if there are two places carrying the same name, then how would a buyer be certain about the exact place where the good in question is being manufactured? Homonyms are common. When a country-level analysis based on the names of 8,410 towns and cities listed in the Census of India 2011 was made, it generated as many as 410 toponymic homonyms. Nearly 5 per cent of the towns and cities of India have the same name as another city, town or place (Figure 7.1).

Among the 'name alikes' close to 50 per cent of them occur within India, 34 per cent are outside India while 17 per cent are such that they crop up both in and outside India (Table 7.1).

Homonyms of the towns and cities of India are spread across 72 countries of the world and have travelled as far as Zambia, Greece, Fiji and Canada. Sharing a common history of language and culture with Nepal, Bangladesh, Pakistan and Sri Lanka, along with Tibet, Iran and

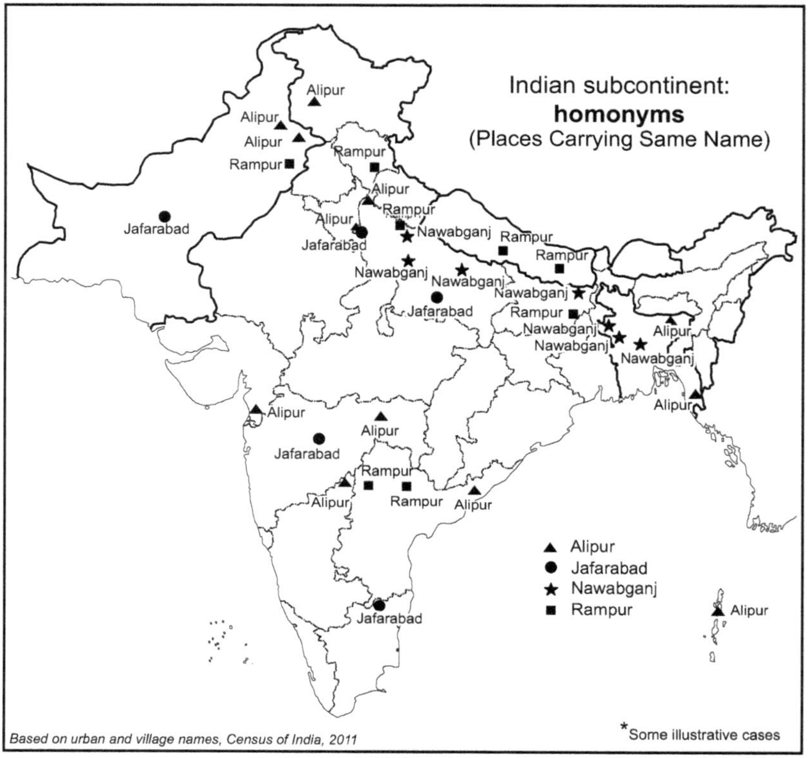

Figure 7.1 Indian subcontinent: homonyms

Table 7.1 India: number of towns and cities with homonyms, 2011

Type	*Number**
Number with homonyms within India only	199 (49.0)
Number with homonyms outside India only	141 (34.0)
Number with homonyms both inside and outside India	70 (17.0)
Total towns and cities with homonyms	410 (100)
Total towns and cities in India	8,410
Homonyms as per age of the total	4.88

Source: Calculated from *Census of India* (2011)

* Figures in bracket denote percentage of all homonym towns.

Afghanistan, bulk of the homonym outside of India occur in these neighbouring countries (Table 7.2).

The problem turns serious when it is seen that of the 410, there are 2 towns with 12 homonyms, 36 towns with 3 , 75 towns with 2 and 251 with 1 homonym (Table 7.3).

There are many ways a homonym could be born, but it seems that when people migrate from one region to another and set up a locality, village

Table 7.2 Places in Asia which are homonyms of towns and cities in India, 2011

Country	*Number of places*
Neighbours of India	
Pakistan	46
Nepal	47
Bangladesh	46
Tibet	1
Afghanistan	7
Sri Lanka	3
Subtotal	150
Countries in Asia other than neighbours*	28
Asia Total	178

Source: Calculated from *Census of India* (2011)

* includes Saudi Arabia, Iran, Indonesia, Malaysia, Philippines, Japan and China among others

Table 7.3 Places outside India which are homonyms of towns and cities in India, 2011

Continent	*Number*	*Percentage of total*
Asia (excluding India)	178	64
Europe	55	20
America	20	7
Africa	19	7
Australia	4	1
Total	276	100

Source: Calculated from *Census of India* (2011)

Number of Indian towns with homonyms outside India is 211.

The 276 places across the world which have homonyms of Indian cities are spread across 72 countries of the world and range as far as Zambia, Greece, Fiji, Canada and others.

or town they tend to give a 'native' name to the new place. The urge to replicate a 'native' name perhaps is an expression of topophilia. Coined from the Greek word *topos* meaning place, with the suffix *philia*, meaning 'love for' , it is well accepted that people foster a close emotional bond with their 'environment'. Thus, topophilia is one way that leads to the birth of homonyms.

Homonyms can mislead and confuse buyers about the origin of goods. Arani, a town in Tamil Nadu, is famous for its silk. It also is the name of a city in Bolivia. Similarly, Agra is a town in Oklahoma, United States. While the chances of Arani in Bolivia weaving silk or Agra in Oklahoma selling the sweet meat *petha* are remote, there is the case of the two Hyderabads. The mutton called Hyderabad haleem belongs to the state of Telangana in India, but Hyderabad is also a city in the Pakistani province of Sind. Since both the Hyderabads have a dominant share of Muslim population and associated cultural similarities it may happen that the 'other Hyderabad' lays a claim on haleem. There is a Srinagar in the state of Jammu and Kashmir, and there is also is another Srinagar in Pauri Garhwal district of Uttarakhand. Both are in the Himalayas, both share a common type of forests, so it could be that the woodcraft traditionally held in esteem from the Srinagar of Kashmir could be imitated and marketed by Garhwal with a label stating 'made in Srinagar'!

Kashmir is a classic case. The political strife between Pakistan and India has given rise to a Kashmir in India and an Azad Kashmir or Occupied Kashmir in Pakistan. This means that consumers may find it hard to decide the origin and locale of production of pashmina or sozani embroidery. The area of cultivation of Basmati rice is Punjab, a region which straddles across both India and Pakistan. Ideally it would have been best if the two countries settled their political differences and sat together at tables where trade is negotiated and provide the 'hearth of the good' its due recognition, price and value. But till the battles are resolved, homonyms would continue to blur the 'origin' of a good. Addressing the issue of homonyms, Geographical Indications article 22 of TRIPS states '. . . territory, region or locality in which the good originates, falsely represents to the public that the good originates in another territory'. It misleads buyers and allows a lesser grade good to ride on one that is more reputed. Another serious challenge to place goods are the generics.

Generics: Like the change of people and names, language is not static. Words can change from proper nouns into common nouns and vice versa. A proper noun refers to a particular place, a specific name, exact thing or a precise idea and so is always capitalised. Linguistically, names of geographic locations are proper nouns; for example Delhi is a city in India. In contrast are common nouns, which are general words for any people, place and thing. A common noun is not distinguished by any superior and noteworthy characteristics. Therefore, when the name of a 'good or product' changes from a proper noun to a common noun it becomes a generic and it loses the hallmark of distinction and particular characteristics of place associated with it. Reduced to a generic, the place and characteristics it imparts to a good are disowned and disregarded. The change from a proper noun to generic causes a serious loss to the 'value' of place goods. In spite of the loss, the drift of genericity is all around us.

Block-printed cottons imported into England around 1630 were called Calicuts. The fabric praised by early travellers to India for its fine texture and beautiful colours originated in Calicut. But soon the name calico came to be applied to all Indian cottons having an equal number of warp and weft threads and subsequently to all plain weave cotton. Bengal was the main producer of lightweight silks called taffeta, a Persian word which means 'twisted woven'. Taffeta is also mentioned in the *Ain-i-Akbari* as silk fabric manufactured 'particularly in the towns of Hooghly and Qasimbazar'. By the turn of the seventeenth century, the English were using taffeta as a generic term for all fine silk fabrics. Kolhapuri is the exquisitely handcrafted chappal or footwear made in Kolhapur, Maharashtra, where they are locally called *pie-taan*. But today kolhapuri denotes a certain 'type of chappal' regardless of its place of production. Lucknow is known for its exquisite style and fine needlework called chikan. It gained an entirely new respectability as it was much preferred and supported by the Mughal rulers. But Lucknow chikan is now more synonymous with a 'type of embroidery' and less with the place of its origin.

Patiala salwars are 'loose trousers' stitched with pleats near its belt. The Patiala salwar has its roots in Patiala, a city in the state of Punjab in India. But today it has become more a type of pyjama than one coming from a particular place. In a similar vein is the English word 'dungaree' for strong cotton working overalls. The Hindi name dungri came probably from a low rocky hill and village on the Bombay Harbour, which was to be the site of Fort Dungree/Dongri. The fort was demolished in 1769 and replaced by Fort George. Fort George too was pulled down and today the name Dongri lives as a street in Mumbai.

Polo was once known as the game of kings. It is therefore no coincidence that the costume for horse riding should have been invented by a king. The attire Jodhpur derives from the once princely state of Jodhpur, located 300 kilometres west of the state capital Jaipur in Rajasthan. It was Sri Pratap Singh, an avid polo player and the younger son of the Maharaja of Jodhpur, who first tailored Jodhpuri in India around 1890. Singh was invited to England during the Diamond Jubilee celebrations of Queen Victoria in 1897. Because the Maharaja created a sensation with the number of polo matches he won, so his Jodhpuri too attracted attention. Nearly 100 years later, when Ralph Lauren presented an exhibit of riding clothes and associated paraphernalia at the Metropolitan Museum of New York in 1984 and released the book *Man and the Horse: An Illustrated History of Equestrian Apparel*, it carried the following description: Jodhpurs are riding breaches that extend to the ankle, often with a foot strap, to be worn with short boots, derived from the name of the state in India. Today Patiala salwar, dungri and Jodhpuri are commonly referred to as 'type of garments' with total disregard to their place of birth.

Genericity is rampant and it comes easy, almost automatically. The process of genericisation is rarely intentional, and it could well be that people unconsciously 'adopt' words within their language with a sense of familiarity, and as the popularity of a 'thing' grows other manufacturers hijack the name and use it to their advantage.

It often has a blurred origin in the mind of the seller and buyer who may use a name as a shorthand to refer to the product. Therefore a person out shopping may ask for Bikaneri and thus refer to a type of salty snack presuming that he is getting the one produced at Bikaner in Rajasthan. In reality this may not be the case, as he may be getting a snack produced elsewhere. Genericity is a bane to place good as it cashes in on the name per se but denounces and trivialises the importance of place.

The problem turns serious when a geographic designator is poached for purposes of profit. The salty spicy Bikaneri is a food produced in cottage industries in Bikaner, Rajasthan, which gives employment to around two and half million people in villages. Although Pepsi has denied it, fear persisted among bhujia manufactures that this multinational company was trying to sell the product under its own brand name 'Pepsi Namkeen', till the India Patent Office confirmed the rights of the Geographical Indications with the genuine manufacturers of Bikaner.

Linguistically names of geographic locations are proper nouns so that they can differentiate between places. When geographical names become common nouns or generics, they are rendered impotent to communicate the origin or the difference in quality between place-related products. Under TRIPS the Origin Regulation in Article 13(2) explicitly states: 'Protected names may not become generic'. Genericity destroys place and product relationship. Once a name degenerates into a generic, it is difficult to reclaim it to its former status, and it usually has to be clawed back aggressively. While genericity dilutes and dispenses with the importance of place relationship, another cause for worry are trademarks.

Trademarks: A trademark is the means by which a business makes itself visible. Trademarks provide their owners with the legal right to prevent others from using a confusingly similar mark. Examples of well-known trademarks are Coca-Cola, Maruti or Air India. Prudent business people register their trademarks with patent offices to gain an official record of their rights to a particular mark. It can happen that a name of a place is the trademark.

The Government of India passed the Trade Mark Act in 1999 to prevent two business firms from acquiring the same trademark. Trademarks which are registered are published in the *Trademarks Journal* of India. When thousands of trademarks registered in India till 2010 were systematically scrutinised, as many as 765 carried a reference to a place. Among these 191 or 25 per cent of the trademarks used the name India and its various versions be it Hindustan or Bharat. Exemplifying this category are trademarks like Bharat Gold, Ashok India, Bharat Super and Hindustan Lever. The use of the name of country in the trademark is largely governed by the consideration of linking production of the good with the country of manufacture. Another category of place-based trademarks are those that take the name of foreign countries into their fold. These comprise 34 per cent of the total and include Boston Chicken, Life America, Hawai and Arctic Ice. The remaining one-third referred to places in India, like Assam Savera or Chambal cement.

There seem to be three main reasons why trademarks use a reference to place.

In the first case the choice is purely arbitrary and is governed simply by a liking for a name with little consideration of the features of the place, but most often than not the name is taken to establish some flavour of the site and situation. In the Trademarks Journal, India, there are 26 companies registered with the trademark Ajanta. A settlement in the Aurangabad district of Maharashtra, Ajanta is famous for its rock edicts and cave paintings. But under the trademark Ajanta are manufactured electrical goods, pharmaceuticals, furniture and sundry other goods which have no association with the Ajanta rock edicts. Moreover, most of these companies are registered in Gujarat and not Maharashtra. It could well be the name Ajanta was chosen to inform the buyers of the perfection of goods. Ajanta paintings after all have a high standard among the world of art. Everest signifies the highest peak and therefore a company that uses this as a trademark wants to project an image that the goods it produces are of the 'highest' standards.

A second and perhaps the more important reason is that names connect to a particular place and create special perception in the minds of people. Therefore, any reference to a particular name results in an immediate recall, recognition, association and approval with people. When marketing their goods, businesses are keen to cash in on this 'image'. Monte Carlo, the capital of Monaco, is famous for its casinos and gambling. Because people perceive that drinking liquor is part and parcel of gambling in a casino, the trade name Monte Carlo was seen as a good option by manufacturers of beer in India. Similarly to capture the glamour associated with the movie business, a firm which manufactures tobacco products in Delhi opted to register the trademark Hollywood! The products, beer in the case of Monte Carlo and tobacco in the case of Hollywood, are not produced in places named in the trademark, but both use the name of the place as a correlate, an association, to advertise the goods. Therefore, in reality these trademarks say nothing about the geographical origin or characteristics of the goods.

A third use of place name in trademarks is more for purposes of misleading people. Producers of aqua drinking water adopt names of Himalayan rivers for purposes of marketing. Ganga Sagar is an island in the delta of the river Ganga about a hundred kilometres south of Kolkata; it is a place where thousands of Hindus gather to take a holy dip at the confluence of the river Ganges and the Bay of Bengal. Capturing this sacred identity is the Ganga Sagar Aqua Pure packaged drinking water plant located in Dehradun.

Cashing in on the cachet of a place good, many brands can use place as a trademark to market different types of goods. Darjeeling, till recently, was used as a trademark for a French brand of lingerie sold in the European Union. The brand Divine Darjeeling was used for coffee, cocoa and tea in Japan. The perfume company Bulgari used Darjeeling Tea fragrance for men in Switzerland (Das, 2003).

Another way to mislead consumers is to sneak in a bit of the original name in the trademark. For several years, the Texas-based company Rice Tec Inc. in the United States has been selling its own Basmati rice using such trademarks as Texmati and Kasmati from Texas, as Calmati from California and even as American Basmati (Dasgupta, 1996). In France, the food company Establishments Haudecoeur La Courneuve has been granted two French trademarks Riz Long Basmati and Riz du Monde. This is being unfair to the original Basmati producers and consumers.

Trademarks can also be visuals and thus mislead through pictures. An ambience of a typical tea estate, terraced gardens, women picking tea and carrying baskets on their backs with a backdrop of mist-covered mountain slopes are tapped by tea producers and packers to convince customers of the place and thereby confirm the quality of origin of tea.

It is thus clear that trademarks which use the name of a place are mischievous, spurious and not only mislead the public but also severely tarnish the image of the geographical tag. While trademarks mislead, a more serious problem is that of imitations.

Imitations: A disturbing fact is that trade in counterfeit products is reaching epidemic proportions. The scale of fakes, duplicates and copycat brands is large and is growing. Within the circles of trade 'copying' has damaging repercussions. Darjeeling is not always what it seems. Throughout the world many types of teas are sold under the fame of Darjeeling (Figure 7.2).

Trade journals and popular media observe that almost 80 per cent of the global trade in Darjeeling tea is counterfeit. Estimates suggest that 40 million kilograms are sold as 'Darjeeling Tea' when the actual production

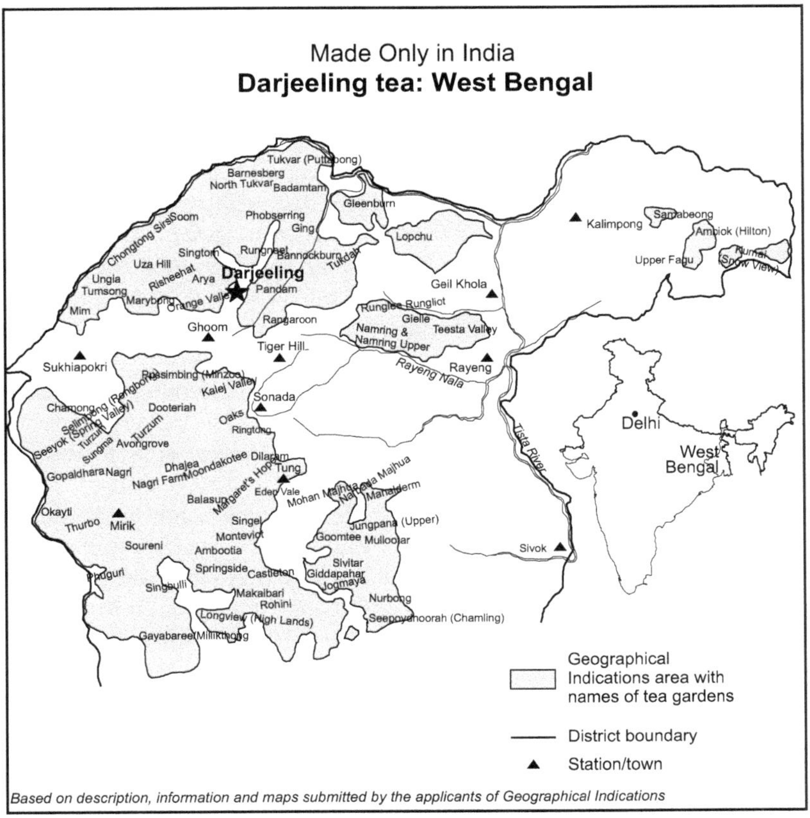

Figure 7.2 Darjeeling tea: West Bengal

capacity is only 10 million. While the statistic is strongly disputed by the Tea Board of India, they agree that there is counterfeiting. Copycat brands employ descriptors such as Lanka Darjeeling or Hamburg Darjeeling; typically, they do not forget to reiterate that their tea is 'Pure Darjeeling'. Chinese imitations of the famous 'Banarasi' sarees are slyly creeping into the Indian market. It is learnt that master craftsmen from Varanasi are being lured to produce imitations of the saree with cheaper Chinese silk. Poor quality imitations are also being manufactured within India, particularly in Surat, Gujarat. Imitations made on power loom cost only one-tenth the price of an original 'Banarasi' saree, thereby posing tough competition. The scenario is such that a large section of weavers and their families in Varanasi are now forced to look for alternative means of livelihood, often in menial jobs.

Even a casual search over the Internet about the sales of Kashmiri pashmina reveals the many sites which market the product as pashminas from Nepal! Media reports that since Nepal mixes polyester and wool while manufacturing pashmina, the country has earned a bad name in the international market (Correspondent, 2007). The Kullu shawl is a handloom product, but 80 per cent of the shawls sold under this name are made in Ludhiana on power looms. There are more than eight varieties of jasmine grown in Karnataka; however, the sweetest and strongest fragrance is of the Mysore jasmine. It therefore is in great demand for decorative purposes and for making garlands. The per plant production of Mysore jasmine flowers is less compared to other popular varieties such as Dendu Malligae, which is extensively grown in the Satyamangala area of Tamil Nadu. Merchants in the Mysore market mislead people by passing on the Dendu Malligae from Tamil Nadu as Mysore Malligae.

Tellicherry and Malabar are the two types of Indian pepper corns. The Tellicherry peppercorns are larger in size than the typical black pepper corns; their colour is not black but rather dark brown and they are more aromatic and strong. The Malabar grade of pepper is the regular black pepper with a slightly greenish hue. The mark Tellicherry is a gold mine of opportunities, and this has led to its misuse in alarming proportions.

Mango buyers are being cheated by traders who sell Karnataka Alphonso with the label of Ratnagiri or Devgadh mango. The manager of the Devgad Taluka Mango Growers Co-operative Society complained: 'Many mango traders all over the country are using the Devgad Alphonso or Devgad Hapus as a generic brand name to sell any variety of mango. This is giving a bad name to the Devgad Alphonso' (Sapre, 2008).

Ilish or Hilsa fish rules the hearts of Bengalis. Bengalis are passionate about the taste of Ilish from the Hooghly or the Padma. But little do most

Bengalis know that 40 per cent of the Ilish available in their market is from the river Tapti at Bharuch, and 10 per cent of what is imported from Bangladesh is from the river Irrawady but is sold as Hilsa from Hooghly (Mazumdar, 2012).

The cases of counterfeit result in serious damage to both the consumers and the legitimate sellers. Customers are misled into believing that they are buying an authentic product with specific qualities and features from a particular place, whereas they are paying for a cheap imitation. Such frauds are construed and constructed by manufacturing companies at large. The genuine producers suffer by losing the benefit of lucrative commercial enterprise, and in the process the reputation of their products is also damaged.

Place tags on products assume greater significance for India in view of the competition from cheaper imitations that are increasingly wedging their way into the fast-changing markets in the era of globalisation. A legal route is often proposed as a solution to counter frauds and counterfeits. But justice comes with a heavy price.

A costly legal route: Surveillance for homonyms, generics or imitations does not come either cheap or easy. Kancheepuram silk sarees are one of the first products in the country to graduate to the level of implementing the security protocol, which includes jail and a provision for imposing a fine on the violators. The security protocol for Kancheepuram silk sarees stipulates that only the authorised manufacturers who at present are 31 in number would be eligible to responsibly draw the benefits of the Geographical Indications tag.

The enforcement strategies adopted by Chanderi fabric include a survey of selling points and supply chains for duplicate Chanderi in different cities of India. Alongside it includes informing dealers regarding legal implications of such misuses and the potential penalties that may come about (Gulati, 2007). Kota Doria Development Hadauti Foundation has developed a logo with the consent of all weavers to prevent sale of fake Kota Doria. This logo is woven on all sarees and fabric to enable the buyer to differentiate real Kota Doria from power loom products. But the battles of litigation are many.

The Mysore Silk Weaving Factory was started in 1912 by the Maharaja of Mysore. Mysore silk is synonymous with the silk produced in the geographical territory of Mysore district. This silk has a distinctive drape, grainy effect and high washability. After the independence of India and the abolition of the princely states, the management of the silk weaving factory was taken over by the Mysore State Sericulture Department, and in 1980–1981 it was transferred to Karnataka Silk Industries Corporation Limited.

Karnataka Silk Industries Corporation got itself a Geographical Indications tag to ensure that it alone could use the name Mysore Silk. In 2005, Karnataka Silk Industries Corporation got a certification from the Indian Standards Organization to safeguard its quality. This was done because the Mysore Silk brand name was being greatly violated all over Karnataka, where spurious material was being sold as crepe silk. The company installed scanning machines in its showrooms for the buyers to actually check the quality of its products. In addition Karnataka Silk Industries Corporation sent legal notices to anyone found misusing their logo (Sen, 2009). The opponents on the other hand contend that since there are many manufacturers and merchants originating from the state of Karnataka, granting registration to the Corporation under the Geographical Indications in India is inappropriate. The legal battle continues.

There is also the experience of Pochampally ikat. In May 2005, it came to the notice of the rights holders that a retailer in Hyderabad was selling imitations of Pochampally ikat sarees and that the retailer was getting its supplies from a Mumbai-based manufacturer and wholesaler. In June 2005, a case was filed in the Delhi High Court against the manufacturing and selling of these imitations. Importantly, this was the first-ever infringement case filed under the Geographical Indications Act in India. The defendants (both the manufacturer and the retailer) accepted the charge of infringement and pleaded for an out-of-court settlement. The defendants confessed their unawareness about the geographical protection of 'Pochampally Ikat' and claimed that they have destroyed fake sarees and pledged that if such sarees are sold in the market they would be ready to pay the requisite penalty (Textiles Committee, 2007).

Among all the registered Geographical Indications, Darjeeling is a model of how it has used the legal framework to battle all odds and get back its geographical name. Darjeeling earned its Geographical Indications status in October 2004, but in order to ensure the authenticity of the tea being exported, the Tea Board set up a compulsory system of certification under the purview of the Tea Act of 1953. Under this system, the licensees must furnish information about the production and manufacture of Darjeeling tea and its sale through auction or otherwise. The Tea Board is thus able to compute and compile the total volume of Darjeeling tea produced and sold in a given period. Moreover, certificates of origin have to accompany all consignments of the Darjeeling tea leaving the shores of India. The procedure includes continuous hygiene tests and a close supervision. Despite such a close watch, Darjeeling has to fight several cases of infringement. In India itself, over 20 legal notices have been served and 15 oppositions have been filed. The effort in enforcing rights and protecting the name

Darjeeling does not come cheap. From 1998 to 2002, the Tea Board had spent US$200,000 on registration and legal fees, fighting infringement in overseas jurisdictions. The cost of hiring watchdogs, fighting court cases and filing legal suits is huge. In a poor country like India many holders of Geographical Indications are groups of artisans or cultivators with limited resources to take on long-drawn legal battles. A mechanism will have to be created to safeguard the Made Only in India. But India is not always the victim and an innocent party. It can be an offender too. Take the case of Scotch Whisky.

Legal battles: the case of Scotch whisky and that of Basmati

The Scotch Whisky Act came into force in the United Kingdom in 1988. To aid the 1988 Act came the Scotch Whisky Order in 1990. According to Rule 3 of the Order, 1990, Scotch whisky means whisky that has been produced at any distillery in Scotland. The whisky must be produced from water and malted barley and be distilled at an alcoholic strength by volume of less than 94.8 per cent. This is necessary to ensure that the distillate has a specific aroma and taste. Moreover the whisky must be matured in oak casks of capacity not more than 700 litres, and the duration for maturating must not be less than 3 years. Lastly, no other substance other than water and spirit caramel must have been added to the whisky. This method of production and maturation ensures the whisky ensures its colour, aroma and taste that is derived from the raw materials. As such if any one of the ingredients is not processed in Scotland or if the entire manufacturing process is not completed in Scotland, the whisky cannot be called Scotch whisky. Moreover, even if a whisky is manufactured in Scotland, it cannot be called a Scotch whisky if any of the requirements of raw material or processing is not fulfilled. Also if a whisky is manufactured in any other country and follows the entire Scottish procedure and technique it still cannot be called Scotch whisky as it has been manufactured outside Scotland. It is important to note here that Scotch whisky is known worldwide to be a whisky produced in Scotland and is also advertised as such.

The Scotch Whisky Association came to learn that Golden Bottling Limited, a company set up in 1994 at Alwar, Rajasthan, was manufacturing and selling whisky by the name Red Scot. Since the name Red Scot whisky gave an impression that it was Scotch whisky, the Scotch Whisky Association sent a legal notice to Golden Bottling Limited on 30 September 2000 asking it to not to use the word 'Scot' in its trade name. However, Golden Bottling Limited paid no heed to the legal notice and continued to sell its whisky under the name 'Red Scot'. The Scotch Whisky Association sent another notice on 26 May 2001 to Golden Bottling Limited requesting it not to pass off its Red Scot whisky as if it was Scotch whisky.

Thereafter it was found that Red Scot whisky had vanished from the market, and this gave an assumption that Golden Bottling Limited had realised its mistake and fallen in line. However, in June 2003, the Scotch Whisky Association found out that Golden Bottling Limited had once again started selling Red Scot whisky. Aggrieved by the acts of Golden Bottling Limited, the Scotch Whisky Association filed a case against it before the Delhi High Court. The Delhi High Court passed an order thereby restraining Golden Bottling Limited from using the word 'Scot' or any other similar word for the whisky manufactured by it. The Delhi High Court also directed Golden Bottling Limited to pay Rs 5,00,000 as damages for the loss suffered by the Scotch Whisky Association due to its acts. In addition it directed Golden Bottling Limited to pay a sum of Rs 3,10,000 towards the cost of litigation incurred by the Scotch Whisky Association.

Basmati is another case of legal entanglements. Rice is an important grain in India and farming communities have developed, sustained and conserved different varieties to suit different tastes and needs. One among the prized is Basmati. It is one of the fastest growing export items of both India and Pakistan. In undivided India, the geographical region of Basmati production spans the banks of the river Indus, in Punjab and Sind across to Kashmir and Himachal Pradesh. The world over Basmati is known as rice that belongs to India and Pakistan. Every year India exports close to four million tonnes of Basmati, while Pakistan touches close to 0.17 million tonnes (www.http://oryza.com/). It is a premium type of rice in trade. In spite of its proven geographical and historical lineage in India and Pakistan, Basmati is still wrapped in legal disputes at the international, national and regional level.

Internationally, RiceTec Inc., a firm in the United States of America, was issued the Patent number 5663484 on Basmati rice grains on 2 September 1997. RiceTec Inc. had attempted to sell its long-grain rice under such brand names as Texmati and Kasmati but not as Basmati. However, if the patent is not revoked, RiceTec Inc. can now sell its rice under the brand name Basmati which would definitely cut into India's and Pakistan's global market share, especially as the rice grown in the United States of America could be sold cheaper than the Indian and Pakistani varieties. It is for this reason that patenting of Basmati by RiceTec Inc is perceived not only as theft of Geographical Indications but also as a direct threat to the livelihood of farm communities in India and Pakistan. After learning of the Basmati patent issued to RiceTec Inc, the Government of India mobilised a high-level inter-ministerial group of experts, including representatives of the ministries and departments of commerce, industry, foreign affairs, Council for Scientific and Industrial Research, Agriculture, Bio-technology, All India Rice Exporters Association and the Indian Council of Agricultural Research. Indians feel that the US government's decision to grant a patent for the prized Basmati rice violates the International Treaty on Trade-Related Intellectual Property Rights and that of Geographical Indications. The clear stand of India is that if the United States of America cannot label their wine as champagne, they should not be permitted to label their rice Basmati.

India and Pakistan who are joining hands to resolve the crisis and have a strong case against RiceTec Inc have also enrolled British traders. According to Howard Jones, marketing controller of the United Kingdom's privately owned distributor Tilda Ltd, 'True Basmati can only be grown in India or Pakistan. We will support them in any way if it is necessary'. The long-simmering issue was largely settled in 2001, when the United States of America granted a narrower patent to the company, RiceTec of Alvin, Texas. While the finer details of the case are yet to unfold the problem for registration of Basmati has not even been solved on home turf.

Heritage, a society formed by farmers, traders, commission agents and millers of Karnal district in Haryana, had filed an application for Geographical Indications for Basmati in August 2004. The application was refused on the grounds that though Basmati is produced in at least six states of India, the applicant society did not represent the interests of all the producers except those in Karnal district of Haryana. The main objection was that besides Punjab, Haryana, Delhi, Himachal Pradesh, Uttarakhand, parts of western Uttar Pradesh and Jammu and Kashmir, Basmati is produced also in Madhya Pradesh. Subsequently, another application was filed by the Agricultural and Processed Food Products Export Development Authority for Basmati. Several oppositions were filed mainly from Madhya Pradesh against the grant of registration of Geographical Indications. The growers of Basmati in Madhya Pradesh made a claim that Basmati has been cultivated in that state since 1900. In support they cited research titled 'scented pearl' by S.C. Ahuja *et al.* which states, 'Basmati cultivation is comparatively a recent phenomenon in Haryana. It was introduced in this part after the partition of India in 1947 when major basmati-growing area was carved out in Pakistan'. The publication further goes on to state that 'Karnal, Panipat, Kaithal, Kurkushetra (erstwhile district Karnal) which are now world famous did not grow even an acre of basmati in 1901' (Ahuja, Panwar, Ahuja, and Gupta, 1995: 10–11). The truth has yet to be uncovered as when the report *Races of Rice* was checked it stated: 'Basmati is a race of rice cultivated throughout the Panjab, said to be the best' (The

Reporter of Economic Products to the Government of India, 1911: 666). The prepartition Panjab of the subcontinent includes Punjab of Pakistan, Punjab of India, Haryana and parts of Himachal Pradesh. This Report does not even mention Madhya Pradesh. The concerns of place goods thus run into issues of defining the area and its boundaries.

Defining boundaries: Geographical studies confirm that regionalisation is arduous and contentious. Deciding what to include is always tricky. Moreover sharp discontinuities are rare, yet if the law of Geographical Indications is to be implemented, boundaries need to be drawn because the tag of indications is confined to a definite area. The criterion for demarcating the boundary is the 'area over which the goods carries the attributes of place'. In this context territories of some goods like Monsooned Malabar Arabica Coffee and Alleppey Green Cardamom cut across two neighbouring states.

Not only do geographical regions disobey administrative and political jurisdictions but even the nomenclature for reference to the concerned area varies. A valley is the physiographic unit for Kangra tea, Assam tea and Kullu shawl, but for Tirupathi laddu and Nilgiri tea it is hills of Tirumala and Nilgiris. The narrow strips of the Brahmaputra and Barak Valleys are where the host plants for Muga cocoons grow abundantly. The 'enclosed region of Malabar' is the area for Monsooned Arabica and Robusta coffee. Within these large territories it is certain locales which are known for the product, but defining the precise boundaries of these can also be controversial among producers. Moreover, pressure may exist to extend the Nashik Valley or Kullu Valley regions beyond what is historically believed to be the area. Producers of grapes in the neighbourhood of Nashik Valley may want to be annexed to this valley to benefit from its superior geographical identity. For such and other reasons the precise boundaries of a place good can be politically and socially controversial (Table 7.4).

Endless also are the changes in the administrative control of an area. It can happen that a new district is formed or even a new state, like the case of Uttarakhand, Jharkhand and now Telangana. So to solve this issue the Geographical Indications Registry at Chennai is now beginning to resort to latitudinal and longitudinal extent of place of production of goods. This mathematical grid is permanent and durable. However, there is need to provide more details of the graticule to locate the exact boundaries of the territory since what matters is not so much the number of states, nor the size, not even the nomenclature, but the fact that the geographical conditions which affect the characteristics of the product should be present throughout the demarcated territory. Further the indications cannot be used on similar goods if they either originate from outside the designated geographical area or, if from within the region, are produced differently (Table 7.5).

Table 7.4 Type of 'place' referred to in the name of goods with Geographical Indications in India

Type	*Number of goods*	*Percentage of total*
District	88	48.89
Town	38	21.11
State	18	10.00
Village	17	9.44
City	11	6.11
Region	7	3.89
Country	1	0.56
Total	180*	100.00

* The remaining 19 goods are 'named' after people or process or technique of production.
Based on *Geographical Indications Journal* No. 1 to 58

Table 7.5 Boundaries of goods with Geographical Indications which cut across more than one state/union territory

Name	Number	State/Union Territory
Monsooned Malabar Arabica Coffee	4	Karnataka, Tamil Nadu, Andhra Pradesh and Orissa
Warli Painting	4	Maharashtra, Gujarat, Dadra and Nagar Haveli and Daman and Diu
Malabar Pepper	3	Kerala, Karnataka, Tamil Nadu
Monsooned Malabar Robusta Coffee	3	Karnataka, Tamil Nadu, Kerala
Phulkari	3	Punjab, Haryana, Rajasthan
Alleppey Green Cardamom	2	Kerala, Tamil Nadu
Eathomozhy Tall Coconut	2	Kerala, Tamil Nadu
Nagpur Orange	2	Maharashtra and Madhya Pradesh

Based on *Geographical Indications Journal* No. 1 to 58

Looking at the range of issues which surround the Geographical Indications, it can be said that the landscape of place goods in India is like two tall parallel mountain ranges.

One range carries problems like setting up marketing structures, building a brand image and convincing customers of the value of a product that is linked with a place. The confusion caused by homonyms, generics and the trademarks that are all out to tarnish the image of the goods and place are additional matters of concern. Adding to the woes are the frauds and imitations. The endless monitoring and surveillance means that lawsuits have to be filed and pursued to bring the offenders to book. All this takes and wastes time, effort and money.

But Geographical Indications are not just about problems. A second mountain range covers the benefits and possibilities like profit, safeguard of environment, preservation of heritage, insurance of quality and health, and the appreciation of diverse and the exotic. There is also the name, fame and gain for place. While these are concerns no doubt, yet the two parallel ranges one of problems and the other of potentialities do not capture the entire terrain. Saddled between the two are the manufacturers and producers of place goods: the spinners, weavers, dyers, tanners, casters, potters, moulders, twisters, printers, tracers, embroiderers and painters. There are also the hunters, gatherers, collectors, trappers, climbers, pluckers, carvers, engravers, polishers and endless more. Since most of the processes are done by hand, it means that the place goods of India are not only rural-based but labour-intensive.

Around 100,000 workers are directly engaged in Firozabad glassware manufacturing with another double the workers indirectly involved in the industry. With 30,000 workers engaged directly in the manufacturing of saddler items and 20,000 workers indirectly engaged, the saddler industry of Kanpur is highly labour-intensive. Saharanpur has more than 300 production units scattered in different parts of the city. The larger among these are registered as the Saharanpur Wood Carving Manufacturing Association. This association has a strength of 38 members. The remaining over 250 small-scale units belong to the traditional Muslim craftsmen. In addition there are approximately 3,500 marginal units which function from their domestic premises. They form the backbone of the massive woodcraft industry and produce 90 per cent of the total bulk (Handa and Jain, 2000). More than 25,000 artisans are engaged in the manufacturing of ceramic products like stoneware, crockery, sanitary ware, hospital ware, chemical porcelain and decorative wares at Khurja. The tea plantations at Darjeeling employ 52,000 people on a permanent basis and an additional 15,000 during the plucking season, making this sector heavily reliant on very cheap labour. The types of communities engaged in the production of place goods undoubtedly are the small farmers, craft manufacturers and tribal people. The majority are women. This is especially true of the textile and handicraft sector both of which contribute to make the bulk of goods registered with a geographical tag in India.

Kutch embroidery, which was registered at Chennai in 2008, is a sustained expression of the textile tradition of the Rabaris, a nomadic tribe in Gujarat. Another nomadic tribe, the Banjara, creates the handicraft and mirror work which makes the Telangana region famous. The Ghadawas are a small artisan group who produce the brass or bell metal objects for which Bastar is known. The name Ghadawa is derived from Ghalana which means to melt. This is the community who craft items by melting the metal using the lost wax technique. Kotpad handloom is a vegetable-dyed fabric woven by the tribal weavers of Kotpad. The pretreatment and dyeing work is done by tribal women. In Mangalagiri, in the Guntur district of Andhra Pradesh, nearly 25 per cent of the weavers are women. Sixty-eight per cent of the registered Geographical Indications of India are in the category of handicrafts, including handlooms and paintings.

Handloom weaving, an occupation of ancient vintage in India, continues to be the main source of livelihood of around 6.5 million people in the country (Ministry of Textiles, 2006). These are the people who seed, water, plant, harvest or make, weave, print, embroider, embellish, and so tender the goods that they are distinctive and are able to carry and courier the stamp of place (Figure 7.3).

While the goods they manufacture and produce are distinctive and also have the potential to fetch premium price, a more relevant question for the true test and future of place goods is contingent upon the state of place and the status of people. What comes to fore is that environmental deterioration of place and the plight of people is dismal.

Ecological degradation: India has experienced a whole-scale degradation of her resources, be it forests, grasslands, soil, water or air since the end of the nineteenth century. The ecological deterioration, be it vanishing forests, eroding soils, polluting air and water, has its impact on the production and quality of goods. This is an extensively researched theme in India and needs no repetition or replication here. The shrinking natural resources and deterioration of the natural environment of India at large cannot spare sites of production of distinctive origin-based goods. This is because the natural environment has no boundaries and what happens in one place flows and impacts other places along the chain. A classic case is that of chemical fertilisers and pesticides. Even though cultivators of a Geographical Indications tag never use chemical fertilisers, yet 'sprays' and washes from neighbourhood farms create a severe threat. The Coorg orange witnessed a steep decline in acreage from about 24,000 hectares in the 1960s to 1,400 hectares now. Each plant that once yielded 50 to 60 kilograms of orange now gives only about 10 kilograms. Production declined drastically when in the wake of a virus attack, coffee growers in the adjacent lands

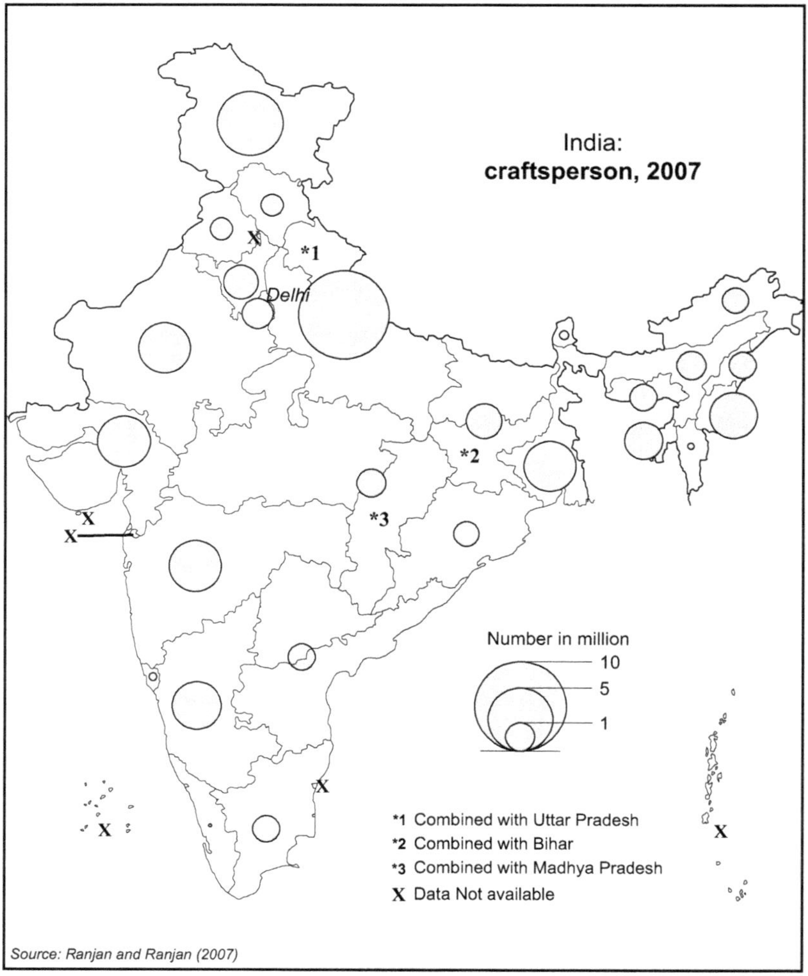

Figure 7.3 India: craftsperson, 2007

made rampant use of pesticides and fertilisers. This led to the destruction of several natural species which at one time were protecting the Coorg orange (Manoj, 2006).

India ranks first among the world's mango-producing countries. It accounts for about half the world's total mango production (2002–2003). India's mango crop is increasingly plagued by black tip, a disease which causes the ends of mango to rot, turning it black from brown. In northern India, the origin of this disease is linked to the coal-fired brick kilns scattered throughout the countryside, which spew clouds of sulphur dioxide and carbon monoxide into the air (Prakash and Khan, 2005). Banana stands second only to mango in terms of area and production among the fruit crops of India. The tasty Nanjanagud Rasabale in Karnataka was earlier cultivated over thousands of acres of land but is now confined to only a few acres within Mysore at Nanjanagud and adjacent districts of Charmarjangar and Mandya. This is attributed to Panama disease in which a fungus attacks the roots of the banana plant. Moreover, when chemical fertilisers or pesticides are applied on the fruits it is seen that the particular taste and smell of the fruit which makes them so special is immediately lost. Farmers, in this case, also allege that as the plants are very sensitive, after the construction of Kabini Canal across the river Kabini, Karnataka, in 1974, the flowers of the banana plant have started withering away (Rathna, 2014). The ecological price of construction of dams and canals are many. In Nanjanagud, Rasabale is finding it hard to maintain its production, and farmers are moving towards other banana varieties such as Pachabala (Robusta) and Elakkibale and Grande 9 which are more productive and profitable in terms of revenue and resistant to diseases like panama wilt and bunchy top (Kumar, 2012).

The Pokkali rice of Kerala has seen a 68 per cent decline in area under cultivation. The total area under Pokkali cultivation was originally estimated to be around 25,000 hectares a few decades ago. The present area has shrunk to roughly 8,000 hectares. In another 2,000 hectares, paddy cultivation is done only when the climatic conditions are favourable. The number of farmers involved in regular Pokkali cultivation is about 11,000. The biggest threat to Pokkali fields comes from real estate boom. In the past five years, real estate prices in Kochi region have skyrocketed, and real estate companies have bought up large tracts of Pokkali fields (Basheer, 2007). The land available for Pokkali rice cultivation is shrinking. Another serious threat is the growing practice of prawn cultivation. Here is the reason: the average production of organic Pokkali per season was two and half to four tonnes from two and half hectares, making a net profit of Rs 3,675 per hectare. After the same fields were subjected to shrimp filtration and farming, the net profit from shrimp cultivation jumped to Rs 22,870 per hectare, six times more than that of paddy cultivation (Shyna and Joseph, 2000).

The greatest damage to the tea gardens has come from climatic variability. Drought has become frequent, rainfall is concentrated in few months and temperature has risen. Darjeeling gardens are volatile; if the climate is adverse during the key months, they are in deep trouble (Wright, 2011).

Ecological degradation, resource depletion, chemical pesticides and encroachments are all taking their toll and become a serious threat to the survival or rejuvenation of places. Within the sweep of the 'environment of change' there are different forms of threat to survival. For example, who in the day of electronic media would engage with a puppet show? In the past, puppeteers moved from village to village, spreading news and entertaining people. Today, the future of puppetry is bleak. It is mostly in the schools in small towns and villages where the puppeteer finds an audience today. Only during the tourist season, which lasts from November to January, are some puppeteers invited to the hotels of the big cities of Rajasthan, like Jaipur, Jodhpur, Jaisalmer, Udaipur and Bikaner to perform. Since demand is low, many of the puppeteers have been forced to abandon their traditional work and have joined music bands, local theatres and even taken to work as labourers in the fields (Dhru, 1990). Today only a handful of about 200 to 250 Bhat puppeteers are living in the Nagaur district and an equal number is spread over in cities of Udaipur, Jodhpur and Jaipur (Figure 7.4). Similar is the case of the Deccan scroll painters.

The Deccan scrolls are the largest in size among the known examples of Indian pigment paintings on cloth. They are about a meter wide and 10 meters long and are normally vertical in format. Up till 1875 the scrolls were executed on cotton cloth of very fine texture and handspun khadi after which millmade cloth was used. Until about 60 years ago painter families lived in several villages and temple towns of Telangana. Today only one family which moved in about 1940 to Cherial village in Warangal district produces scrolls (Vishwanadha, 2006).

The weaving of Navagund durries is a slowly dying art and only seven families still weaving this durrie stay in a corner of the town and have a total of nine looms of which two are idle. As a matter of fact, durrie weaving seems to have reached a stage where it fails to provide enough earnings to weavers to maintain their families (Figure 7.5).

The weaving of Sambalpuri sarees is a case to reckon with. It was the late prime minister Indira Gandhi who became the first brand ambassador of these Sambalpuri sarees, adorning them at public functions. Soon the women newscasters of the national television channel Doordarshan followed this trend, and in the 1980s Sambalpur became the toast of the upper crust for its sarees. But less than a quarter century later, the weavers left the trade to pull rickshaws. 'It is a peculiar case where the product is in demand, but the creator is struggling,' says handloom researcher' (Sahu, 2009).

'We weave five sarees a month. Seven years ago, we used to get Rs 1,000 to Rs 1,300 per saree. Now, it is barely Rs 500', shares Narayan Meher,

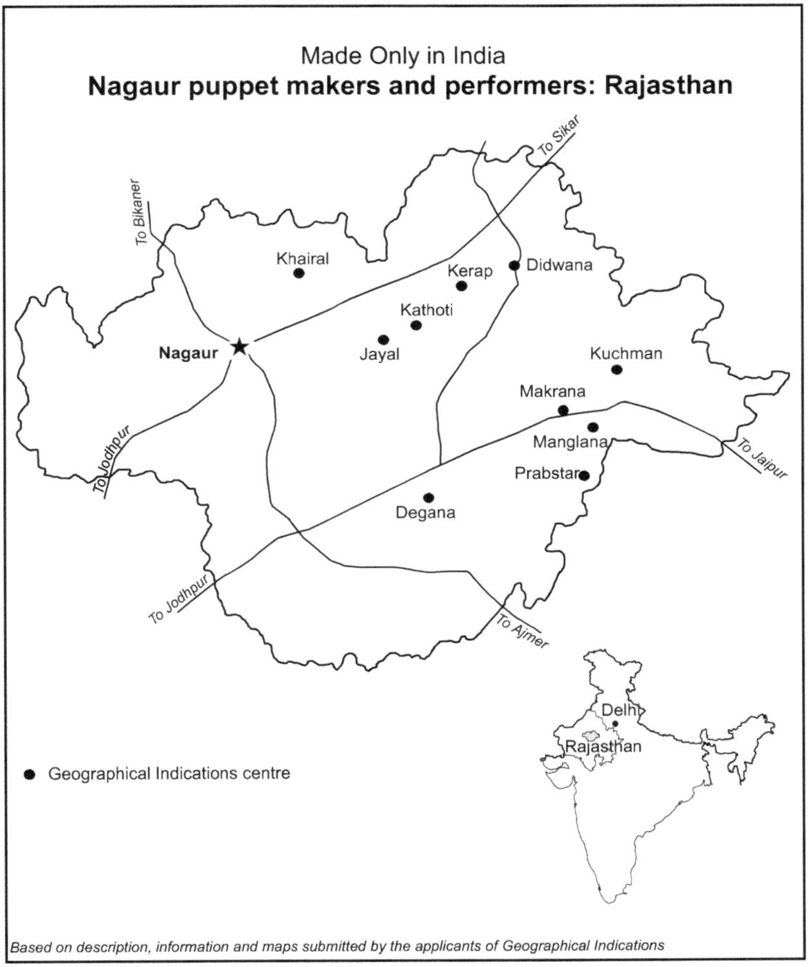

Figure 7.4 Nagaur puppet makers and performers: Rajasthan

46, an artisan in Sagarpalli village, a hub of Sambalpuri sarees, about 300 kilometres west of Bhubaneswar. Earlier the artisans got the threads and dyes from the cooperatives which then also marketed the finished products. The cooperative movement, initiated mainly in Bargarh, 59 kilometres from Sambalpur, had emerged as India's biggest weavers' cooperative with more than 16,000 members. But due to financial irregularities the cooperatives have since collapsed. The result is that trade

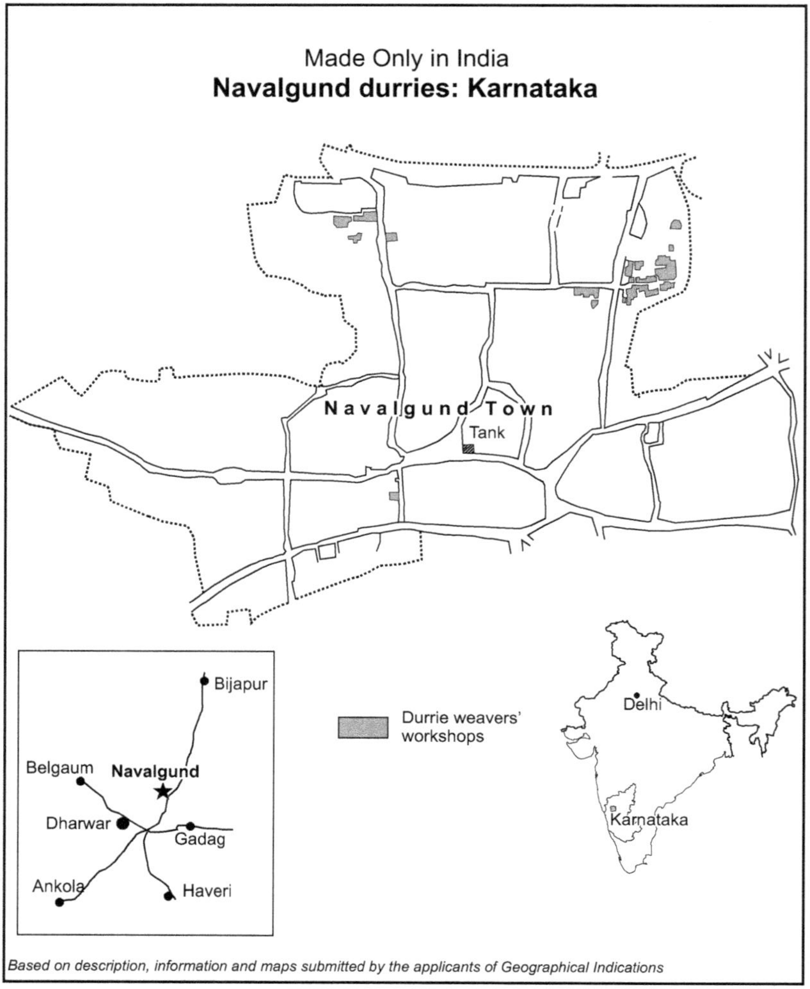

Figure 7.5 Navalgund durries: Karnataka

in Sambalpuri saree has gone back to the middleman, who markets the sarees. The case of such exploitation and corruption is rampant across the country, and Sambalpur is not the lone victim. The producers of many place goods languish in abject poverty.

The fundamental fact of life for artisans is their poverty. There is a carpet belt in India consisting of Varanasi, Mirzapur, Jaunpur and Allahabad districts, with Bhadohi, located in district of Varanasi, as the nucleus. A survey conducted in 79 households selected from three villages in the Bhadohi-Mirzapur carpet belt revealed that the occupation of carpet weaving though remunerative in the past had recently become nonprofitable at present due to low wages. Of the 64 practising households, nearly three–quarter considered carpet weaving less lucrative because their income is insufficient to support their families. About the same proportion of households do not want their children to take up this occupation as the wages paid are low and there is no adequate reward for the amount of hard labour put in by them. The weavers are mostly dependent on loans from the manufacturers, which leaves them vulnerable to exploitation by the manufacturers (Ram, Singh and Chandra, 1989).

In Pochampally or the 'silk city' of Telangana nearly 50 per cent of the families were living below the poverty line in 2003. Of these nearly 25 per cent were struggling with acute poverty (Textiles Committee, 2007). While the average size of the weavers' families was five, the mean annual income of a household ranged from Rs 8,000 to Rs 10,000. This would be a paltry sum of Rs 28 per day per household, a fact which puts the poverty pale at shame. The concerns for India clearly are many and complex. While homonyms can be carefully redrafted, generics clawed back and imitations tracked and bought to book through the court the issues of rampant ecological degradation and poverty are deeper and require imaginative solutions. What the Geographical Indications Act has rekindled is that place matters because place gathers.

8

GEOGRAPHICAL INDICATIONS

Place gathers

Geographical Indications brings out the fact that place is a strong contender and winning candidate in the context of goods. The Geographical Indications confirm that place matters because place gathers. Place is a receptacle where the physical and human, tangible and intangible, the diverse and the intense, the experiences and emotions come together. Empowering the collection are the intentions, energies and forces which resonate in place. What gathers and what this gathering does creates different places. To illustrate, a place which promises learning is a congregation of books, classrooms, libraries and to the seekers and imparters of knowledge, a sacred place is the gathering of tranquillity where the symbols and chants, the priests and prayers are in dominance. In a similar vein place-laden goods are the outcome of the gathering of diverse factors which allow the 'origin' goods. Place goods germinate in wide habitats. The nurturing of place goods is not confined to a particular site or situation, latitude or altitude, cultural or income groups. There are goods like the Pokkali rice in the backwaters of Kerala, Pashmina shawls and Darjeeling tea in the Himalayas and the Bikaneri bhujia that hail from the Thar desert. Such is the centring that the major, if not the entire, process of production and manufacturing of the goods is confined within the place. The saree-weaving centres be it that of Kancheepuram or Banaras are dense with looms, threads, dyers and weavers. Within the locus of Kangra, Nilgiri, Darjeeling and Assam estates live the pruners, pickers, collectors, sorters and packers of tea. Common to Basmati and Pokkali are the people who plough, transplant, water, weed, harvest, thresh, grade, pack and market the rice. Such is the role of place that at each step of producing, processing and manufacturing, the people adhere to the same rules. The role of place sets the rule of place. The rules are such that these are places which are engaged in the process of production which are deviant from those followed at large. Here dominate the handcrafted in comparison to the machine made. Whereas the use of chemicals is more prevalent, such places are committed to engage with the organic realm. While most places are geared towards mass production these are places with self-imposed limits to growth. Moreover whereas the activity in most places is that of hurry (and worry) and waste, these are places which gather, guide and beckon for the need to be spaced out in thrift, thought and time. These characteristics build what the Japanese would call a treasuring view and Buddha the mindfulness due. The paisley embroidered on the Pashmina, the strokes of gesso on the Tanjore paintings, the vibrancy of the Kancheepuram spark and speak of creativity gathered in a place.

The good captures the entirety of place. Mysore agarbathi is about the identification, recognition, collection and processing of the fragrance of numerous plants growing in the deciduous forests of teak, sandalwood and rosewood; the Monsoon Arabica coffee drinks the wind, heat, humidity of the monsoons in the Western Ghats. What is it if not the 'sum' of the place which is captured in the fragrance of Basmati or the Malligae or in the aroma of Alleppey green cardamom and Darjeeling tea or in the soft silkiness of Pattamadai of Tirunelveli or the pale hue in the Pahari paintings.

Place sediments time and place goods mirror and capture changing India. The Bobbili veena, Nagercoil jewellery, Tirupathi laddu and the umpteen varieties of sarees are symbolic of the ancient, traditional and the temple era; the Bidriware, Lucknow chikkan, Firozabad glassware, Hyderabad haleem are iconic reminders of the legacy of the Mughals, while the tea and coffee plantations remind us of the colonial investment with place. The nurturing of place goods changed according to needs and demands. In ancient times, temples were locales of place goods; during the Mughal period they were housed in the 'royal' court, but in colonial times patrons were abolished and attempts were made to locate the production in the newly industrialising 'black towns'. The latter led to the demise of place goods. In fact it is a wonder that in spite of the multiple forces unleashed to destroy place goods in India right from the period of the eighteenth century well into the twentieth and up to the twenty-first centuries, Indian artists and craftsmen still try to preserve and create distinctive origin goods. But history is proof to the fact that many place goods were lost without compensation or voice for the people in place. The tragedy should not be repeated. The present Geographical Indication laws within TRIPS should in no way repeat, word by word, the colonial situation when India's place goods were injured in exactly those areas where they could best compete. If the colonists had blatantly plagiarised the textiles and ruined the handicrafts of India with the grave consequences on the people of India, then today most, if not all, the 'areas' of place goods face the threat of pollution while the people in these places are troubled by poverty. Moreover there is need to watch out constantly for the frauds, homonyms and the generics. But there is hope when allegiance gathers within a place for the place. This is evident from the fact that the Geographical Indications Act bestows power of ownership not to a lone farmer, weaver or artisan, not to a single person or company. It gives ownership to all producers of the good within a particular territory. It is the people in the area along with facilitating organizations which come together to facilitate a registration under the Geographical Indications Act. The applicants could band together as cooperatives, associations, state departments, development commissioners and a range of other bodies. The registration of Pochampally ikat was the collective effort of the Textiles Committee, Directorate of Handlooms and Textiles of the state government of Andhra Pradesh, Weavers Service Centre and Andhra Pradesh Technology Development Centre. The application for Lucknow chikan craft was filed by a group comprising of stakeholders, civil society organizations as well as government bodies like the Lucknow Chikan Handicraft Association, Shilp Sadhana and Uttar Pradesh Export Corporation Limited. They are a place-based collective. They define the rules which govern the production and process to uphold the Geographical Indications. They are the custodians of all the factors that cohere to make a place good. Such is the role of place that it fosters deep attachment and builds so strong an identity that Bikaner claws back its bhujia from Pepsi, Basmati resists its cloning, Darjeeling wages many legal battles to combat its poachers while many others go to court to get back their 'place' back. The case of Darjeeling and Scotch whisky are proof that the Geographical Indications Act as a place-based armour has great potential, but its range of uses must be known and put to practice. The concerns are many and make no mistake a registration at Chennai, a certification and a label are not the solution to many a deeper problem. To make the Act worthy there is need to act worthy. The Geographical Indications Act brings out the issues of uniqueness, contextuality and place perspective. It reiterates the fact that place matters because place gathers. Place in India cannot be isolated from India as a place. Either way, there is need to give thought, serious thought, to the Made Only in India, for they make India, India.

APPENDICES

Appendix 1 Year wise Number of Goods Registered with Geographical Indications, 2004–2014

Year	*Name of the Good (Number of Registered Goods)*
2004	Aranmula Kannadi, Chanderi Sarees, Darjeeling Tea, Pochampally Ikat **(4)**
2005	Bhavani Jamakkalam, Bidriware, Channapatna Toys and Dolls, Coimbatore Wet Grinder, Coorg Orange, Kalamkari, Kancheepuram Silks, Kangra Tea, Kasuti Embroidery, Kota Doria, Kotpad Handloom Fabric, Kullu Shawl, Madurai Sungudi, Mysore Agarbathi, Mysore Rosewood Inlay, Mysore Sandal Soap, Mysore Sandalwood Oil, Mysore Silk, Mysore Traditional Paintings, Salem Fabric, Solapur Chaddar, Solapur Terry Towel **(22)**
2006	Madhubani Painting, Mysore Betel Leaf, Nanjanagud Banana, Orissa Ikat **(4)**
2007	Allahabad Surkha Guava, Alleppey Coir, Appliqué (Khatwa) Work of Bihar, Ganjifa Cards of Mysore, Hadagali Malligae, Ilkal Sarees, Karnataka Bronze Ware, Kondapalli Bommalu, Malabar Pepper, Muga Silk of Assam, Mysore Malligae, Nakshi Kantha, Navalgund Durries, Navara Rice, Palakkadan Matta Rice, Sikki Grass Work of Bihar, Silver Filigree of Karimnagar, Sujini Embroidery Work of Bihar, Temple Jewellery of Nagercoil, Thanjavur Art Plate, Thanjavur/ Tanjore Painting, Udupi Malligae **(22)**
2008	Agates of Cambay, Alleppey Green Cardamom, Andhra Pradesh Leather Puppetry, Arani Silk, Assam (Orthodox) Tea, Bagh Prints of Madhya Pradesh, Bastar Dhokra, Bastar Iron Craft, Bastar Wooden Craft, Bell Metal Ware of Datia and Tikamgarh, Blue Pottery of Jaipur, Brass Broidered Coconut Shell Crafts of Kerala, Budithi Bell and Brass Craft, Chamba Rumal, Coorg Green Cardamom, Dharwad Pedha, East India Leather, Eathomozhy Tall Coconut, Feni, Kani Shawl, Kashmir Pashmina, Kashmir Sozani Craft, Kathputlis of Rajasthan, Konark Stone Carving, Kovai Kora Cotton Sarees, Kutch Embroidery, Leather Toys of Indore, Lucknow Chikan Craft, Machilipatnam Kalamkari, Maddalam of Palakkad, Malda Fazli Mango, Malda Khirsapati (Himsagar) Mango, Malda Lakhasmanbhog Mango, Molakalmuru Sarees, Molela Clay Work,

(*Continued*)

Appendix 1 (Continued)

Year	*Name of the Good (Number of Registered Goods)*
	Monsooned Malabar Arabica Coffee, Monsooned Malabar Robusta Coffee, Naga Mircha, Nilgiri (Orthodox) Tea, Nirmal Furniture, Nirmal Paintings, Nirmal Toys and Craft, Orissa Pattachitra, Pipli Appliqué Work, Pokkali Rice, Salem Silk known as Salem Venpattu, Sankheda Furniture, Santiniketan Leather Goods, Screw Pine Crafts of Kerala, Sirumalai Hill Banana, Swamimalai Bronze Icons, Thanjavur Doll, Uppada Jamdani Sarees, Virupakshi Hill Banana **(54)**
2009	Appemidi Mango, Balaramapuram Sarees and Fine Cotton Fabrics, Banaras Brocades and Sarees, Cannanore Home Furnishings, Devanahalli Pomello, Kamalapur Red Banana, Mango Malihabadi Dusseheri, Puneri Pagadi, Sanganeri Hand-Block Printing, Santipore Saree, Tangaliya Shawl, Tirupathi Laddu, Vazhakulam Pineapple **(13)**
2010	Bikaneri Bhujia, Byadagi Chilli, Central Travancore Jaggery, Champa Silk Saree and Fabrics, Cheriyal Paintings, Gadwal Sarees, Guntur Sannam Chilli, Handmade Carpet of Bhadohi, Hyderabad Haleem, Kasaragod Saree, Khandua Saree and Fabrics, Kinnauri Shawl, Kuthampully Sarees, Mahabaleshwar Strawberry, Nashik Grapes, Nashik Valley Wine, Paithani Saree and Fabrics, Payyannur Pavithra Ring, Pembarthi Metal Craft, Phulkari, Sandur Lambani Embroidery, Surat Zari Craft, Wayanad Gandhakasala Rice, Wayanad Jeerakasala Rice **(24)**
2011	Bagru Hand-Block Print, Baluchari Saree, Bhalia Wheat, Bobbili Veena, Chendamangalam Dhotis and Set Mundu, Dhaniakhali Saree, Ganjam Kewda Flower, Ganjam Kewda Rooh, Gir Kesar Mango, Gopalpur Tussar Fabrics, Kachchh Shawls, Kashmir Papier Mache, Kashmir Walnut Wood Carving, Khatamband, Kinhal Toys, Siddipet Gollabama, Tirukanur Papier Mache Craft, Udupi Mattu Gulla Brinjal, Venkatagiri Sarees, Villianur Terracotta Works **(20)**
2012	Agra Durrie, Bangalore Blue Grapes, Berhampur Patta (Phoda Kumbha) Saree and Joda, Bhagalpur Silk, Bomkai Saree and Fabrics, Chettinad Kottan, Dhalapathar Parda and Fabrics, Farrukhabad Prints, Habaspuri Saree and Fabrics, Lucknow Zardozi, Madurai Malli, Maheshwar Sarees and Fabrics, Mangalagiri Sarees and Fabrics, Nachiarkoil Kuthvilakku (Nachiarkoil Lamp), Narayanpet Handloom Sarees, Pattamadai Pai (Pattamadai Mats), Sambalpuri Bandha Saree and Fabrics, Thanjavur Veenai, Toda Embroidery **(19)**
2013	Dharmavaram Handloom Pattu Sarees and Paavadas, Firozabad Glass, Kaipad Rice, Kalanamak Rice, Kangra Painting, Kannauj Perfume, Kanpur Saddlery, Kolhapur Jaggery, Moirang Phee, Moradabad Metal Craft, Nagpur Orange, Patan Patola, Saharanpur Wood Craft, Shaphee Lanphee, Thewa Art Work, Wangkhei Phee, Warli Painting **(17)**
2014	0
Total	**199**

Based on *Geographical Indications Journal* No. 1 to 58

Appendix 2 Distribution of Geographical Indications, 2004–2014, by Categories as per the Geographical Indications of Goods (Registration and Protection) Act, 1999

Class No.	*Category of Geographical Indications*	*Number of Registered Goods*
3	Bleaching preparations and other substances for laundry use; cleaning; polishing; scouring and abrasive preparations; soaps; perfumery, essential oils, cosmetics, hair lotions, dentifrices	5
6	Common metals and their alloys; metal building materials; transportable buildings of metal; materials of metal for railway tracks; nonelectric cables and wires of common metal; ironmongery, small hems of metal hardware; pipes and tubes of metal; safes; goods of common metal not included in other classes; ores	11
7	Machines and machine tools; motors and engines (except for land vehicles); machine coupling and transmission components (except for land vehicles); agricultural implements other than hand-operated; incubators for eggs	1
8	Hand tools and implements (hand-operated); cutlery; side arms; razors	2
14	Precious metals and their alloys and goods in precious metals or coated therewith, not included in other classes; jewellery, precious stones, horological and other chronometric instruments	6
15	Musical instruments	3
16	Paper, cardboard and goods made from these materials, not included in other classes; printed matter; bookbinding material; photographs; stationery; adhesives for stationery or household purposes, artists' materials; paint brushes; typewriters and office requisites (except furniture); instructional and teaching material (except apparatus); plastic materials for packing (not included in other classes); playing cards; printers' type; printing blocks	12
18	Leather and imitations of leather, and goods made of these materials and not included in other classes; animal skins, hides, trunks and travelling bags; umbrellas, parasols and walking sticks; whips; harness and saddler	5
19	Building materials (nonmetallic), nonmetallic rigid pipes for building; asphalt, pitch and bitumen; nonmetallic transportable buildings; monuments, not of metal	4
20	Furniture, mirrors, picture frames; goods (not included in other classes) of wood, cork, reed, cane, wicker, horn, bone, ivory, whalebone, shell, amber, mother-of-pearl, meerschaum and substitutes for all these materials, or of plastics	20

(Continued)

Appendix 2 (Continued)

Class No.	*Category of Geographical Indications*	*Number of Registered Goods*
21	Household or kitchen utensils and containers (not of precious metal or coated therewith); combs and sponges; brushes (except paint brushes); brush-making articles; articles for cleaning purposes; steel wool; unworked or semi-worked glass (except glass used in building); glassware, porcelain and earthenware not included in other classes	9
22	Ropes, string, nets, tents, awnings, tarpaulins, sails, sacks and bags (not included in other classes) padding and stuffing materials (except of rubber or plastics); raw fibrous textile materials	1
23	Yarns and threads, for textile use	9
24	Textiles and textile goods, not included in other classes, bed and table covers	60
25	Clothing, footwear, headgear	47
26	Lace and embroidery, ribbons and braid; buttons, hooks and eyes, pins and needles; artificial flowers	12
27	Carpets, rugs, mats and matting, linoleum and other materials for covering existing floors; wall hangings (nontextile)	18
28	Games and playthings, gymnastic and sporting articles not included in other classes; decorations for Christmas trees	10
29	Meat, fish, poultry and game; meat extracts; preserved, dried and cooked fruits and vegetables; jellies, jams, fruit sauces; eggs, milk and milk products; edible oils and fats	2
30	Coffee, tea, cocoa, sugar, rice, tapioca, sago, artificial coffee; flour and preparations made from cereals, bread, pastry and confectionary, ices; honey, treacle; yeast, baking powder; salt, mustard; vinegar, sauces (condiments); spices; ice	22
31	Agricultural, horticultural and forestry products and grains not included in other classes; live animals; fresh fruits and vegetables; seeds, natural plants and flowers; foodstuffs for animals, malt	29
33	Alcoholic beverages (except beers)	2
34	Tobacco, smokers' articles, matches	1
Total		291*

* A single Geographical Indication good can be registered in more than one class. The classification of goods is listed in the Fourth Schedule of the *Geographical Indications Rules, 2002*. The goods mentioned in the Fourth Schedule only provide a means by which the general content of numbered international classes can be quickly identified. Therefore, 199 Geographical Indications goods when distributed in different classes add up to 291.

Classes without a single case of registration of the good

Class No.	*Category of Geographical Indications*
1	Chemical used in industry, science, photography, agriculture, horticulture and forestry; unprocessed artificial resins, unprocessed plastics; manures, fire extinguishing compositions; tempering and soldering preparations; chemical substances for preserving foodstuffs; tanning substances; adhesive used in industry
2	Paints, varnishes, lacquers; preservatives against rust and against deterioration of wood; colorants; moderants; raw natural resins; metals in foil and powder form for painters; decorators; printers and artists
4	Industrial oils and greases; lubricants; dust absorbing, wetting and binding compositions; fuels (including motor spirit) and illuminants, candles, wicks
5	Pharmaceutical, veterinary and sanitary preparations; dietetic substances adapted for medical use, food for babies, plasters, materials for dressings; materials for stopping teeth, dental wax; disinfectants; preparation for destroying vermin; fungicides, herbicides
10	Surgical-medical-dental-veterinary apparatus-artificial limbs-eyes-teeth-orthopaedic articles-suture materials
11	Apparatus – lighting-heating-steam generating-cooking-refrigerating-drying ventilating-water supply-sanitary purposes
12	Vehicles; apparatus for locomotion by land, air or water
13	Firearms, ammunitions and projectiles; explosives; fireworks
17	Rubber; gutta percha, gum, asbestos, mica and goods from these materials not included in other classes; plastics in extruded form used in manufacture; packing, stopping, insulating materials; flexible pipes, not of metal
32	Beers, mineral and aerated waters and other nonalcoholic drinks; fruit drinks and fruit juices; syrups and other preparations for making beverages

Based on *Geographical Indications Journal* No. 1 to 58

Appendix 3 Goods Registered with Geographical Indications by Categories as per the Geographical Indications of Goods (Registration and Protection) Act, 1999

Class	*Category*	*Registered Goods (No.)*
3	Bleaching preparations and other substances for laundry use; cleaning; polishing; scouring and abrasive preparations; soaps; perfumery, essential oils, cosmetics, hair lotions, dentifrices	1. Ganjam Kewda Rooh 2. Kannauj Perfume 3. Mysore Agarbathi 4. Mysore Sandal Soap 5. Mysore Sandalwood Oil
6	Common metals and their alloys; metal building materials; transportable buildings of metal; materials of metal for railway tracks; nonelectric cables and wires of common metal; ironmongery, small hems of metal hardware; pipes and tubes of metal; safes; goods of common metal not included in other classes; ores	1. Bastar Dhokra 2. Bastar Iron Craft 3. Bell Metal Ware of Datia and Tikamgarh 4. Bidriware 5. Budithi Bell and Brass Craft 6. Karnataka Bronze Ware 7. Moradabad Metal Craft 8. Nachiarkoil Kuthvilakku (Nachiarkoil Lamp) 9. Pembarthi Metal Craft 10. Silver Filigree of Karimnagar 11. Swamimalai Bronze Icons
7	Machines and machine tools; motors and engines (except for land vehicles); machine coupling and transmission components (except for land vehicles); agricultural implements other than hand-operated; incubators for eggs	1. Coimbatore Wet Grinder
8	Hand tools and implements (hand-operated); cutlery; side arms; razors	1. Kashmir Walnut Wood Carving 2. Silver Filigree of Karimnagar
14	Precious metals and their alloys and goods in precious metals or coated therewith, not included in other classes; jewellery, precious stones, horological and other chronometric instruments	1. Agates of Cambay 2. Payyannur Pavithra Ring 3. Silver Filigree of Karimnagar 4. Temple Jewellery of Nagercoil 5. Thanjavur Art Plate 6. Thewa Art Work
15	Musical instruments	1. Bobbili Veena 2. Maddalam of Palakkad 3. Thanjavur Veenai

(*Continued*)

Appendix 3 (Continued)

Class	*Category*	*Registered Goods (No.)*
16	Paper, cardboard and goods made from these materials, not included in other classes; printed matter; bookbinding material; photographs; stationery; adhesives for stationery or household purposes, artists' materials; paint brushes; typewriters and office requisites (except furniture); instructional and teaching material (except apparatus); plastic materials for packing (not included in other classes); playing cards; printers' type; printing blocks	1. Cheriyal Paintings 2. Ganjifa Cards of Mysore 3. Kangra Painting 4. Kashmir Papier Mache 5. Kondapalli Bommalu 6. Madhubani Painting 7. Mysore Traditional Paintings 8. Nirmal Paintings 9. Orissa Pattachitra 10. Thanjavur/ Tanjore Painting 11. Tirukanur Papier Mache Craft 12. Warli Painting
18	Leather and imitations of leather and goods made of these materials and not included in other classes; animal skins, hides, trunks and travelling bags; umbrellas, parasols and walking sticks; whips; harness and saddler	1. Andhra Pradesh Leather Puppetry 2. East India Leather 3. Kanpur Saddlery 4. Santiniketan Leather Goods 5. Silver Filigree of Karimnagar
19	Building materials (nonmetallic), nonmetallic rigid pipes for building; asphalt, pitch and bitumen; nonmetallic transportable buildings; monuments, not of metal	1. Khatamband 2. Konark Stone Carving 3. Mysore Rosewood Inlay 4. Nakshi Kantha
20	Furniture, mirrors, picture frames; goods (not included in other classes) of wood, cork, reed, cane, wicker, horn, bone, ivory, whalebone, shell, amber, mother-of-pearl, meerschaum and substitutes for all these materials, or of plastics	1. Aranmula Kannadi 2. Bastar Wooden Craft 3. Bobbili Veena 4. Brass Broidered Coconut Shell Crafts of Kerala 5. Budithi Bell and Brass Craft 6. Chettinad Kottan 7. Kashmir Papier Mache 8. Kashmir Walnut Wood Carving 9. Khatamband 10. Kinhal Toys 11. Kondapalli Bommalu 12. Mysore Rosewood Inlay

(*Continued*)

Appendix 3 (Continued)

Class	*Category*	*Registered Goods (No.)*
		13. Nakshi Kantha 14. Nirmal Furniture 15. Nirmal Paintings 16. Saharanpur Wood Craft 17. Sankheda Furniture 18. Sikki Grass Work of Bihar 19. Silver Filigree of Karimnagar 20. Warli Painting
21	Household or kitchen utensils and containers (not of precious metal or coated therewith); combs and sponges; brushes (except paint brushes); brush-making articles; articles for cleaning purposes; steel wool; unworked or semi-worked glass (except glass used in building); glassware, porcelain and earthenware not included in other classes	1. Bastar Dhokra 2. Bastar Iron Craft 3. Bidriware 4. Blue Pottery of Jaipur 5. Budithi Bell and Brass Craft 6. Firozabad Glass 7. Molela Clay Work 8. Pembarthi Metal Craft 9. Villianur Terracotta Works
22	Ropes, string, nets, tents, awnings, tarpaulins, sails, sacks and bags (not included in other classes) padding and stuffing materials (except of rubber or plastics); raw fibrous textile materials	1. Cannanore Home Furnishings
23	Yarns and threads, for textile use	1. Banaras Brocades and Sarees 2. Cannanore Home Furnishings 3. Champa Silk Saree and Fabrics 4. Gopalpur Tussar Fabrics 5. Khandua Saree and Fabrics 6. Muga Silk of Assam 7. Mysore Silk 8. Orissa Ikat 9. Surat Zari Craft
24	Textiles and textile goods, not included in other classes, bed and table covers	1. Appliqué (Khatwa) Work of Bihar 2. Arani Silk 3. Bagh Prints of Madhya Pradesh 4. Bagru Hand-Block Print 5. Balaramapuram Sarees and Fine Cotton Fabrics 6. Baluchari Saree 7. Banaras Brocades and Sarees

(*Continued*)

Appendix 3 (Continued)

Class	*Category*	*Registered Goods (No.)*
		8. Berhampur Patta (Phoda Kumbha) Saree and Joda
		9. Bhagalpur Silk
		10. Bhavani Jamakkalam
		11. Bomkai Saree and Fabrics
		12. Cannanore Home Furnishing
		13. Chamba Rumal
		14. Champa Silk Saree and Fabrics
		15. Chanderi Sarees
		16. Dhalapathar Parda and Fabrics
		17. Dhaniakhali Saree
		18. Dharmavaram Handloom Pattu Sarees and Paavadas
		19. Farrukhabad Prints
		20. Gadwal Sarees
		21. Gopalpur Tussar Fabrics
		22. Habaspuri Saree and Fabrics
		23. Ilkal Sarees
		24. Kachchh Shawls
		25. Kalamkari
		26. Kancheepuram Silks
		27. Kashmir Pashmina
		28. Khandua Saree and Fabrics
		29. Kinnauri Shawl
		30. Kota Doria
		31. Kotpad Handloom fabric
		32. Kovai Kora Cotton Sarees
		33. Kullu Shawl
		34. Lucknow Chikan Craft
		35. Machilipatnam Kalamkari
		36. Madurai Sungudi
		37. Maheshwar Sarees and Fabrics
		38. Mangalagiri Sarees and Fabrics
		39. Molakalmuru Sarees
		40. Muga Silk of Assam
		41. Mysore Silk
		42. Nakshi Kantha
		43. Orissa Ikat
		44. Orissa Pattachitra
		45. Paithani Saree and Fabrics
		46. Patan Patola
		47. Pipli Appliqué Work
		48. Pochampally Ikat
		49. Salem Fabric

(Continued)

Appendix 3 (Continued)

Class	*Category*	*Registered Goods (No.)*
		50. Salem Silk known as Salem Venpattu
		51. Sambalpuri Bandha Saree and Fabrics
		52. Sandur Lambani Embroidery
		53. Sanganeri Hand-Block Printing
		54. Santipore Saree
		55. Siddipet Gollabama
		56. Solapur Chaddar
		57. Solapur Terry Towel
		58. Tangaliya Shawl
		59. Toda Embroidery
		60. Uppada Jamdani Sarees
25	Clothing, footwear, headgear	1. Arani Silk
		2. Bagru Hand-Block Print
		3. Balaramapuram Sarees and Fine Cotton Fabrics
		4. Baluchari Saree
		5. Banaras Brocades and Sarees
		6. Bhagalpur Silk
		7. Champa Silk Saree and Fabrics
		8. Chendamangalam Dhotis and Set Mundu
		9. Dhaniakhali Saree
		10. Dharmavaram Handloom Pattu Sarees and Paavadas
		11. Farrukhabad Prints
		12. Gopalpur Tussar Fabrics
		13. Kalamkari
		14. Kancheepuram Silks
		15. Kani Shawl
		16. Kasaragod Saree
		17. Khandua Saree and Fabrics
		18. Kota Doria
		19. Kovai Kora Cotton Sarees
		20. Kuthampully Sarees
		21. Lucknow Chikan Craft
		22. Machilipatnam Kalamkari
		23. Madurai Sungudi
		24. Maheshwar Sarees and Fabrics
		25. Mangalagiri Sarees and Fabrics
		26. Moirang Phee
		27. Muga Silk of Assam
		28. Mysore Silk
		29. Nakshi Kantha

(*Continued*)

Appendix 3 (Continued)

Class	*Category*	*Registered Goods (No.)*
		30. Narayanpet Handloom Sarees 31. Orissa Ikat 32. Paithani Saree and Fabrics 33. Patan Patola 34. Pochampally Ikat 35. Puneri Pagadi 36. Salem Silk known as Salem Venpattu 37. Sambalpuri Bandha Saree and Fabrics 38. Sandur Lambani Embroidery 39. Sanganeri Hand-Block Printing 40. Shaphee Lanphee 41. Siddipet Gollabama 42. Tangaliya Shawl 43. Toda Embroidery 44. Uppada Jamdani Sarees 45. Venkatagiri Sarees 46. Wangkhei Phee 47. Warli Painting
26	Lace and embroidery, ribbons and braid; buttons, hooks and eyes, pins and needles; artificial flowers	1. Banaras Brocades and Sarees 2. Champa Silk Saree and Fabrics 3. Kashmir Sozani Craft 4. Kasuti Embroidery 5. Kutch Embroidery 6. Lucknow Chikan Craft 7. Lucknow Zardozi 8. Phulkari 9. Sandur Lambani Embroidery 10. Silver Filigree of Karimnagar 11. Sujini Embroidery Work of Bihar 12. Toda Embroidery
27	Carpets, rugs, mats and matting, linoleum and other materials for covering existing floors; wall hangings (nontextile)	1. Agra Durrie 2. Alleppey Coir 3. Andhra Pradesh Leather Puppetry 4. Bhavani Jamakkalam 5. Cannanore Home Furnishings 6. Hand Made Carpet of Bhadohi 7. Kalamkari 8. Kashmir Walnut Wood Carving 9. Kinhal Toys 10. Kondapalli Bommalu 11. Machilipatnam Kalamkari 12. Muga Silk of Assam

(Continued)

Appendix 3 (Continued)

Class	*Category*	*Registered Goods (No.)*
		13. Mysore Rosewood Inlay 14. Navalgund Durries 15. Pattamadai Pai (Pattamadai Mat) 16. Pochampally Ikat 17. Screw Pine Craft of Kerala 18. Tangaliya Shawl
28	Games and playthings, gymnastic and sporting articles not included in other classes; decorations for Christmas trees	1. Andhra Pradesh Leather Puppetry 2. Channapatna Toys and Dolls 3. Kathputlis of Rajasthan 4. Kinhal Toys 5. Kondapalli Bommalu 6. Leather Toys of Indore 7. Mysore Rosewood Inlay 8. Nirmal Toys and Craft 9. Silver Filigree of Karimnagar 10. Thanjavur Doll
29	Meat, fish, poultry and game; meat extracts; preserved, dried and cooked fruits and vegetables; jellies, jams, fruit sauces; eggs, milk and milk products; edible oils and fats	1. Dharwad Pedha 2. Hyderabad Haleem
30	Coffee, tea, cocoa, sugar, rice, tapioca, sago, artificial coffee; flour and preparations made from cereals, bread, pastry and confectionary, ices; honey, treacle; yeast, baking powder; salt, mustard; vinegar, sauces (condiments); spices; ice	1. Alleppey Green Cardamom 2. Assam (Orthodox) Tea 3. Bikaneri Bhujia 4. Byadagi Chilli 5. Central Travancore Jaggery 6. Coorg Green Cardamom 7. Darjeeling Tea 8. Guntur Sannam Chilli 9. Kaipad Rice 10. Kalanamak Rice 11. Kangra Tea 12. Kolhapur Jaggery 13. Malabar Pepper 14. Monsooned Malabar Arabica Coffee 15. Monsooned Malabar Robusta Coffee 16. Navara Rice 17. Nilgiri (Orthodox) Tea 18. Palakkadan Matta Rice 19. Pokkali Rice 20. Tirupathi Laddu 21. Wayanad Gandhakasala Rice 22. Wayanad Jeerakasala Rice

(*Continued*)

Appendix 3 (Continued)

Class	*Category*	*Registered Goods (No.)*
31	Agricultural, horticultural and forestry products and grains not included in other classes; live animals; fresh fruits and vegetables; seeds, natural plants and flowers; foodstuffs for animals, malt	1. Allahabad Surkha Guava
		2. Appemidi Mango
		3. Bangalore Blue Grapes
		4. Bhalia Wheat
		5. Coorg Orange
		6. Devanahalli Pomello
		7. Eathomozhy Tall Coconut
		8. Ganjam Kewda Flower
		9. Gir Kesar Mango
		10. Hadagali Malligae
		11. Kamalapur Red Banana
		12. Madurai Malli
		13. Mahabaleshwar Strawberry
		14. Malda Fazli Mango
		15. Malda Khirsapati (Himsagar) Mango
		16. Malda Lakhasmanbhog Mango
		17. Mango Malihabadi Dusseheri
		18. Muga Silk of Assam
		19. Mysore Betel Leaf
		20. Mysore Malligae
		21. Naga Mircha
		22. Nagpur Orange
		23. Nanjanagud Banana
		24. Nashik Grapes
		25. Sirumalai Hill Banana
		26. Udupi Malligae
		27. Udupi Mattu Gulla Brinjal
		28. Vazhakulam Pineapple
		29. Virupakshi Hill Banana
33	Alcoholic beverages (except beers)	1. Feni
		2. Nashik Valley Wine
34	Tobacco, smokers' articles, matches	1. Bidriware

Appendix 4 Foreign Goods Registered and Awaiting Registration for Geographical Indications in India

Country	*Registered*	*Awaiting Registration*
France	Champagne, Cognac (2)	Alsace, Anjou, Armagnac, Beaujolais, Bordeaux, Bourgogne, Brie de Meaux, Calvados, Camembert en Normandie, Canard à foie gras du Sud-Ouest, Chablis, Châteauneuf du Pape, Comté, Côtes de Provence, Côtes du Rhône, Côtes du Roussillon, Emmental de Savoie, Essential Oil of Lavender from Upper Provence, Graves, Haut Médoc, Huîtres Marennes Oléron, Jambon de Bayonne, Languedoc, Margaux, Médoc, Pays d'Oc, Pruneaux d' Agen, Reblochon, Roquefort, Saint Émilion, Sauternes, Touraine, Val de Loire, Vinohradnícka oblast' Tokaj **(34)**
Spain	NA	Alicante, Azafrán de la Mancha, Baena, Bierzo, Brandy de Jerez, Cataluña, Cava, Empordà, Jerez-Xérès-Sherry, Jumilla, La Mancha, Málaga, Manzanilla Sanlúcar de Barrameda, Navarra, Penedés, Priorat, Queso Manchego, Rías Baixas, Ribera del Duero, Rioja, Rueda, Sierra de Cazorla, Sierra de Segura, Somontano, Toro, Utiel-Requena, Valdepeñas, Valencia **(28)**
Italy	Prosciutto di Parma "Parma Ham" (1)	Aceto Balsamico di Modena, Asigo, Barbaresco, Bardolino Superiore, Barolo, Brunello di Montalcino, Chianti, Conegliano Valdobbiadence Prosecco, Dolcetto d'Alba, Franciacorta, Gorgonzola, Grana Padano Grappa, Lambrusco di Sorbara, Lambrusco Grasparossa di Castelvetro, Montepulciano d'Abruzzo, Parmigiano Reggiano, Prosciutto Toscano, Provolone Valpadana, Soave, Taleggio, Toscano, Vino Nobile di Montepulciano **(23)**
Greece	NA	Elia Kalamatas, Feta, Kalamata, Lesvos, Mytilini, Masticha Chiou / Chios Gum Mastic, Naoussa, Nemea, Ouzo, Peza Irakliou Kritis, Retsina of Attiki, Samos, Sitia Lasithiou Kritis, Tsipouro / Tsikoudia **(13)**
Germany	NA	Bayerisches Bier, Franken, Hopfen aus der Hallertau, Korn, Lübecker Marzipan, Mittelrhein, Mosel-Saar-Ruwer, Münchener Bier, "Nürnberger Bratwürste / Nürnberger Rostbratwürste", Rheingau, Rheinhessen **(11)**

(*Continued*)

Appendix 4 (Continued)

Country	*Registered*	*Awaiting Registration*
Hungary	NA	Pálinka, Tokaj, Törkölypálinka **(3)**
Austria	NA	Inländerrum, Jägertee / Jagertee / Jagatee **(2)**
Cyprus	NA	Commandaria, Zivania **(2)**
Czech Republic	NA	Českobudějovické pivo, Žatecký chmel' **(2)**
Finland	NA	Finnish Berry Liqueur, Vodka of Finland **(2)**
Ireland	NA	Irish Cream, "Irish Whiskey / Whisky / Uisce Beatha Eireannach" **(2)**
Poland	NA	Polska Wodka, Wódka Ziolowa z Niziny Pólnocnopodlaskiej / Herbal vodka from the North Podlasie Lowland **(2)**
Sweden	NA	Svensk Vodka / Swedish Vodka **(1)**
Portugal	Porto, Douro (2)	0
Mexico	Tequila (1)	0
Peru	Peruvian Pisco (1)	0
Scotland	Scotch Whisky (1)	0
USA	Napa Valley (1)	0
Total	**9**	**125**

Based on www.ipindiaservices.gov.in/GirPublic/DetailsGIR.aspx, July 2004–May 2014

BIBLIOGRAPHY

Achaya, K. T. (1998). *Historical dictionary of Indian food.* Delhi: Oxford University Press.

Agrawal, Y. (1995). Benares brocades: varying themes. In J. Dhamija (Ed.), *The woven silks of India* (pp. 105–122). Bombay: Marg Publication.

Agarwal, S., and Michael J. B. (2005). *Emerging issues for geographical indication branding strategies.* MATRIC Research Paper. Iowa: Iowa State University.

Ahmad, I. (2005). Court rulings of eggs and beef. *Economic and Political Weekly*, 40(48), 4989–5146.

Ahmad, M. (2003). *Remarks at the creation of the 'Organization for an International Geographical Indications Network' (ORIGIN).* Brussels: World Intellectual Property Organisation.

Ahmad, M. (2010). *Linking people, places and products: a guide for promoting quality linked to geographical origin and sustainable geographical indication.* Rome: Food and Agriculture Organisation.

Ahmad, R. (2000). Trivia and science of Indian Monsoon Coffee. *Indian Coffee*, 64(4), 3–7.

Ahuja, S. C., Panwar, D. V. S., Ahuja, U., and Gupta, K. R. (1995). *Basmati rice: the scented pearl.* Hisar: Chaudhari Charan Singh Haryana Agricultural University.

Akhtar, J. D. (1897). *A history of ancient geography.* Delhi: ESS Publication.

Almeida, H. de, and Gilpin, G. H. (2006). *Indian renaissance: British romantic art and the prospect of India.* Burlington, VT: Ashgate Publishing Limited.

Ames, F. (1999). *The Kashmiri shawl.* New York: The Asia Society.

Anand, A. (1998). *Bazar India.* London: University of California Press.

Anand, Mulk Raj. (1954). Chamba Rumals. *Marg*, 7(4), 35–40.

The art of Khatamband. (2006, March 31). *Kashmir Newz.*

Asopa, V. N. (2007). *Tea industry of India: the cup that cheers has tears* (Working Paper No. 2007–07–02). Ahmedabad: Indian Institute of Management.

Assadi, M. (2006). Karnataka the muted anti–reservation agitation. *Economic and Political Weekly*, 41(29): 3146.

Babur, Padshah Zahir al-Din Muhammad. (1921). *Babur Nama*, Volume 2. Eng. tr. A. S. Beveridge, London: Luzac and Company, p. 584.

Bachelard, G. (1958). *The poetics of space* (M. Jolas, Trans.). Boston: Beacon Press.

Baden–Powell, B. H. (1894). The silver workers of Cutch. *Journal of Indian Art and Industry*, 5(45), 59–62.

Baeumer, L. 1999. *Protection of geographical indications under WIPO treaties and questions concerning the relationship between those treaties and the TRIPS agreement*. Geneva: World Intellectual Property Organisation.

Bagchi, S. (2001a). India and the World Trade Organisation: sectarian interests versus the public good. *Economic and Political Weekly*, 36(2), 90–93.

Bagchi, S. (2001b). Understanding World Trade Organisation. *Economic and Political Weekly*, 36(51), 4718.

Bagchi, S. (2001c). What happened at Doha World Trade Organisation. *Economic and Political Weekly*, 36(52), 4782–4785.

Baker, A. F. (1932). The textile industries of Kashmir. *Journal of the Royal Society of Arts*, 80(4134), 309–326.

Balabanlilar, L. (2009). The Emperor Jahangir and the pursuit of pleasure. *Journal of the Royal Asiatic Society (Third Series) 19*, 173–186.

Banerji, N. N. (1900). The cotton fabrics of Bengal. *Journal of Indian Art and Industry*, 8(68), 65–72.

Barbosa, D. (1518). *The book of Duarte Barbosa: an account of the countries Bordering on the Indian Ocean and their inhabitants*. London: Hakluyt Society, 1918–21; Nendeln, Liechtenstein: Kraus Reprint, 1967.

Barnes, R. (1990). Indian trade cloth in Egypt: the Newberry Collection. In *Textiles in Trade: Proceedings of the Textile Society of America Biennial Symposium* (pp. 178–187). Washington DC, Los Angeles: Textile Society of America.

Baroncelli, E. Fink, C. and Smarzynska Javorcik, B. (2004). *The global distribution of trademarks: some stylised facts* (World Bank Policy Research Working Paper No. 3270). Washington DC: World Bank.

Basham, A. L. (1961). *The wonder that was India: a survey of the history and culture of the Indian Sub-Continent before the coming of the Muslims*. London: Sidwick and Johnson Publishers.

Basheer, K. P. M.(2007, August 26). The shrinking fields of Pokkali. *The Hindu*.

Bayly, C. A. (1995). The Age of Hiatus: the North Indian economy and society, 1830–50. In A. Siddiqui (Ed.), *Trade and finance in colonial India 1750–1860* (pp. 218–249). Delhi: Oxford University Press,.

Beattie, A. (2009). *False economy: a surprising economic history of the world*. London: Viking Penguin Books.

Benedict, A. (1983). *Imagined communities: reflections on the origin and spread of nationalism*. London: Verso.

Bentham, J. (1789). *An introduction to the principals of morals and legislation*. Oxford: Clarendon Press.

Berard, L., and Marchenay, P. (1996). Tradition, regulation and intellectual property: local agricultural products and foodstuffs in France. In S. B. Brush and D. Stabinsky (Eds.), *Valuing local knowledge: indigenous peoples and intellectual property rights*. Washington, DC: Island Press.

Berger, C. (2003). *Geographical indications: a business opportunity and a rural development tool.* France: Food and Rural Affairs, Ministry of Agriculture.

Berizzi, P. (1997). *The impact of community protection measures introduced by regulation (EEC).* Parma: 52nd European Association of Agricultural Economics Seminar.

Bernier, F. (1891). *Travels in the Mogul Empire, A.D. 1656–1668.* Edinburgh: A. Constable, Printers to Her Majesty, at the Edinburgh University Press.

Bernstein, W. J. (2008). *A splendid exchange: how trade shaped the world.* New York: Atlantic Monthly Press.

Bhardwaj, O. P. (1986). *Studies in the historical geography of Ancient India.* Delhi: Sundeep Prakashan.

Bhattacharjea, A. (2001). Competition policy: India and the WTO. *Economic and Political Weekly,* 36(51), 4710–4713.

Bhattacharya, A. (1977). *Historical geography of ancient and early medieval Bengal.* Calcutta: Sanskrit Pustak Bhandar.

Bhattacharya, N. N. (1988). *Ancient Indian history and civilization: trends and perspectives.* New Delhi: Manohar Publications.

Bhattacharya, P. K. (1977). *Historical geography of Madhya Pradesh from early records.* New Delhi: Motilal Banarasidass.

Bhavani, E. (1968). *Decorative designs and craftmanship of India.* Bombay: D. B. Taraporevala Sons and Co. Pvt. Ltd.

Bheda, C. (1986). *Documentation on Navalgund Durries. Project V: Winter–Summer.* Ahmedabad: National Institute of Design.

Bheda, C. (1992). *Navalgund Durries of Karnataka.* Ahmedabad: National Institute of Design.

Bhowmik, S. K. (2005). Tea plantation workers' strike: workers lose out on wages. *Economic and Political Weekly,* 40(38), 4103–4105.

Birdwood, Sir G. C. M. (1878). *Paris Universal Exhibition of 1878: handbook to the British Indian section.* London, Paris: Offices of the Royal Commission.

Birdwood, Sir. C. M. (1880). *The industrial arts of India.* Oxford: Chapman and Hall.

Biswas, S. S. (1981). *Terracotta art of Bengal.* Delhi: Agam Kala Prakashan.

Blakeney, M. (1999a). *Round Table Conference on World Property Intellectual Rights and Traditional Knowledge.* Paper prepared for World Intellectual Property Organisation WIPO/IPTK/RT/99/3.

Blakeney, M. (1999b). *What is traditional knowledge? Why should it be protected? Who should protect it? For whom? Understanding the value chain.* Geneva: World Intellectual Property Organisation.

Blakeney, M. (2001a). *Geographical indications and TRIPS.* Geneva: Quaker United Nations Office.

Blakeney, M. (2001b). Proposals for the international regulation of geographical indications. *The Journal of World Intellectual Property,* 4(5),630–652.

Blenerhassett, A. (1915). The cotton fabrics of the Central Provinces. *Journal of Indian Art and Industry, 17*(132), 41–44.

Borpujari, J. G. (1995). The impact of the transit duty system in British India. In A. Siddiqui (Ed.), *Trade and finance in colonial India 1750–1860* (pp. 321–344). Delhi: Oxford University Press.

Bose, T. K. (2002). *Vegetable crops*. Calcutta: Naya Prokash.

Bowrey, T. (1903). *A geographical account of countries round the Bay of Bengal, 1669–1679*. Cambridge: Hakluyt Society.

Braham, E. (2002). Towards a theory of values–based labelling. *Agriculture and Human Values*, *19*(4), 349–350.

Brahmamuni, Swami. (1960). *Vedic vandana*. New Delhi: Sarva Deshiko Arya Prathinidhi Sabha.

Brendon, B. A. (1899). *A monograph on the woollen fabrics of the Bombay Presidency*. Cambridge: Cambridge University Press.

Bronson, B. (1983). An industrial miracle in a golden age: the 17th-century cloth exports of India. In *Bulletin of the Field Museum of Natural History*, *54* (1), 12–25.

Broude, T. (2005). Taking 'trade and culture' seriously: geographical indications and cultural protection in WTO Law. *Journal of International Economic Law*, *26* (4): 623–692.

Brunhes, J (1947). *Human Geography*. New York: Rand Mc Nally and Company.

Business Times Bureau. (2001). Bengal government spins a woeful pattern for weavers. *Times of India*. Retrieved August 2012 from http://timesofindia.indiatimes.com/business/india–business/Bengal–govt–spins–a–woeful–pattern–for–weaver/articleshow/42349490.cms#ixzz1D42HbOEi.

Carvalho, P. M. (2008). *Luxury for export artistic exchange between India and Portugal Around 1600*. Boston: Isabella Stewart Gardner Museum.

Casey, Edward. (1998). *The fate of place: a philosophical history*. Berkeley: University of California Press.

Census of India. Bibliography of Indian arts and crafts. (1961). Delhi: Manager of Publications.

Census of India. Bibliography of small-scale and cottage industries and handicrafts. (1961). Delhi: Manager of Publications.

Census of India. Fairs and festivals of Gujarat. (1961). Delhi: Manager of Publications.

Census of India. Fairs and festivals of Kerala. (1961). Delhi: Manager of Publications.

Census of India. Folkart of Kumaon. (1961). Delhi: Manager of Publications.

Census of India. Handicrafts and artisans of Madras State. (1961). Delhi: Manager of Publications.

Census of India. Handicrafts and artisans of Pondicherry State. (1961). Delhi: Manager of Publications.

Census of India. Handicrafts of Nagaland. (1961). Delhi: Manager of Publications.

Census of India. Monograph series. (1961). Delhi: Manager of Publications.

Census of India. Selected crafts of Andhra Pradesh. (1961). Delhi: Manager of Publications.

Census of India. Selected crafts of Bihar. (1961). Delhi: Manager of Publications.

Census of India. Selected crafts of Delhi. (1961). Delhi: Manager of Publications.

Census of India. Selected crafts of Gujarat. (1961). Delhi: Manager of Publications.

Census of India. Selected crafts of Himachal Pradesh. (1961). Delhi: Manager of Publications.

Census of India. Selected crafts of Kerala. (1961). Delhi: Manager of Publications.

Census of India. Selected crafts of Madhya Pradesh. (1961). Delhi: Manager of Publications.

Census of India. Selected crafts of Maharashtra. (1961). Delhi: Manager of Publications.

Census of India. Selected crafts of Manipur. (1961). Delhi: Manager of Publications.

Census of India. Selected crafts of Mysore. (1961). Delhi: Manager of Publications.

Census of India. Selected crafts of Rajasthan. (1961). Delhi: Manager of Publications.

Census of India. Selected crafts of Uttar Pradesh. (1961). Delhi: Manager of Publications.

Census of India. Selected crafts of West Bengal and Sikkim. (1961). Delhi: Manager of Publications.

Census of India. Selected handicrafts of Assam. (1961). Delhi: Manager of Publications.

Census of India. Survey of traditional crafts of Orissa. (1961). Delhi: Manager of Publications.

Census of India. The tribes of Orissa. (1961). Delhi: Manager of Publications.

Census of India. Jewellery and ornaments in India: a historical outline. (1971). Delhi: Office of Registrar General.

Census of India. M *series: basketry and mat weaving in India.* (1971). Delhi: Government of India.

Census of India. Ritual terracottas and terracotta toys of Darbhanga. (1971). Delhi: Ministry of Home Affairs, Office of Registrar General.

Census of India. Special study report on Bhuta Cult in South Kanara District, Mysore. (1971). Delhi: Controller of Publications.

Census of India. Tribal wood-carving in India. (1971). Delhi: Office of Registrar General.

Census of India. Handicraft survey report on Banjara Embroidery. (1981). Delhi: Directorate of Census Operations.

Census of India. Handicrafts survey report, Gujarat. (1981). Delhi: Controller of Publications.

Census of India. Handicrafts survey report, Bhadohi, Uttar Pradesh. Woolen carpet industry: a rural-based traditional handicraft. (1981). Delhi: Controller of Publications.

Census of India. Series 22, Part X–D: Uttar Pradesh – handicraft survey report, Bhadohi. (1981). (Eds.) R. K. Ram, R. K. Singh, and Gopal Chandra. New Delhi: Controller of Publications.

Census of India. Primary census abstract. (2011). New Delhi: Government of India.

Central Statistical Organisation. (2007). *Statistical abstract India 2007* (43rd ed.). Calcutta: Ministry of Statistics and Programme Implementation, Government of India, Pallav Publishers.

Chadha, K. L, and Awasthi, R. P. (2005). *The Apple – Improvement, production and post harvest management.* New Delhi: Malhotra Publishing house.

Chakrabrati, D. K. (1990). *The external trade of the Indus civilization.* New Delhi: Munshiram Manoharlal Publishers Ltd.

Chand, R., *et.al.* (2001). Subsidies and support in agriculture. *Economic and Political Weekly*, 36(32), 4710–4713.

Chand, R. *et.al.* (2004). World Trade Organisation and oilseeds sector. *Economic and Political Weekly*, 39(6), 533–537.

Chanda, O. C. (1998). *Textiles, costumes and ornaments of western Himalayas*. New Delhi: Indus Publishing Company.

Chandar Meher, K. (1995). *The Orissan art of weaving*. Cuttack: Jagannath Processes.

Chandiramani, N. (2002). Legal factors in TRIPS. *Economic and Political Weekly*, 37(3), 200–203.

Chari, S. M. (1988). *Fundamentals of Visistadvaita Vedanta: a study based on Vedanta Desika's Tattva–Mikta Kalapa*. New Delhi: Motilal Banarasidass.

Chaturvedi, S. (2002). *India, the European Union and geographical indications: convergence of interests and challenges Ahead*. Paper presented at 'Centre De Sciences Humaines, EC Delegation, Fundacao Oriente, JNU European Union Studies Project and Kondrad Adenauer Foundation Seminar on India, The European Union, and the WTO', Delhi, 1 6–17 October.

Chaturvedi, S., and Nagpal, G. (2003). WTO and product-related environmental standards: Emerging issues and policy options. *Economic and Political Weekly*, 38(1), 66–74. Chaudhari, K. (2005). *Economic history of India from eighteenth to twentieth century*. Bombay: Centres for Studies of Civilization.

Chaudhuri, K. N. (1978). *The trading world of Asia and the English East India Company: 1660–1760*. New York: Cambridge University Press.

Chaudhuri, K. N. (1995). India's foreign trade and the cessation of the East India Company's trading activities, 1828–40. In A. Siddiqui (Ed.), *Trade and finance in colonial India 1750–1860* (pp. 290–320). Delhi: Oxford University Press.

Chaudhuri, S. (2002). TRIPS agreement and amendment of Patents Act in India. *Economic and Political Weekly*, 37(32), 3354–3455.

Chaulia, S. (2002). Social clause in WTO. *Economic and Political Weekly*, 37(7), 613–615.

Chikar Marmian, J. (1993). *Parthains: a romance in brocades*. Delhi: Bharatiya Book Corporation.

Childe, V. G. (1951). *Man makes himself*. London: Watts and Company.

Chimini, B. S. (2000). WTO and environment. *Economic and Political Weekly*, 35(20), 1752–1761.

Chimini, B. S. (2002). WTO and environment legitimisation of unilateral trade sanctions. *Economic and Political Weekly*, 37(2), 133–139.

Chishti, S. (2000). World trade and labour. *Economic and Political Weekly*, 35(30), 2669.

Chishti, S. (2001). India and the World Trade Organisation. *Economic and Political Weekly*, 36(14), 1246–1248.

Choudhary, M. L., and Sindhu, S.S. (2001). *Commercial flowers production*. New Delhi: Indian Agricultural Research Institute.

Choudhary, S. (1993). *Economic history of colonialism*. Delhi: Inter India Publication.

Christopher, W. (2000). *The arts of Kutch*. *Bombay*: Marg Publication.

Cocker, H. and Pizetti, I. (1968). *Flowers–a guide for your garden*. New York: Harry N. Abrams Inc.

Cole, H. H. (1874). *Catalogue of the objects of Indian art exhibited in the South Kensington Museum*. London: Chapman and Hall.

Colonial and Indian Exhibition. (1886). *Empire of India: special catalogue of exhibits by the Government of India and private exhibitors*. London: William Clowes and Sons.

Coomaraswamy, A. K. (1909). *The Indian craftsman*. London: Probsthain and Co.

Cooper, I. (1996). *Arts and crafts of India*. London: Thames and Hudson.

Correspondent. (1985, December 16). The counterfeit trade: illegal copies threaten host industries and can endanger consumers. *Business Week*.

Correspondent. (1999, March 6). A stitch in time. *The Telegraph*.

Correspondent. (2003a). Cancun fiasco: belling the cat. *Economic and Political Weekly*, *38*(38), 3963–3964.

Correspondent. (2003b). WTO: heavy baggage for cancun. *Economic and Political Weekly*, *38*(36), 3748–3749.

Correspondent. (2005a). A confusing patent law for India. *Economic and Political Weekly*, *40*(6), 1576–1578.

Correspondent. (2005b). What went wrong ahead of Hong Kong?. *Economic and Political Weekly*, *40*(48), 4987–4989.

Correspondent. (2007, August 7). Pashmina exports fall. *The Himalayan Times*.

Correspondent. (2008). High stakes in the WTO mini–ministerial. *Economic and Political Weekly*, *43*(29), 14–16.

Craig, G. (2007). *Guinness World Records*. Vancouver: Jim Pattision.

Crill, R. (1995). Vaishnavite silks: the figured textiles of Assam. In J. Dhamija (Ed.), *The woven silks of India* (pp. 37–47). Bombay: Marg Publication.

Cripps, F. (2005). Financial imbalances in the world economy. *Economic and Political Weekly*, *40*(52), 5453.

Cunningham, A. (1963). *The Ancient geography of India*. Varanasi: Indological Book House.

Cunningham, D. *et al*. (2005). Role of certificates of origin in the Access and Benefit Sharing (ABS) provisions of the convention of biological diversity', Roundtable Discussion by the Smithsonian Institution and UNU – Institute of Advanced Studies, Washington DC, September 9. Retrieved June 2012 from http://www.researchgate.net/publication/237433728_The_feasibility_practicality_and_cost_of_a_certificate_of_origin_system_for_genetic_resources_Preliminary_results_of_comparative_analysis_of_tracking_material_in_biological_resource_centres_and_of_proposals_for_a_certification_scheme.

Curchod, F. (2003). *Geographical indications: point of view of governments*. San Francisco: Worldwide Symposium on Geographical Indications.

Dara, W. (2002). Extension of stronger geographical indications protection: against the interests of developing countries? *Bridges, Between Trade and Sustainable Development*, 6(4), 17–18.

Darjeeling Tea Association. Retrieved May 2011 from www.darjeelingtea.com.

Darwin, J. (2007). *After Tamerlane the global history of empire since 1405*. London: Penguin Books.

Das Gupta, A. (1995). The medieval merchant. In A. Siddiqui (Ed.), *Trade and finance in colonial India 1750–1860* (pp. 107–141). Delhi: Oxford University Press.

Das, K. (2010). Prospects and challenges of geographical indications in India. *The Journal of World Intellectual Property*, *13*(2), 148–201.

Das, N. K. (2003). *Geographical indications: the experience of Indian tea producers–protection of Darjeeling Tea*. Paper presented at *Worldwide Symposium on Geographical Indications*, at San Francisco, California.

Dasgupta, P. P. (1994). Towards a new economics science. *Elsevier Science*, *23*(11), 487–521.

Dasgupta, S. (1996). Ours and theirs. *Down to Earth*, *5* (July 15), 13–14.

Deodhar, Y. S. (2002). Educational services. *Economic and Political Weekly*, *37*(19), 1791–1794.

Department of Commerce, Government of India. (2009). *Export Data Commodity Wise, 2008–2009*. Retrieved August 2013 from http://commerce.nic.in/eidb/ecomq.asp.

Desai, R. B. (2006, November 1). Life of Bidriware artisans looking up. *The Hindu*.

Dhamija, J. (1995). Paithani weaves: an ancient tapestry art. In J. Dhamija (Ed.), *The woven silks of India* (pp. 77–90). Bombay: Marg Publication.

Dhamija, J. and Jain, J. (1989). *Handwoven fabrics of India*. Ahmedabad: Mapin Publishing Pvt. Ltd.

Dhar, B. (2001). Doha: a developing country perspective. *Economic and Political Weekly*, 36(46 and 47), 4343–4347.

Dhru, S. (1990). Kathputli. In *Textile designer*. Ahmedabad: Knowledge Management Centre, National Institute of Design.

Directorate General of Commercial Intelligence and Statistics. (1985). *Monthly statistics of the foreign trade of India: Vol.1.Exports and re-exports*. Delhi: Government of India.

D'Mello, B. (2005). Development round, neo–liberal development. *Economic and Political Weekly*, 40(49), 5146–5148.

Dominique, B., *et al.* (2000). *Protected designations of origin and protected geographical indications in Europe: regulation or policy*. Switzerland: European Commission.

Douay–Rheims (Trans.) (2010). *The Vulgate Bible: Vol 1. The Pentateuch*. S. Edgar (Ed.). Cambridge, MA: Harvard University Press.

Downes, D., and Laird, S. (1999). *Innovative mechanisms for sharing benefits of biodiversity and related knowledge: case studies on geographical indications and trademarks*. Geneva: UNCTAD BioTrade Initiative.

Draco, M. (2012). *Magic crystals, sacred stones: the magical lore of crystal minerals and gemstones*. Alresford: Axis Mundi Books.

Dubey, M. (2006). WTO's Hong Kong conference: an appraisal. *Economic and Political Weekly*, 36(1), 15–19.

Dunn, H. A. (2004). Geographic indications at issue in Idaho Spud Case. *National Law Journal*, 26(21), 10–12

Dutfield, G. (1999). *Intellectual property rights trade and biodiversity: the case of seeds and plant varieties*. Background Paper Written for the IUCN Project on the Convention on Biological Diversity and the International Trade Regime, Intersessional Meeting on the Operations of the Convention (Montreal, Canada, 28–30 June).

Echols, G. (1984). *Indian carpets*. London: Thames and Hudson.

Echols, M. A. (2003). Geographical indications for Food, TRIPS, and the Doha development agenda. *Journal of African Law, 47*(2), 199–220.

Editorials. (2001a). A maturer World Trade Organisation. *Economic and Political Weekly, 36*(46), 4323–4324.

Editorials. (2001b). Wrong on World Trade Organisation. *Economic and Political Weekly, 36*(45), 4235–4236.

Editorials. (2003). Intellectual property thorny issue. *Economic and Political Weekly, 38*(21), 2001.

Editorials. (2005). Controversial choice change of guard at WTO. *Economic and Political Weekly, 40*(21), 2116.

Editorials. (2007). Deal–making at the WTO. *Economic and Political Weekly, 42*(5), 339–340.

Editorials. (2008a). Contravening the Doha mandate. *Economic and Political Weekly, 43*(15), 5.

Editorials. (2008b). Manufacturing a WTO agreement. *Economic and Political Weekly, 43*(10), 6.

Elenour, K. (2002). *Geographical indications and trademarks: IP or 'Feta–Complo'?* Alexandria: Patent and Trademark Office.

Escudero, S. (2001). *International protection of geographical indications and developing countries*. Trade-Related Agenda, Development and Equity Working Paper 10. Geneva: WTO.

Felix, A, and Grazioli, A. (2002). Geographical indications beyond wines and spirits: a roadmap for a better protection for geographical indications in the WTO/TRIPS agreement. *The Journal of World Intellectual Property*, 5(6), 865–897.

Fink, C., and Smarzynska, B. (2000). *Possible solutions for conflicts between trademarks and geographical indications and for conflicts between homonymous geographical indications*. Geneva: World Intellectual Property Organisation.

Fink, C., and Smarzynska, B. (2002). *Trademarks, geographical indications and developing countries*. Washington, DC: World Bank.

Foster, W. (Ed.). (1921). *Early travels in India 1583–1619*. London: Oxford University Press.

Francis, M. S. (1997). *Folk embroidery and traditional handloom weaving*. Cuttack: A.P.H Publishing Corporation.

Francis, P. (1986). Baba Ghor and the Ratanpur Rakshisha. *Journal of the Economic and Social History of the Orient*, 29(2) 198–205.

Francis, P. (Jr.). (2002). *Asia's maritime bead trade: 300 B.C. to the present*. Honolulu: University of Hawaii Press.

Friedmann, H. (1993). The political economy of food: a global crisis. *New Left Review, 197*, 29–57.

Friedman, T. L. (2005). The world is flat: a brief history of the twenty–first century. New York: Farrar, Straus and Giroux. Furber, H. (1995). Trade and politics in Madras and Bombay. In A. Siddiqui (Ed.), *Trade and finance in colonial India 1750–1860* (pp. 66–98). Delhi: Oxford University Press.

Gadgil, M., and Guha, R. (1993). *This fissured land: an ecological history of India*. Berkeley: University of California Press.

Gandhi, M. K. (1909). *Hind Swaraj or Indian Home Rule* (1938 ed.). Ahmedabad: Navajivan Publishing House.

Gandhi, M. K. (1962). *Village swaraj*. Compiled by H. M. Vyas. Ahmedabad: Navijian Publishing House.

Ganguli, R. (2007, May 31). Two Kerala pepper varieties to get GI tags. *The Economic Times*.

The Ganjifa Art. (2014). Retrieved June 2014 from http://www.kamat.com/kalranga/art/ganjifa.htm.

Geographical Indications of Goods (Registration and Protection) Act. (1999). Act No. 48 of 1999. New Delhi: Ministry of Law, Justice and Company Affairs.

Geographical Indications Registry. (2004–2014). *Geographical Indications Journal* No. 1 to 58. Chennai: Intellectual Property India.

George, S. P., Bastian, D., Radhakrishan, N. V., and Aipe, K. C. (2005). Evaluation of aromatic rice varieties in Wayanad, Kerala. *Journal of Tropical Agriculture*, 43(1–2), 67–69.

Gervais, D. (1998). *The TRIPS agreement: drafting history and analysis*. London: Sweet and Maxwell.

Geuze, M. (1999). *Protection of geographical Indications under the TRIPS agreement and related work of the World Trade Organisation*. Geneva: World Intellectual Property Organisation.

Ghosal, S. (2005, May 8). Ace adman reads tea leaves. *The Telegraph*.

Ghosh, A. (1985). The lost wax process. *India Magazine*. Cited in *Geographical Indications Journal*, *51*, September 30, 2013, p. 27.

Ginsburg, J. C. *et al.* (2007). *Trademark and unfair competition law*. New York: N.Y. Foundation Press.

Giovannucci, D., Josling, T., Kerr, W., O'Connor, B., and Yeung, M. T. (2009). *Guide to geographical indications: linking products and their origins*. Geneva: International Trade Centre.

Glazier, R. (1899). *A manual of historic ornament*. London: Mayfield Publications.

Goel, M. (2005). Indian Railways: on wheels of death. In Anu Kapur *et al.* (Eds.), *Disasters in India: studies of grim reality*. New Delhi: Rawat Publications.

Gokhale, B. G. (1961). *Indian thoughts through the Ages: a study of some dominant concepts*. Bombay: Asia Publishing House.

Gokhale, B. G. (1995). *Ancient India: history and culture*. Bombay: Popular Prakashan.

Goldberg, S. (2001). Who will raise the white flag? The battle between the United States and the European Union over the protection of geographical indications. *University of Pennsylvania Journal of International Economic Law*, *22*(1), 107–151.

Goldstein, L. J. (1976). *Historical knowing*. Austin: University of Texas Press.

Gombar, V., and Reddy, Ch P. (2009, October 21). GI protection: gain for some, pain for others. *Business Standard*.

Gopal, S. (1975). *Commerce and crafts in Gujarat*. New Delhi: People's Publishing House.

Gopalakrishnan, N. S. (2002). Protection of traditional knowledge: the need for a sui generis law in India. *The Journal of World Intellectual Property*, 5(5), 725–742.

Gopalakrishnan, N. S, Nair, P. S., and Babu, A. K. (2007). *Exploring the relationship between geographical indications and traditional knowledge: an analysis of the legal tools for the protection of geographical indications in Asia* (Working Paper). A Study Commissioned by the International Centre for Trade and Sustainable Development (ICTSD), Switzerland.

Government of India. (1918). *Annual statement of the sea-borne trade of British India 1916–1917* (Vol. 2). Calcutta: Superintendent of Government Press.

Government of Madhya Pradesh and United Nations Industrial Development Organization Cluster Development Programme. (2003). *A diagnostic study of artisans, the handloom weaving cluster of Chanderi, Madhya Pradesh*. Retrieved May 2012 from www.smallindustryindia.com.

Government of Madhya Pradesh and United Nations Industrial Development Organization Cluster Development Programme. (2006). *End of project report: handloom cluster of Chanderi, Madhya Pradesh*. Retrieved June 2013 from http://clusterobservatory.in/report/EPR%20Final%20report%20-%20Chanderi%20no%20ph.doc.

Grant, C. (2005). Geographic indicators: implications for Africa. Tarlac Trade Brief No. 6/ 2005.

Gray, A. (Trans.) (1887). *The voyage of François Pyrard of Laval to the East Indies, the Maldives, the Moluccas, and Brazil, 1619*. London: Hakluyt Society.

Grazioli, A. (2002). *The protection of geographical indications*. Los Angeles: Bridges Publications.

Grevers, F. (1999). *Topical issues of the protection of geographical indications*. Geneva: World Intellectual Property Organization.

Grossman, G. M. and Shapiro, C. (1988). Counterfeit – product trade. *American Economic Review*, *78*(1), 59–75.

Grove, R. H. (1995). *Green imperialism: colonial expansion, tropical island edens and the origin of environmentalism, 1600–1860*. Cambridge: Cambridge University Press.

Guenther, E. (1948). *The essential oils*. New York: D. Van Nostrand Co.

Guerra, J. L. (2004). *Geographical indications and biodiversity: bridges joining distant territories*. San Francisco: International Centre for Trade and Sustainability–Bridges.

Gulati, M. (2007). The magic of Chanderi. In *Workshop on relevance, importance and operation of geographical indication*. New Delhi: Centre for WTO Studies, Indian Institute of Foreign Trade and EU India Trade and Investment Development Programme.

Gustavo, C. (2003). *Trade: 'Geographical indications' a new snag in agricultural talks*. New York: Global Information Network.

Gyles, M. F. (1947). Nero fiddled while Rome burned. *The Classical Journal*, *42*(4), 211–217.
Handa, O. C. (1998a). *Textile-based arts and crafts: cotton products*. New Delhi: Indus Publishing Company.
Handa, O. C. (1998b). *Textile-based arts and crafts: woollen products*. New Delhi: Indus Publishing Company.
Handa, O. C. (1998c). *Textiles, costumes and ornaments of the western Himalayas*. New Delhi: Indus Publishing Company.
Handa, O. C, and Jain, M. (2000). *Wood handicraft: a study of its origin and development in Saharanpur*. New Delhi: Indus Publishing Company.
Hankin, N. B. (2003). *Hanklyn-janklyn: a rumble–tumble guide to some words, customs, and quiddities Indian and Indo-British*. Delhi: India Research Press.
Hansen, S., and Vanfleet, J. (2003). *Traditional knowledge and intellectual property: a handbook on issues and options for traditional knowledge holders in protecting their intellectual property and maintaining biological diversity*. New York: American Association for the Advancement of Science.
Hare, R. A. P. (1957). *Best food from India*. London: Arco Publications Ltd.
Hariharan, S. (2001). Economy of Broach during the seventeenth century: gains from bleaching activity. *Indian Historical Review*, *28*(1 and 2), 68–83.
Hariharan, S. (2002). *Cotton textiles and corporate buyers in Cottonopolis*. Delhi: Manak Publications.
Harris, H. T. (1908). *Monograph on the carpet weaving industry in southern India*. Madras: Government Press.
Havell, E. B. (1928). *Indian sculpture and paintings*. Moscow: Ripol Classic Publishing House.
Hayne, E. (2005). *Manual of summit of SAARC Countries at Dhaka*. Dhaka: SAARC.
Hazarika, R. K., and Boro, K. (2006). *Textile designs of the Boros of North-East India, intangible cultural heritage of India series* (Vol. 3). Bhopal: Indira Gandhi Rashtriya Manav Sangrahalaya.
Hendley, T. H. (2011). *Memorials of the Jeypore Exhibition 1883: Vol. 1. Industrial Art*. Ahmedabad: Mapin Publishing.
Hill, R. (1881). *Manual of the Coimbatore District*. Madras: Government Press.
Himanshu, P. R. (1986). *Monastery and guild commerce under the Satavahans*. New Delhi: Oxford University Press.
Höpperger, M. (2000). *International protection of geographical indications: the present situation and prospects for future development*. Geneva: World Intellectual Property Organisation.
Howe, S. E. (1946). *In quest of spices*. London: Hebert Jenkins.
Hughes, J. (2006). Champagne, Feta, and Bourbon: the spirited debate about geographical indications. *Hastings Law Journal*, *58*(2), 299–386.
Hunter, W. W. (1885). *Imperial Gazetteer of India*. London: Trubner and Co.
Hunter, W. W. (1912). *A History of British India*. London: Longmans, Green and Co.
Imperial Gazetteer of India. (1908). Embroideries. In *Vol. 3 – The Indian Empire, Economic* (pp. 218–222). London: Oxford, Clarendon Press.

Imperial Gazetteer of India. (1909–1931). *Volume 1 – The Indian Empire, Descriptive*. London: Oxford, Clarendon Press.

Imperial Gazetteer of India. (1909–1931). *Volume 2 – The Indian Empire, Historical*. London: Oxford, Clarendon Press.

Imperial Gazetteer of India. (1909–1931). *Volume 3 – The Indian Empire, Economic*. London: Oxford, Clarendon Press.

Imperial Gazetteer of India. (1909–1931). *Volume 4 – The Indian Empire, Administrative*. London: Oxford, Clarendon Press.

Imperial Gazetteer of India. (1909–1931). *Volume 5 – Abazai–Arcot*. London: Oxford, Clarendon Press.

Imperial Gazetteer of India. (1909–1931). *Volume 6 – Argaon–Bardwan*. London: Oxford, Clarendon Press.

Imperial Gazetteer of India. (1909–1931). *Volume 7 – Bareilly–Berasia*. London: Oxford, Clarendon Press.

Imperial Gazetteer of India. (1909–1931). *Volume 8 – Berhampore–Bombay*. London: Oxford, Clarendon Press.

Imperial Gazetteer of India. (1909–1931). *Volume 9 – Bomjur–Central India*. London: Oxford, Clarendon Press.

Imperial Gazetteer of India. (1909–1931). *Volume 10 – Central Provinces–Coopta*. London: Oxford, Clarendon Press.

Imperial Gazetteer of India. (1909–1931). *Volume 11 – Coondapoor–Edwardesabad*. London: Oxford, Clarendon Press.

Imperial Gazetteer of India. (1909–1931). *Volume 12 – Einme–Gwalior*. London: Oxford, Clarendon Press.

Imperial Gazetteer of India. (1909–1931). *Volume 13 – Gyaraspur–Jais*. London: Oxford, Clarendon Press.

Imperial Gazetteer of India. (1909–1931). *Volume 14 – Jaisalmer–Kara*. London: Oxford, Clarendon Press.

Imperial Gazetteer of India. (1909–1931). *Volume 15 – Karachi–Kotayam*. London: Oxford, Clarendon Press.

Imperial Gazetteer of India. (1909–1931). *Volume 16 – Kotchandpur–Mahavinyaka*. London: Oxford, Clarendon Press.

Imperial Gazetteer of India. (1909–1931). *Volume 17 – Mahbubabad–Moradabad*. London: Oxford, Clarendon Press.

Imperial Gazetteer of India. (1909–1931). *Volume 18 – Moram–Nayagarh*. London: Oxford, Clarendon Press.

Imperial Gazetteer of India. (1909–1931). *Volume 19 – Nayakanthatti–Parbhani*. London: Oxford, Clarendon Press.

Imperial Gazetteer of India. (1909–1931). *Volume 20 – Pardi–Pusad*. London: Oxford, Clarendon Press.

Imperial Gazetteer of India. (1909–1931). *Volume 21 – Pushkar–Salween*. London: Oxford, Clarendon Press.

Imperial Gazetteer of India. (1909–1931). *Volume 22 – Samadhiala–Singhana*. London: Oxford, Clarendon Press.

Imperial Gazetteer of India. (1909–1931). *Volume 23 – Singhbhum–Trashi–Chod–Zong*. Oxford: Clarendon Press.

Imperial Gazetteer of India. (1909–1931). *Volume 24 – Travancore–Zira*. Oxford: Clarendon Press.

Imperial Gazetteer of India. (1909–1931). *Volume 25 – Index*. Oxford: Clarendon Press.

Imperial Gazetteer of India. (1909–1931). *Volume 26 – Atlas 1909*. Oxford: Clarendon Press.

Imperial Gazetteer of India. (1909–1931). *Volume 26 – Atlas 1931*. Oxford: Clarendon Press.

Intergovernmental Group on Tea. (2006). Policy developments in the world tea market: economic impact of maximum residue levels and ISO 3720 quality standard. FAO's Committee on Commodity Problems, *17th Session*. Nairobi, Kenya, November 29–December 1.

Irwin, J. (1955). Indian textile trade in the 17th century (western India). *Journal of Indian Textile History*, *1*(1), 4–33.

Irwin, J. (1974). *The Kashmir shawl (Victoria and Albert Museum Monograph, No. 29)*. London: Her Majesty's Stationery Office.

Ismail, F. (2004). World Trade Organisation July package from a development perspective. *Economic and Political Weekly*, 39(46 and 47), 4977–4980.

Jain, M. (2000). *Wood handicraft*. New Delhi: Indus Publishing Company.

Jaiswal, K. A. (2003). WTO Agreement on SPS. *Economic and Political Weekly*, *38*(5), 4737–4742.

Jaitley, J. (1990a). *Crafts of Jammu, Kashmir and Ladakh (Living traditions of India)*. Ahmedabad: Mapin Publishing.

Jaitley, J. (1990b). *The craft traditions of India*. New Delhi: Lustre Press Pvt. Ltd.

James, C. (2003). What's in a name?', *USA Today*, Retrieved 25 June 2011 from http://usatoday30.usatoday.com/money/economy/trade/2003-09-09-names_x.htm.

Jan, G. (1975). *Vedic literature*. Wiesbaden: Otto Harrasso Witz.

Jayakar, P. (1950–51). Cotton printing of Gujarat and Kathiawar. *Marg* 4(4).

Jha, V. R. (1995). Kanchivani: the saris of Kanchipuram. In J. Dhamija (Ed.), *The woven silks of India* (pp. 91–96). Bombay: Marg Publication.

Johason, J. K. (1988). Determinants and effects of the use of 'Made in' Labels. *International Marketing Review*, 6(1), 47–58.

Josling, T. (2006). The war on terror: geographical indications as a trans-Atlantic trade conflict. *Journal of Agricultural Economics*, *57*(3), 337–363.

Jung, A. (1977). *When a place becomes a person*. New Delhi: Vikash Publishing House.

Kanth, R. (2004). World Trade Organisation: advantage, G–20. *Economic and Political Weekly*, 39(34), 3795–3798.

Kapur, A. (1995). *Paradise in peril: an ecological profile of the Kashmir Valley*. Delhi: Allied Publishers.

Karpinski, C. (1963). Kashmir to Paisley. *The Metropolitan Museum of Art Bulletin*, *22*(3), 116–123.

Kautilya. (2000). *The Arthashastra* (Ed.), L. N. Rangarajan. Delhi: Penguin Classics.
Kelegama, S., and Mukherji, I. (2003). WTO and South Asia. *Economic and Political Weekly*, *38*(37), 3864–3867.
Keshav, A. (1943). *Trade of India*. Bombay: Vincent Chambers.
Khaldun, Ibn. (1967). *The Muqaddimah: an introduction to history*. Princeton: Princeton University Press.
Khatau, A. (2003). *Epicure's vegetarian cuisines of India*. Mumbai: Popular Prakashan.
Khor, M. (2005). WTO's Hong Kong conference: imbalanced outcome. *Economic and Political Weekly*, *40*(52),5448–5452.
Khor, M. (2006). Failure of WTO Geneva mini–ministerial: New deadline and challenges. *Economic and Political Weekly*, *41*(29), 3143–3145.
Khor, M. (2008a). Behind the July failure of WTO Talks on Doha. *Economic and Political Weekly*, *43*(33), 35–40.
Khor, M. (2008b). Imbalances remain in the WTO texts of 6 December 2008. *Economic and Political Weekly*, *43*(52), 8–11.
King, B. M. (2005). *Silk and empire*. Manchester: Manchester University Press.
Kipling, J. L. (1886). Indian Ivory Carving. *Journal of Indian Art and Industry*, *1*(7), 49–53.
Kochhan, R. (2000). *Vedic people: their history and geography*. New Delhi: Orient Longman Limited.
Kosambi, D. D. (1965). *The culture and civilisation of ancient India in historical outline*. London: Routledge, Kegan Paul.
Kramrisch, S. (1956). Artist, patron and public in India. *The Far Eastern Quarterly*, *15*(3), 335–342.
Krishnamurthy, R. (2009, October 30). Tracing a creative journey, *The Hindu*.
Kulke, H., and Rothermund, D. (2009). *A History of India* (5th ed.). Kiel and Heidelberg: Routledge.
Kumar, D. (2002). *Kebabs, chutneys and breads*. Kolkata: UBS Publishers.
Kumar, N. (2001a). World Trade Organisation regime, host country policies and global patterns of MNE activity. *Economic and Political Weekly*, *36*(1), 39–50.
Kumar, N. (2001b). WTO's emerging investment regime. *Economic and Political Weekly*, *36*(33), 3151–3158.
Kumar, N. (2003). Investment on WTO agenda. *Economic and Political Weekly*, *38*(30), 3177–3188.
Kumar, N. (1988). *The artisans of Banaras: popular culture and identity 1880–1986*. Delhi: Orient Longman.
Kumar, P. (2012). *Indigo plantations and science in colonial India*. New York: Cambridge University Press.
Kumar, R. K. (2012, January 6). Nanjangud Rasabale, over and out? *The Hindu*.
Kumar, R., and Naik, V. (2003). Case studies: Darjeeling Tea – challenges in the protection and enforcement of intellectual property rights. Retrieved August 2011 from http://www.wipo.int.
Ladaniya, M. S. (2008). Citrus fruit – biology, technology and evaluation. Amsterdam: Elsevier.

Lal, P. (1968). *Indian recipes*. Slough: Foulsham.
Lalbhai, R. (1995). Ashavali saris of Ahmedabad. In J. Dhamija (Ed.), *The woven silks of India* (pp. 105–107). Bombay: Marg Publication.
Lall, S. (1999). India and Pakistan: geographical indications – the Basmati issue. In *International Trademark Association Annual Meeting*. Seattle.
Lalwani, K. C. (1982). *Philosophy of Vedas*. Ulhasnagar: Talreja Publication.
Lamy, P. (2003). *Creation of the Organisation for an International Geographical Indications Network*. Brussels: Origin Publishers.
Latimer, C. (1915). Carpet making in the Punjab. *Journal of Indian Art and Industry*, *17*(131), 17–26.
Law, B. C. (1967). *Historical geography of ancient India*. New Delhi: Orient Reprint.
Linschoten, J. H. van (1885). *The voyage of John Huyghen van Linschoten to the East Indies* (Vols. 2, from the old English translation, 1598) (Eds.), A. C.Burnell and Pieter A. Tiele. London: Hakluyt Society; Delhi: Asian Educational Service (Reprint 1988).
Locke, John. (1690). Two Treatise of Government, cited in Volume V of 1823 edition *The works of John Locke*, 10 volumes. London: Thomas Davison.
Lotter, D. W. (2003). Organic agriculture. *Journal of Sustainable Agriculture*, *21*(4), 59–128.
Loureiro, M. L., and McCluskey, J. J. (2000). Assessing consumer response to protected geographical identification labelling. *Agribusiness*, *16*(3), 309–320.
Lukermann, F. (1964). Geography as a formal intellectual discipline and the way in which it contributes to human knowledge. *The Canadian Geographer*, 8(4), 167–172.
Mackay–Smith, A., Druesedow, J. R., and Ryder, T. (1984). *Man and the horse: an illustrated history of equestrian apparel*. New York: The Metropolitan Museum of Aart, Simon and Schuster.
MacKenzie, J. M. (Ed). 1990. *Imperialism and the natural world*. Manchester: Manchester University Press.
The Madrid Agreement for the Repression of False or Deceptive Indication of Source of Goods, Contracting parties. (1995). Geneva: World Intellectual Property Organisation.
Mahert, M. (2001). On Vino Veritas? Clarifying the use of geographic references on American wine labels. *California Law Review*, 89(6), 1881–1925.
Mahindru, S. N. (1982). *Spices in Indian life*. Delhi: Sultan Chand and Sons.
Malalasekera, G. P. (1983). *Dictionary of Pali proper names*. New Delhi: Oriental Books.
Malavika, T. V. (2006, April 9). Intellectual property? Right! *The Hindu*.
Malpas, J. (1999). *Place and experience: a philosophical topography*. Cambridge: Cambridge University Press.
Malpas, J. (2006). *Heidegger's topology: being, place, world*. Cambridge, MA: MIT Press.
Mani, B. R. (1987). *The Kushan civilization*. Delhi: B. R. Publishing Corporation.
Manoj, P. (2006, March 22). GI tag may help revive Coorg Orange cultivation. *The Hindu*.

Mansingh, S. (1996). *Historical dictionary of India*. London: Scarecrow Press.
Marshall, P. J. (1995). The internal trade of Bengal. In A. Siddiqui (Ed.), *Trade and finance in colonial India 1750–1860* (pp. 142–185. Delhi: Oxford University Press,.
Mathew, J. C. (2002). World trade and Indian banking sector: the road ahead. *Economic and Political Weekly, 37*(24), 2315–2321.
Mathew, K. S. (1986). *Portuguese and the Sultanate of Gujarat (1500–1573)*. Delhi: Mittal Publication.
Mathur, A. R. (2004). *Indian shawls: mantles of splendour*. Delhi: Rupa and Co.
Mathur, S. (2000). *Indian sweets*. Ahmedabad: Prabhat Prakashan.
Mazumdar, J. (2012, July 21). Hook, line and sinking. *The Times of India Crest Edition*,.
McCrindle, J. W. (1987). *Ancient India as described in classical literature*. Patna: Eastern Book House.
Meher, M. S. (2007, February 27). Kannur's Manchester moment: a rebirth. *Kerala Calling*, pp. 10–11.
Mehera, K. (1994). *The global re-structuring of agro-food systems*. Ithaca, NY: Cornell University Press.
Mehta, M. (1991). *Indian merchants and entrepreneurs in historical perspective*. Delhi: Academic Foundation.
Meltzer, E. K. (2002, June/ July). Pass the Parmesan? What you need to know about geographical indications and trademarks. *Virginia Lawyers Weekly*, pp. 18–23.
Meltzer, E. K. (2003). *Examples of foreign geographical indications protected in the United States*, United States Patent and Trademark Office.
Ministry of Textiles. (2006). *Development schemes for handloom sector, 9th Report, Standing Committee on Labour, 14th Lok Sabha*. New Delhi: Government of India.
Mishra, Rahul. (2006). Kota Doria Fabric – The fabric of the future. Retrieved June 2012 from http://www.bharattextile.com/articles/15.2.kota–doria–fabric–the–fabric–of–the.html#ixzz1D4DcqnXQ.
Mishra, V. (2001). TRIPS, product patents and pharmaceuticals. *Economic and Political Weekly, 24*(3), 4464–4467.
Misra, L. (1964). Sanganer printing. *Marg 18*(1), 25.
Mohanty, B. C. (1980). *Applique craft of Orissa*. Ahmedabad: Calico Museum of Textiles.
Monserrate, Father Antonio. (1922). *The commentary of Father Monserrate S.J. on his journey to the court of Akbar*. Trans. J.S. Hoyland and S.N. Banerjee. London: Second Reprint (2003) New Delhi: Asian Educational Service.
Mookerjee, A. (1990). *Designs in Indian textiles*. Calcutta: Sree Saraswaty Press Ltd.
Mookerji, B. N. G. (1894). The silk industries of Moorshedabad. *Journal of Indian Art and Industry, 5*(38),1–8.
Moorcroft, W, and George, T. (1841). *Travels in the Himalayan provinces of Hindustan and the Panjab; in Ladakh and Kashmir; in Peshawar, Kabul, Kunduz, and Bokhara (1819–1825)* (Vol. 2). London: J. Murray.
Moraes, D. (1976). *The open eyes: a journey through Karnataka*. Bangalore: The Directorate of Information and Publicity.

Moran, W. (1993a). *Rural space as intellectual property*. Auckland: Department of Geography, University of Auckland.

Moran, W. (1993b). The wine appellation as territory in France and California. *Annals of the Association of American Geographers* 83(4), 694–717.

Moxham, R. (2003). *Tea: addiction, exploitation and empire*. London: Constable.

Mukherjee, B. N. (1992). *External trade of early North–Eastern India*. New Delhi: Vikash Publishing House.

Mundy, P. (1907). *The travels of Peter Mundy in Europe and Asia: 1608–1667 Vol. 1*. Cambridge: Hakluyt Society.

Mundy, P. (1914). *The travels of Peter Mundy in Europe and Asia: 1608–1667 Vol. 2*. Cambridge: Hakluyt Society.

Mundy, P. (1919). *The travels of Peter Mundy in Europe and Asia: 1608–1667 Vol. 3*. Cambridge: Hakluyt Society.

Musungu, S. F. (2008). The protection of geographical indicators and the Doha Round: strategic and policy consideration for Africa. Retrieved June 2012 from http://quno.org/geneva/pdf/economic/Issues/QUNO–PROTECTION%20OF%20GEOGRAPHICAL%20INDICATIONS–AFRICA.pdf.

Lalitha, N. 2004. Intellectual property protection for plant varieties issues in focus. *Economic and Political Weekly*, 39(19), 1921–1927.

Naeed, J. (2006). *The Kashmiri shawl*. Ahmedabad: Mapin Publishing.

Nair, L. N. (2003, October 3). Forgotten agenda from Doha. *The Economic Times*.

Nair, L. R., and Kumar, R. (2005). *Geographical indications: a search for identity*. New Delhi: Lexis–Nexis Butterworths.

Nanda, N. (2003). WTO and trade facilitation. *Economic and Political Weekly*, 38(26), 2622–2625.

Nanda, N. (2004). World Intellectual Property Organisation patent agenda. *Economic and Political Weekly*, 39(39), 4310.

Narayan, S. (1995). *Shakahari*. Delhi: Metropolitan Book Company.

Naryan Sharkar, J. (1991). *Private traders in medieval India: British and Indian*. Kolkata: Noya Prakash.

Nath, A., and Wazciarg, F. (1987). *Living traditions of India: arts and crafts of Rajasthan*. Ahmedabad: Mapin Publishing.

National Council for Applied Economic Research. (1977). *Techno–Economic Survey of Darjeeling Tea Industry*. Delhi: NCAER.

Nazareth, S. (2004). Weaponisation and loss of cultural identity. *Economic and Political Weekly*, 39(18), 1791–1792.

Newton, B. (1998). *Manchester Royal Jubilee Exhibition Old Trafford, 1887*. London: Trafford Leisure Services.

Nicholas, B. (1992). *Tangail Sarees of Bengal*. Ahmedabad: National Institute of Design.

Nireekshak. (2000). Media watch: unnecessary controversy. *Economic and Political Weekly*, 35(48), 4166–4167.

Nolan, R. (2003). *International food wars*. New York: Foreign Policy Association and Global Policy Forum.

O'Connor, B. (2004). *The Law of Geographical Indications*. London: Cameron May.
OXFAM. (2002). The tea market – a background study. Retrieved 24 June 2011 from http://www.maketradefair.com/assets/english/TeaMarket.pdf.
Paine, S. (1990). *Embroidered textiles: traditional patterns from five continents*. London: Thames and Hudson.
Pandey, B. P. (1999). *Economic botany*. New Delhi: S. Chand and Co.
Parikh, M., Michael, R., and Aditi, R. (1992). *Jala weaving of Benaras, craft documentation series*. Ahmadabad: National Institute of Design.
Parvir, N. (2003). *Shawls of the East*. New York: PDN Publishing.
Patrawala, F. H., and Bharadwaj, M. (1998). *The Indian kitchen*. London: Kyle Cathie.
Percival, M. (1923). *The chintz book*. New York: Frederick A. Stokes Company.
Pillai, R. M., Pillai, S. G. K., and Damodaran, A. D. (2002). The lost: wax casting of icons, utensils, bells and other items in South India. *Journal of Metallurgy*, 54(10), 12–16.
Pires, Tome. (1515/1944). *The Suma Oriental of Tome Pires*. Vol. 2 trans. A. Cortesao. London: Hakluyt Society.
Pius, M. (2001). *Portuguese Cochin and maritime trade of India 1500–1663*. New Delhi: Pavilion Books Limited.
Plessis, I. du. (2003). EU wants to have its feta and eat it. *Futures and Commodity Market News*. Retrieved from Tradingcharts.com Inc.
Prabhavananda, Swami. (1983). *Vedic religion and philosophy*. Mylapore: Sri Ramakrishna Math.
Prager, F. D. (1950). The early growth and influence of intellectual property. *Journal of the Patent Office Society*, 34(2), 106–140.
Prakash, O., and Khan, R. M. (2005). *A tryst with mango*. New Delhi: A.P.H. Publishing Corporation.
Prasad, A. (1960). *Sarva deshiko arya prathinidhi sabha*. New Delhi: Vedic Vandana.
Prasad, A. (1971). *Vedic thoughts*. New Delhi: Vedic Vandana.
Prasad, S. (1986). *Terracottas of Bengal*. New Delhi: B.R Publishing Corporation.
Pratap, R. (2003). WTO panel report on Indian steel. *Economic and Political Weekly*, 38(11), 1021–1023.
Puri, L. (2003). Tackling militancy in Jammu. *Economic and Political Weekly*, 38(31), 3243–3455.
Raghavachar, S. S. (1988). *Studies in Vedanta*. Mysore: Mysore University Printing Press.
Rai, A., and Ranjan, A. (1992). *Chikankari embroidery of Lucknow, craft documentation series*. Ahmedabad: National Institute of Design.
Rai, R. (1962). *The vedic index of names and subjects*. Varanasi: Chowkhamba Vidyabhavan.
Rai, R. (1995). *Tandoor*. New York: Overlook Press.
Rajannan, B. (1992). *Salem cyclopedia: a cultural and historical dictionary of Salem District*. Salem: Institute of Kongu Studies.
Raju, P. T. (1936). *Indian thoughts and its development*. New York: Henry Holt and Company Publishers.

Rajwade, A. V. (2001). Universal banking: some issues. *Economic and Political Weekly*, 36(45), 3243–3455.

Rakitov, A., and Chambell, C. H. (1987). *Historical knowledge: a system epistemological approach*. Moscow: Progress Publishers.

Rakob, E. M. (1995). Baluchari textiles: pictorial brocades. In J. Dhamija (Ed.), *The woven silks of India* (pp. 61–76). Bombay: Marg Publication.

Ram, R. K., Singh, R. K. and Gopal, C. (1989). Uttar Pradesh: Handicraft Survey Report: Bhadohi Woolen Carpet Industry (A Rural-based Traditional Handicraft), Census of India 1981, Series 22; Part X-D. Delhi: Controller of Publications, Census of India.

Ramaswamy, V. (1985). *Textiles and weavers in medieval South India*. Delhi: Oxford University Press.

Randhawa, M. S., and Galbraith, J. K. (1968). *Indian painting: the scene, theme and legends*. Delhi: Oxford and IBH Publishing Co. Pvt. Ltd.

Rangarajan, M. (Ed.). (2007). *Environmental issues in India: a reader*. New Delhi: Pearson–Longman.

Rangekar, D. (2002). The pros and cons of geographical indication protection. *Bridges, between Trade and Sustainable Development*, 6(3), 3–6. Retrieved June 2012 from http://ictsd.org /downloads/bridges/bridges6–3.pdf.

Rangekar, D. (2003). *Geographical indications: a review of proposals at the TRIPS Council*. Geneva: UNCTAD/ICTSD Capacity Building Project on Intellectual Property Rights and Sustainable Development.

Rangel Ortiz, H. (1999). *Geographical indications in recent treaty law in the Americas: NAFTA, Latin American Free Trade Agreements, MERCOSUR, the Andean Community and the Central American Protocol*. Geneva: World Intellectual Property Organization.

Ranjan, A. (2004). *Handmade in India*. Delhi: National Institute of Design.

Ranjan, A., and Ranjan, M. P. (2007). *Crafts of India: handmade in India*. New Delhi: Council of Handicrafts Development Corporations and Office of the Development Commissioner Handicrafts, Ministry of Textiles.

Ranjan, V. (2008). Arguing with Sen on nationalism. *Economic and Political Weekly*, 43(10), 4.

Ranjan, V. (2009). Applicable law in the dispute settlement body of the WTO. *Economic and Political Weekly*, 44(15), 23–27.

Rao, C. H. H. (2001). WTO and viability of Indian Agriculture. *Economic and Political Weekly*, 36(36), 3453–3457.

Rao, G. S. (1954). *Indian words in English: a study in Indo–British cultural and linguistic relations*. Oxford: Clarendon Press.

Rao, N. C. (2002). Patents for biotechnology inventions in TRIPS. *Economic and Political Weekly*, 37(22), 2126–2129.

Rao, N. C. (2003). *Geographical indications in Indian context: a case study of Darjeeling tea*. New Delhi: ICRIER.

Rao, N. C. (2005). Geographical indications in Indian context: a case study of Darjeeling tea. *Economic and Political Weekly*, 40(42), 4545–4550.

Rao, N. C. (2006). Para 6 of WTO Doha Declaration: non solution of TRIPS problem. *Economic and Political Weekly, 41*(4), 301–302. Rathna, K. (2014). Yalakki Banana comes to the rescue to Nanjangud farmers. Retrieved 13 June 2014 from http://odysseyonapen.blogspot.in/2014_04_01_archive.html.

Raustiala, K. S. (2007). Global struggle over the geographic indications. *European Journal of International Law, 18*(2), 337–356.

Ravishankar, A., and Archak, S. (2000). Intellectual property rights and agricultural technology. *Economic and Political Weekly, 35* (27), 2446–2451.

Raychaudhuri, H. G. (1928). The study of ancient Indian geography. *Indian Historical Quarterly, 4*.

Relph, E. (1976). *Place and placelessness*. London: Pion.

The Reporter of Economic Products to the Government of India (Ed). (1911). *Races of rice in India: the agricultural ledger* (Vol. 16). Calcutta: Superintendent Government Printing.

Richards, F. J. (1918). *Salem District Gazetteer*. Madras: Government Press. Retrieved June 2012 from http://www.archive.org/details/p1salemrich01richuoft.

Richards, J. F. (1993). *The Mughal Empire*. Cambridge: Cambridge University Press.

Roberts, D., *et al.* (2001). *The role of product attributes in the agriculture negotiations*. The International Agricultural Trade Research Consortium, Commissioned Paper No. 17.

Roberts, P. E. (1995). *Historical geography of India*. Jaipur: Printwell.

Roest, K. de, and Alberto, M. 2002. Reconsidering 'traditional' food: the case of Parmigiano Reggiano cheese. *Sociologica Ruralis*, 40(4), 439–451.

Ross, Dunn. (2005). *The adventure of Ibn Battuta: a Muslim traveller of the 14th century*. Los Angeles: University of California Press.

Rossi, B. (1998). *From the ocean of painting: India's popular paintings, 1589 to the present*. New York and Oxford: Oxford University Press.

Roy, B. P. (2008). Vrksayurveda in ancient India. In L. A. S. Gopal (Ed.), *History of agriculture in India (up to C.1200 AD)*. Delhi: Concept Publishing Company.

Roy, T. (1999). *Traditional industry in the economy of colonial India*. *Cambridge studies in Indian history and society series*. Cambridge: Cambridge University Press.

Rohini, S. (2001). Anti-dumping probe: a case study in steel. *Economic and Political Weekly*, 36(48), 4447–4449.

Sahai, S. (2001). TRIPS review: basic rights must be restored. *Economic and Political Weekly*, 36(31), 2918–2919.

Sahu, P. R. (2009, September 5). High demand cannot save Sambalpuri Sarees. *Hindustan Times*.

Sangar, P. (1993). *Growth of the English trade under Mughals*. New Delhi: South Asia Books.

Sapre, O. (2008). The lovely Devgad Alphonso Mangoes. Retrieved June 2014 from http://devgad–alphonso–mangoes.blogspot.in/.

Saraf, D. N. (1982). *Indian crafts development and potential*. Delhi: Vikash Publishing House.

Saraf, D. N. (1987). *Arts and crafts Jammu and Kashmir*. New Delhi: Abhinav Publication.

Satapathy, C. (2000a). Implementation of WTO agreement on customs valuation. *Economic and Political Weekly, 35*(25), 2098–2100.

Satapathy, C. (2000b). WTO panel rulings on anti-dumping. *Economic and Political Weekly, 35*(48), 4164–4165.

Satapathy, C. (2000c). WTO panel rulings on anti-dumping – II. *Economic and Political Weekly, 35*(48), 4298–4300.

Satapathy, C. (2001a). Undervalued imports and public interest. *Economic and Political Weekly, 36*(4), 445–447.

Satapathy, C. (2001b). Valuation of undervalued and dumped imports. *Economic and Political Weekly, 36*(2), 98–100. Satapathy, C. (2002). Trade facilitation: a Singapore issue knocking at World Trade Organisation's door. *Economic and Political Weekly, 37*(17), 1587–1589.

Satapathy, C. (2003). Beyond Cancun: back to the basics. *Economic and Political Weekly, 38*(40), 4203.

Sathyan, B. N. (1966). *Mysore State Gazetteer: Bijapur District*. Bangalore: Government Press, Karnataka.

Schoff, W. (Trans. and Anno.) (1912). *The periplus of the Erythraean Sea: Travel and trade in the Indian Ocean by a merchant of the first century*. New York, London, Bombay, and Calcutta: Longmans, Green and Company.

Scholberg, H. (2001). *The Gazetteers of British India, 1833–1962*. Leiden, Netherlands: IDC Publishers.

Schwartz, P. R. (1956a). French documents on Indian cotton painting: (1): The Beaulieu, m.s. 1734. *Journal of Indian Textile History, 2*, 5–23.

Schwartz, P. R. (1956b). French documents on Indian cotton painting: (2): New light on old material. *Journal of Indian Textile History, 3*, 15–44.

The Scotch Whisky Association v. Golden Bottling Limited. (2006). Delhi High Court. (129 (2006) DLT 423, 2006 (32) PTC 656 Del).

Scott, P. (1993). *The book of silk*. London: Thames and Hudson.

Sen Gupta, Pi. (1980). *The art of Indian cuisine: everyday menus, feasts and holiday banquets*. Boston: Dutton Adult.

Sen, S. N. (1988). *Ancient Indian history and civilization*. New Delhi: Wiley Eastern Limited.

Sen, S. (2009, December 3). Silk Route. *India Today*.

Shah, K. T. (1923). *Trade, tariffs and transport in India*. London: P.S. King and Son Ltd.

Shamashastry, R. (Trans.) (1909). *Kautilya's Arthashastra*. Bangalore: Bangalore Government Press.

Shanmugavelu, K. G. (1998). *Viticulture in India*. Agra: Agra Botanica.

Sharma, D. (2004). WTO and agriculture. *Economic and Political Weekly, 39*(20), 1997–1998.

Sharma, R. (2003). *Medicinal plants – an encyclopaedia*. Delhi: Daya Publishing house.

Shaw, Susan A. and Carter, Sara. (1993). The Strathclyde University Food Project: marketing, relationships and structures. *British Food Journal*, 95 (10), 3–10.

Shyna, P. A., and Joseph, S. 2000. *A microanalysis of problems of displaced women agricultural labourers with special emphasis to the Pokkali Fields of Vypinkara*. Kerala

Research Programme on Local Level Development. Thiruvananthapuram: Centre for Development Studies.

Siddiqui, A. (1995). The business world of Jamsetjee Jejeebhoy. In A. Siddiqui (Ed.), *Trade and finance in colonial India 1750–1860* (pp. 186–217). Delhi: Oxford University Press.

Sikdar, S. (1997). *Outcasting of the traditional science and technology practitioners*. New Delhi: National Institute of Science Technology and Development Studies.

Simkin, C. G. F. (1968). *Traditional trade of Asia*. Oxford: Oxford University Press.

Singh, A. K. (2006). *Flower crops cultivation and management*. New Delhi: New India Publishing Agency.

Singh, R. N. (2005). *Mango*. New Delhi: Indian Centre for Agricultural Research.

Singh, R. (2010). *The fabric of our lives: the story of Fabindia*. New Delhi: Penguin Books India.

Singh, S. P. (1992). *Fruit crops for wasteland*. Jodhpur: Scientific Publishers.

Singh, S. (2003). Green business prospects. *Economic and Political Weekly*, *38*(31), 3240–3243.

Singh, U. K. (2006). POTA and the case of Raja Bhaiya. *Economic and Political Weekly*, *41*(1), 19.

Singh, U. (2008). *A history of ancient and early medieval India: from the Stone Age to the 12th century*. New Delhi: Pearson Education India.

Sinha, N. K. (1995). The Armenian traders in Bengal. In A. Siddiqui (Ed.), *Trade and finance in colonial India 1750–1860* (pp. 99–106). Delhi: Oxford University Press.

Srinivasan, R. K. (2007). Intellectual Property Rights and traditional knowledge. *Economic and Political Weekly*, *42*(27), 2866–2870.

Srinivasan, S. (2000). Pharmaceuticals, WTO and Seattle round. *Economic and Political Weekly*, *35*(5), 249–253.

Srivastava, C. S. (2003). Geographical indications and legal framework in India. *Economic and Political Weekly*, *38*(38), 4022–4032.

Srivastava, J. (2005). NGO's at World Trade Organisation. *Economic and Political Weekly*, *40*(19), 1952–1957.

Srivastava, S. C. (2005). Case study 16: protecting the geographical indication for Darjeeling. In P. Gallagher, A. Stoler, and P. Low (Eds.), *Managing the challenges of WTO participation*. Cambridge: Cambridge University Press.

Steuart, Sir J. (1995). The principles of money applied to the present state of the coin of Bengal. In A. Siddiqui (Ed.), *Trade and finance in colonial India 1750–1860* (pp. 61–65). Delhi: Oxford University Press.

Sundaresan, C. S. (2001). Multilateral trade and dairy commodity markets. *Economic and Political Weekly*, *36*(34), 3311–3315.

Surya Rekha, n.d. *Sung in a certain style north Indian light classical vocal music: Thumri and its allied forms*. Sponsored by ITC Sangeet Research Academy, India.

Talley, W. K. (2000). Ocean container shipping: impacts of technological improvement. *Journal of Economic Issues*, *34*(2), 933–948.

Tamaskar, B. G. (1985). *Contributions to historical geography of India*. New Delhi: Inter India Publications.

Taneja, M. (1979). *The Indian epicure*. London: Mills and Boon.

Tate, W. B. (1994). The development of the organic industry and market: an international perspective. In N. H. Lampkin and S. Padel (Eds.), *The economics of organic farming*. Wallingford, England: CAB.

Tavernier, J. B. (1889). *Travels in India* (2nd ed. 1925, Vols. 2) V. Ball (Trans.). London: Macmillan and Company, London: Oxford University Press.

Tea Board of India. (2002a). Average yields of tea in India. Retrieved May 2011 from http://teaboard.gov.in/.

Tea Board of India. (2002b). Tea statistics 2000–2001. Retrieved May 2011 from http://teaboard.gov.in/.

Tea Board of India. (2006). Protection of Darjeeling Tea as a geographical indication. Retrieved May 2011 from http://teaboard.gov.in/.

Tea Board of India. Indian tea industry. Retrieved May 2011 from http://teaboard.gov.in/.

Textiles Committee. (2007). *Pochampally Ikat: a comparative market analysis of pre and post registration periods under Geographical Indications Act*. Mumbai: Ministry of Textiles, Government of India.

Thamarajakshi, R. (2002). Doha Declaration and agriculture in developing countries. *Economic and Political Weekly*, 37(1), 23–27.

Thapa, Y. B. (2003). *Commodity case study: competitiveness and policy issues in the tea sector of Nepal*. Nepal: FAO/MoAC, WTO Project.

Theideg, F., and Sylvander, B. (2000). Welcome to the club? An economical approach to geographical indications in the European Union. *Agarwirtschaft*, 49(12), 428–437.

Thévenod-Mottet, E. (2002). *The protection of geographical indications and multilateral systems: a cultural clash*. Paper presented at the DOLPHINS Meeting, Florence, Italy, September, 10–12.

Thoman, R. S., and Conkling, E. C. (1967). *Geography of international trade*. Englewood Cliffs, NJ: Prentice Hall.

Timberg, T. A. (1995). Hiatus and incubator: indigenous trade and traders, 1837–1857. In A. Siddiqui (Ed.), *Trade and finance in colonial India 1750–1860* (pp. 250–264). Delhi: Oxford University Press.

Thomson, J. O. (1948). *History of ancient geography*. Cambridge: University Press.

Thorn, S. F. (2003). Implications of the extension of protections for geographical indications in the WTO. Grocery manufacturers of America statement made before the Committee on Agriculture, US House of Representatives, July 22.

Thorpers, T. (1922). *Thorpes dictionary of chemistry*. California: Longman Green.

Thu–Lang, T. W. (2000). *Recent developments in the council for TRIPS (WTO)*. Geneva: World Intellectual Property Organization.

Tozer, H. F. (1897). *A history of ancient geography*. Delhi: ESS Publication (Reprint, 1975).

Tripathi, A. (1995). Indo-British trade between 1833 and 1847 and the commercial crisis of 1847–8. In A. Siddiqui (Ed.), *Trade and finance in colonial India 1750–1860* (pp. 265–289). Delhi: Oxford University Press.

Tuan, Yi–Fu. (1974). *Topophilia: a study of environmental perceptions, attitudes, and values*. New York: Columbia University Press.

Tucker, R. P. (2011). *A forest history of India*. Delhi: Sage Publications Pvt. Ltd.

Tunzelmann, G. N. von. (1995). Technology and industrial progress: the foundations of economic growth, England. Retrieved November 2013 from www.gov/Record/236.

Tyabji, L. (2007). *Threads and voices*. Mumbai: Marg Publication.

Vasudeva, P. K. (2000). EU–Canada patents row. How does it affect India? *Economic and Political Weekly*, *35*(19), 1616–1618.

Vicziany, M. (1995). Bombay merchants and structural changes in the export community 1850 to 1880. In A. Siddiqui (Ed.), *Trade and finance in colonial India 1750–1860* (pp. 345–382). Delhi: Oxford University Press.

Vishwanadha, A. (2006). Cheriyal paintings. Retrieved March 2012 from http://ekdesh.blogspot.in/2006/06/cheriyal–paintings.html.

Wachendorf, V. von. (2007). *Tea*. United Kingdom: Parragon Inc.

Wagle, S. (2003). *Geographical indications TRIPS and promoting human development in Asia, and the development dimensions of the Sri Lankan geographical indication of Camellia sinensis (Ceylon Tea)*. Hanoi: UNDP Asia Trade Initiative.

Wagner, P., and Mikesell, M.W. (Eds.). (1962). *Readings in cultural geography*. Chicago: University of Chicago Press.

Warmington, E. H. (1995). *The commerce between the Roman Empire and India*. New Delhi: Munshiram Manoharlal.

Watal, Jayashree. (2001). *Intellectual property rights in the WTO and developing countries*. The Hague: Kluwer Law International.

Watson, J. F. (1866). *The textile manufactures and the costumes of the people of India*. London: Printed for the India Office, by George Edward Eyre and William Spottiswoode.

Watson, J. (1876). *The imperial museum for India and the colonies*. London: W. H. Allen and Co.

Waza, S., and Waza, R. (2001). *Wazwaan*. New Delhi: Roli Books.

Weiss, P. (2010). *Patent policy: legal–economic effects in a national and international framework*. London: Routledge.

Wickramasinghe, U. (2001). Preparing for Doha WTO meeting. *Economic and Political Weekly*, *36*(28), 2630–2635.

WIPO. (1999). *Symposium on the International Protection of Geographical Indications*, Eger, Hungary, October 24 and 25, 1997. Publication No. 760(E). Geneva: WIPO.

WIPO International Bureau. (2001). *Geographical indications: historical background, nature of rights, existing systems for protection and obtaining effective protection in other countries*. Geneva: Standing Committee on the Law of Trademarks, Industrial Designs and Geographical Indications, 6th session, March 12–16.

WIPO International Bureau. (2002). *What is geographical indications*. Retrieved February 2013 from http://www.wipo.int/about-ip/en/index.html.

WIPO Standing Committee on the Law of Trademarks, Industrial Design and Geographical Indications (SCT) and WTO. (1997). *Overview of existing international notification and registration systems for geographical indications relating to wines and*

spirits. IP/C/W/85, IP/C/W/85/Add.1. Wright, Gillian. (2011). *The Darjeeling Tea Book*. Delhi: Penguin India.
WTO. (1999). *Preparations for the 1999 ministerial conference – the TRIPS agreement*. Communication from Kenya on Behalf of the Africa Group. WT/GC/W/302.
WTO. (2001). *Review under Article 24.2 of the application of the provisions of the section of the TRIPS agreement on geographical indications: summary of the responses to the checklist of questions* (IP/C/13 and add.1). IP/C/W/253.
WTO. (2004). *World trade report 2004*. Geneva: World Trade Organization.
Yasmin, E., and Bhat, F. A. (2013). An evaluation of handicraft sector of J and K – a case study of District Budgam. *European Academic Research, 1*(4), 367–381.
Yeung, M. T., and Kerr, W. A. (2008). *Increasing protection of GIs at the WTO: clawbacks, greenfields and monopoly rents*. Canadian Agricultural Trade Policy Research Network Working Paper 2008–2002.
Yule, H. (Trans.). 1920. *The travels of Marco Polo*. Henri Cordier (Ed. and Annot.). London: John Murray.

INDEX

Note: Page Locators with *f* and *t* indicates figures and tables

For Product Safety Concerns and Information please contact our EU representative GPSR@taylorandfrancis.com
Taylor & Francis Verlag GmbH, Kaufingerstraße 24, 80331 München, Germany

www.ingramcontent.com/pod-product-compliance
Ingram Content Group UK Ltd.
Pitfield, Milton Keynes, MK11 3LW, UK
UKHW022110190926
475702UK00013B/1365
9780815395935